In Forest Fields

A Unique Guide to Personal Prayer

By

Rabbi Shalom Arush

Chut Shel Chessed Institutions

POB 50226, Jerusalem, Israel

Telephone - 972-2-5812210

Distribution:

Tel: 972-52-2240696

www.myemuna.com

Design and Layout:
Eye See Productions
972-2-5821453

ISBN

978-965-91342-4-3

Printed in Israel

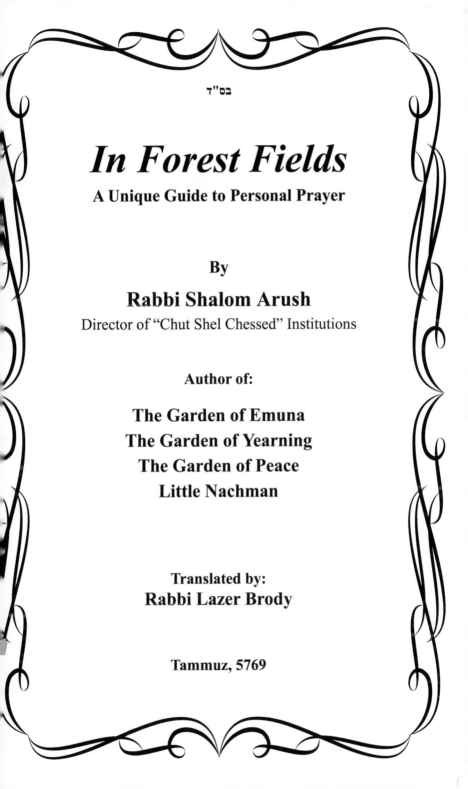

בס"ד

In Forest Fields
A Unique Guide to Personal Prayer

By

Rabbi Shalom Arush
Director of "Chut Shel Chessed" Institutions

Author of:

The Garden of Emuna
The Garden of Yearning
The Garden of Peace
Little Nachman

Translated by:
Rabbi Lazer Brody

Tammuz, 5769

Approbations

The following are excerpts from the approbations that this generation's leading rabbinical figures wrote for **B'Sde Yaar**, the original Hebrew version of **In Forest Fields**:

Rabbi Ovadia Yossef,
Rishon Letzion and President of The Council of Torah Sages:

"**In Forest Fields** is the work of an artist, the Prince of Torah, the brilliant and pious Rabbi Shalom Arush, may he merit long and happy days, who has assembled in his purity a golden treasure of wonderful spiritual arousal…"

Rabbi Naftali Moscowitz, the Melitzer Rebbe:

"I am full of praise for the new book of my esteemed friend, the righteous Rabbi Shalom Arush shlit'a, entitled **In Forest Fields,** which is wonderfully inspiring in the areas of prayer and gratitude to Hashem. This book explains the proper way to pour out one's heart to Hashem… whoever reads this book will undoubtedly feel enhanced strength and courage to engage in the holy endeavor of personal prayer, for there is nothing like it to bring hearts closer to Hashem."

Rabbi Eliezer Berland,
Rosh Yeshiva of Shuvu Banim Breslev, Jerusalem

"I have been moved to the core of my soul by reading **In Forest Fields**…One has an absolute obligation to seek G-d day and night, just as King David did in Ephrata and in forest fields…

By way of *hitbodedut* (personal prayer), one can not only attain his own soul correction and well bring the entire world closer to G-d, thereby nullifying all sorrow and calamity…One therefore has an absolute obligation to purchase this book and distribute it the world over!"

Behold, we have heard it in Ephrata

and have found it in forest fields!

Psalm 132:6

Contents

Chapter Two: For I Am Compassionate   77

Chapter Three: Learning Hitbodedut   103

Chapter Four: The Truest Connection   123

Chapter Five: Self Composure   **163**

Chapter Six: Connecting to the Source   **185**

Chapter Seven: The Attainable Good Life   **211**

Chapter Eight: Hope for Hashem!   279

Chapter Nine: The Foundation of Prayer   311

Chapter Ten: I Call to You All Day Long   319

Chapter Eleven: Take Your Words Along 339

Author's Foreword

This book tells about one of the greatest gifts The Almighty gave to mankind – personal prayer, what we call in Hebrew *hitbodedut*. A number of factors stimulated me to write this book, but a comment that our holy Rebbe Nachman of Breslev made about himself was my most profound influence.

Rebbe Nachman reached a spiritual level that was beyond human comprehension. His entire waking hours were devoted to Torah and prayer. He lived a life of phenomenal personal regiment and holiness. He purified his body with week-long fasts and immersion in icy-cold lakes in the middle of the Ukrainian winter. We can't begin to relate to his holiness and his greatness in Torah. Yet, Rebbe Nachman said that nothing propelled him forward in the service of Hashem like *hitbodedut*, simply speaking to Hashem in his own jargon.

Rebbe Nachman also said that all the great *tzaddikim*, the righteous men with whom he spoke, testified that they too attained what they attained by virtue of *hitbodedut*, speaking to Hashem with the innocence and simplicity that a son speaks to a father.

Our generation is not built for asceticism. Self-abnegation would bring most of us to sadness rather than to the joy that's needed to serve Hashem. Rebbe Nachman's advice of personal prayer is therefore the perfect answer for the people of our generation and the best guarantee for spiritual growth, emotional health, happiness, and fulfillment.

This book teaches all about *hitbodedut* – how to use the wonderful tool of personal prayer to get close to Hashem and thereby attain long-lasting personal satisfaction and happiness that cannot possibly be attained by any other means.

In recent years, I meet more and more people that have been learning Rebbe Nachman's teachings about *hitbodedut*. Many have listened to my CDs, where I speak extensively on this subject. Also, my previous books – The Garden of *Emuna*, The Garden of Yearning, and The Garden of Peace – deal extensively with *hitbodedut* as the foundation of faith and service of Hashem. Many readers since have made *hitbodedut* an integral portion of their daily routine.

On one hand, numerous readers have begun to speak to Hashem in personal prayer on a daily basis. Yet, they've been asking me quite a few important questions and sending me requests for further instruction as to the best way to implement personal prayer. What should a person talk about? What's the best way to do personal prayer? What is a person supposed to feel during a personal prayer session? The questions are vital and need answers, which made my writing this book a solemn obligation.

The final critical influence that prodded me to bring the ideas in this book to printed fruition is my own personal experience. Nothing was so conducive to my own spiritual growth as *hitbodedut*. Since the time when I took my first steps in Torah and *teshuva*, I've been speaking to Hashem as much as I can in daily personal prayer. Nothing has been so beneficial for me.

With Hashem's loving grace, I traverse our beloved homeland from north to south bringing our people closer to Hashem. On a given week, one might find me in Kiryat Arba, Yerucham, Dimona, Ashdod, Natanya, and Haifa. If I weren't travelling so much, I could certainly write more. So why do I travel so much? To encourage people to devote an hour a day to personal prayer! With personal prayer, a person will undoubtedly attain his or her individual redemption from stress, emotional pressures, and the type of depression that is so rampant among the people of this generation.

Personal prayer not only hastens one's individual redemption, but the overall *Geula*, or full redemption of our people as well.

Rebbe Nachman implores us (*Likutei Moharan*, I:79) to avoid being an obstacle that delays the *Geula*. We do that by investing daily time in personal prayer, self-evaluation, and the resulting self-improvement.

While in personal prayer on Rebbe Nachman's holy gravesite in Uman, Ukraine during Rosh Hashanna of 5768 (2007), I was aroused to implement the project of writing a book about *hitbodedut* right away. As soon as I returned to Israel, I began immediately, with the help of my trusty student assistants, to boil down years of scattered teachings on the subject to one concise, practical, and reader-friendly guide to personal prayer.

I named this book, "**In Forest Fields**," by virtue of advice I received from my esteemed rabbi and spiritual guide, Rabbi Eliezer Berland shlit'a. When I approached him to request his approbation for this book, he quoted King David in Psalm 132, verse 6, and said, "Behold, we have heard it in Ephrata and have found it **in forest fields**." Traditionally, since time immemorial, people have been doing personal prayer in the field, as the Torah testifies (*Breishit* 24:63), "And Isaac went out to speak [to Hashem] in the field." The fields and the forests are wonderful places for personal prayer and attaining the type of tranquility and self-composure that we all aspire for.

I thank Hashem for all His unfathomable lovingkindness. I am nothing but a quill in His loving hands. I hope and pray that this book will be beneficial to all those who seek Hashem. My entire wish in life is that people come close to Hashem and taste the sweet life of *emuna*.

My sincere gratitude goes to my spiritual guide and rabbi, Rabbi Eliezer Berland shlit'a, from whose sweet waters I drink. He brought me close to *teshuva* and to Breslever Chassidut.

An unlimited debt of thanks goes to my wife, a blessed woman of valor, Miriam Varda, may Hashem bless her with a long, happy and healthy life – my partner in life and my very best friend. Her power and her merit are the source of all of my success, for she deserves all the credit for my accomplishments.

Many thanks to all my staff and students who assisted in the preparation of this book – recorders, editors, typists, our internet staff, printers and distributors. Special thanks go to my dear pupils Rabbi Yaakov Hertzberg and his wife Esther, may Hashem bless them, who have merited from above in assisting me with the composition of my books.

My blessings and appreciation go to my faithful friend and pupil, Rabbi Eliezer Raphael (Lazer) Brody, for the translation of this book and for his tireless dedication in spreading my teachings around the globe.

In the name of Hashem, may we do and succeed!

Shalom Arush
Jerusalem,
Tammuz, 5768

Translator's Foreword

My esteemed and beloved rabbi and spiritual guide Rabbi Shalom Arush says that this generation's number-one problem is self-persecution: people fail to realize their own fantastic qualities. Deep inside, despair and depression are taking their toll, telling people that they're not good enough and that no one loves them.

Here's the good news: Your beloved Father in Heaven has more gratification from your prayers, dear reader, than He has from those of the loftiest angels. These are not my words, but the words of Rabbi Chaim Ben Attar, the holy "Ohr HaChaim" (Ohr HaChaim on Numbers, 16:22), who says:

"These are the levels of that which Hashem desires: first, the praises and songs that the Heavenly Hosts give Him. Above them are the praises and songs that the souls of the great righteous men give Him. But more than anything, Hashem loves the prayers of those souls who now occupy the material world, those who are prevented from knowing Him because of the constraints of their flesh-and-blood body. Yet, they strengthen themselves in love of Hashem to speak to Him, thank Him, and praise Him – this is loftier and more cherished by Him than anything, as is brought forth in the Zohar and in the words of our sages."

Stop and think for a moment: we already have a guarantee from the Torah that Hashem loves every one of us (see Deuteronomy 23:6). But, as soon a person in this lowly physical world overcomes the obstacles in his or her way to set aside time for *hitbodedut*, or personal prayer, he or she becomes more cherished to Hashem than Moses and King David! Personal prayer is consequently the master key for unlocking Divine abundance of every type, material and spiritual.

Our holy Rebbe and teacher Rebbe Nachman of Breslev, may his saintly and blessed memory intercede in our behalf, teaches all about personal prayer. Rabbi Shalom Arush masterfully brings Rebbe Nachman's teachings to this generation's eye level.

Rabbi Shalom Arush is literally changing the world. His international bestseller and first English-translated book, **The Garden of *Emuna***, made its debut less than three years ago, but has already been translated into five other languages as well (with more on the way, G-d willing). At the time of this writing, **The Garden of *Emuna*** has neared the circulation milestone of nearly one million copies, having helped people from all walks of life to find true happiness and inner peace. Rabbi Arush's **The Garden of Peace** - a men's guide to marriage that first appeared in English last year – has saved thousands of marriages, has improved many more, and has also reached a healthy six-figure distribution status.

Hashem has granted me the rare privilege of basking in the light of Rabbi Shalom Arush for over a dozen years already, both as the dean of the Ashdod branch of his renowned rabbinical seminary, "Chut Shel Chessed" and as his English "voice", translator and understudy. More than anyone I've ever seen, Rabbi Shalom meticulously practices what he preaches. He is the undisputed pillar of *emuna* and personal prayer in this generation.

This book will definitely improve your relationship with G-d. But even more so, it will improve your relationship with yourself, by putting you in contact with your own soul. Rabbi Arush teaches us the vital basics of *hitbodedut* – the when, where, why, and how of speaking to G-d in our own personal and intimately individual way. It's a book you'll always want by your side.

With Hashem's loving guidance, I have tried my utmost to preserve the flavor, intent, and beautiful simplicity of Rabbi Shalom's original style. Even so, any deficiency in this book is surely that of the translator and not of the author.

For the reader's convenience, I've included a practical glossary in the back of this book for non-English words that appear frequently throughout the text.

My sincere thanks and blessings go to (alphabetically) Yosef Berman, Natan Einhorn, Gita Levy, Layah Ornish and Shlomo Akiva (Shelly) Perluss for their dedicated assistance in translating, proofreading, rewriting, and making **In Forest Fields** a reality.

I wish to express my deepest gratitude to Rabbi Shalom Arush himself, who so selflessly has illuminated my mind and soul with his noble teachings. May Hashem bless him, his family, and his pupils with the very best of spiritual and material abundance always.

My cherished wife Yehudit deserves the credit for this book and for everything else I do. May Hashem bless her with long and happy days, success, and joy from all her offspring. May they walk courageously in the path of Torah and *emuna* until the end of time, amen.

With a song of thanks to the Almighty and a prayer for the full and speedy redemption of our people Israel,

Rabbi Lazer Brody,
Ashdod,
Tammuz 5769

"Loftier than anything is hitbodedut, for as a person turns his gaze from worldly matters, he frees his heart from lust. King David already spoke in praise of hitbodedut when he said (Psalm 55:7) 'O that I had the wing of a dove that I would fly away and find rest; behold, I would wander afar in the wilderness.' The Prophets Elijah and Elisha frequented the mountains in personal prayer, and our early sages of blessed memory walked in their footsteps, for they found this the most conducive avenue to perfection and withdrawal from the vanities of their contemporaries."

Rabbi Moshe Chaim Luzzato,
"The Path of the Just", Chapter 15

Chapter One:
The Power of Purification

The Creator gave us a magnificent gift – a daily hour of *hitbodedut*, or personal prayer in solitude. Anyone who desires to taste the sublime sweetness of paradise on earth should accustom himself speaking to Hashem in personal prayer for an hour every single day, as we shall learn in this book.

Prayer is one's personal redemption. One who masters the art of prayer – especially personal prayer – breaks the chains of exile and has attained his individual redemption. To understand this concept further, let's take a look at Rebbe Nachman's famous tale about "The Master of Prayer" (We strongly suggest reading "The Master of Prayer" in its entirety, which is one of Rebbe Nachman's famous "Thirteen Tales"):

The Master of Prayer taught the masses about prayer and Divine service. He'd teach his pupils to devote their lives to prayer and to sanctifying Hashem's Holy Name. Amazingly, his magnetic outreach was on a one-on-one basis. The Master of Prayer would enter a town or village and begin talking to one person about the true meaning of life on this earth. Quickly, the townsman or villager would realize that there's no purpose to anything in the world except for serving our Creator. Subsequently, The Master of Prayer would take the townsman or villager to his encampment out in the wilderness.

Rebbe Nachman tells about a great wind that created chaos and dispersed people all over the face of the earth. The people then gathered together in groups to search for the purpose of life. Each group made its respective mistake. One group thought that prestige was the main goal of life. Another group made power its objective. A third group pursued licentiousness, and a fourth group put its emphasis on oratory prowess. Each group had its silly ideology showing that its erroneous goal was the purpose of life on earth. Yet, the group that made the worst mistake was the cult that entertained a lust for money to the extent that wealth became its idolatry.

One group attained life's true purpose and made prayer its objective.

The king and his pure and holy ministers and servants were also dispersed among the four corners of the earth at the time of the great wind. The Master of Prayer was one of the king's men. In time, the king's men reunited, predominantly in virtue of the Master of Prayer's efforts. Once they were all together, they were faced with purifying the world of the lusts and mistaken ideologies to which they had succumbed. Even though all the king's men were pure of heart, the Master of Prayer led the purification process of the world. He was the emissary to each country, showing the locals the error of their ways.

The "Master of Prayer" tale teaches us that prayer is the key to both each person's personal redemption and to the collective redemption of the entire world. In fact, prayer is synonymous with redemption, for only the Master of Prayer had the power of uplifting the various populations from their respective follies and false ideologies.

Why was the Master of Prayer the only one capable of correcting the world? What did he have that the king's other righteous ministers didn't have? The Master of Prayer was entirely immersed in prayer; he was able to teach everyone how to pray. Therefore, the entire world needed him. The Master of Prayer purified the entire world by way of prayer.

One must understand that "redemption" is synonymous to "prayer". The Master of Prayer redeemed the entire world by teaching people how to pray. This will be the future scenario of *Moshiach*, may he come speedily and in our days. He too will teach everyone how to pray and thereby perfect their *emuna*. Rebbe Nachman of Breslev once said that when *Moshiach* comes, everyone will be devoting an hour a day to personal prayer just as everyone today puts on tefillin in the morning. In Hebrew, the letters that spell "*Moshiach*" are that same exact letters that spell "*Mesiach*", one who converses.

The Kabbalah states that the first two thousand years of the world revolve around the creation of the world. The second two thousand years revolve around human development, and the third two thousand years – which the current generation is a part of – revolve around the spread of prayer in the world.

Learning to Speak

Moshiach's chief concern will be teaching people how to speak to Hashem and thereby return wholeheartedly to Him. *Moshiach* will tell each person, "Go speak with Hashem! Ask Him to have compassion on you and to help you do *teshuva*. Ask Him to free your mind from the follies of this world." Each person has an evil inclination that tries to fill a person's brain with nonsense. One must ask Hashem's help in overcoming the evil inclination, for our sages tell us that a person doesn't sin unless the spirit of nonsense enters his brain.

The Master of Prayer was the only one that could redeem and purify the world since he was the one who prayed for the whole world. Not only that, but he instructed all his disciples to pray for the whole world. In addition, he traversed the world teaching people how to pray. Mankind attains its goal when each individual recognizes and acknowledges The Creator to the extent that each person prays on his own personal level. This is a much loftier achievement than merely having *Moshiach* or a few righteous men praying for the world.

In conclusion, in that the Master of Prayer brings the entire world to pray, he hastens the Messianic Age and the full redemption of the world. On an individual level, since prayer uplifts a person from the level of nonsense and the evil inclination's influence, and brings a person closer to Hashem and to true *teshuva,* prayer leads to one's personal redemption. Therefore, prayer and redemption are synonymous.

The Simplicity of *Emuna*

Hitbodedut is a prime indication of *emuna.* One who believes in Hashem will speak to Hashem and vice versa.

The simplicity of *emuna* means connecting with Hashem. Communication is the principal connection. Therefore, one who speaks to Hashem connects with Hashem.

Since Hashem is our loving Father in Heaven, one who fails to establish a connection with Hashem is like a person without a father, in other words, an orphan. Just as an orphan's life is difficult, living without a connection with our Father in Heaven is virtually unbearable. Rebbe Nachman of Breslev said that one who lives without *emuna* – the pure and simple belief in Hashem that connects a person to Hashem – has a life that's not worth living. Conversely, one who lives with *emuna* lives a life of pleasance and gratification, for he has a merciful Father in Heaven to lean on and depend on for all his needs, big or small, material and spiritual. When one believes that Hashem is always there, he confides in Him, speaks to Him, and asks for His advice in every matter.

In You we trust

Knowing that Hashem is with us constantly – 24 hours a day – and that He listens to us, assists us in whatever we do and rescues us from all peril, we realize that Hashem is much more than a father. The classic book of Jewish ethics "Duties of the Heart" says that one can trust only in Hashem, for only Hashem can fulfill the seven conditions of trust, as follows:

Hashem has compassion on you;

Hashem doesn't ignore your needs, nor does His constant Divine Providence ever neglect you;

He is strong and invincible, and no one can stop Him from fulfilling your request;

He knows all your needs, even the ones that you are not aware of;

His Divine Providence never leaves you; from your first day on earth through your last day on earth, He is with you.

He alone determines your fate, and no one other than Him can help you or hurt you.

His generosity and loving-kindness know no bounds, both for the deserving and for the undeserving.

This is the simplicity of *emuna*: You are a creation and the Creator is with you all the time. He listens to you, heeding every word you say. Therefore, a person of *emuna* must live his *emuna*, namely, he must know that he can always turn to Hashem. Even if one is so-called "religious", without a connection to Hashem, one lacks the main element of spirituality.

Talking to Hashem in your own words is a declaration of faith that surpasses all logic, intellectual arguments, proofs, and explanations. When you speak to Hashem, He is surely with you.

The Main Connection

Speech is our main connection to Hashem. Hashem therefore enables us to speak to Him whenever we want, anytime. Even a person is the lowest possible spiritual level or situation in life can talk to Hashem. As previously mentioned, speaking to Hashem is the prime manifestation of *emuna*. Since *emuna* is one of the "constant mitzvoth" – in other words, a mitzvah that we perform 24 hours a day – then Hashem enables us to speak to Him whenever we want, 24 hours a day. Rebbe Nachman of Breslev writes (*Likutei Moharan* II:84): "Know that the main connection to Hashem is by way of prayer, for prayer is the gate that leads to Hashem." Once more, prayer means to speak with Hashem. The Rambam says (see Rambam, Laws of Prayer) that prayer is basically speaking to Hashem in one's own words, conversing with Hashem, expressing gratitude, and asking for all of one's needs taking nothing for granted.

The obligation of prayer is none other than an incentive for us to cultivate a close relationship with Hashem. The main connection to Hashem is by way of speech. In the case of personal prayer, this connection becomes beautifully intimate in that each person can determine the time, place, language, dialect, and length of conversation. This type of from-the-heart dialogue with Hashem was practiced by our ancestors way before Moses received the Torah on Mount Sinai. Hashem's accessibility to each of us has been our source of strength and encouragement through two thousand years of exile and diaspora. The medium of personal prayer is centuries older than the prescribed prayers we pray today. In fact, the prescribed prayers were established by the Sages of the Great Assembly so that the oppressed and exiled masses wouldn't forget how to pray altogether.

Arousing the heart

Hitbodedut – personal prayer in one's own words – has the power of arousing the heart to yearn for and seek Hashem. Rabbi Yisrael Nachman Anshin of blessed memory once told the story of how he was travelling on a bus when he overheard two old men conversing with each other. One told the other that he had once spent the night by the holy gravesite of Rebbe Elazar, the son of Shimon Bar Yochai, in Miron. While lying on an adjacent bench with his eyes closed about to go to sleep, he heard a simple-looking Jew pleading with Hashem in sincere personal prayer all night long. The old man told his friend that he was so moved that he couldn't eat for the next twenty four hours.

On a subsequent trip to Miron, the old man again encountered the simple-looking Jew that prayed all night long beside Rebbe Elazar's gravesite. He discovered the young man's name – Reb David Stempler, a Breslever *Chassid* and a factory worker from Tel Aviv that eked out a meager living sewing burlap sacks. The old man told his friend, "I've heard thousands of sermons and preachers in my life, but nothing ever aroused me to yearn for Hashem like that young man's personal prayers."

The above story tells us just how much personal prayer can arouse the heart. Here was a simple Jew pleading with Hashem in his own words, oblivious to anyone else and certainly unaware that anyone else heard him. His pleas to Hashem in sincere innocence had the power to stimulate and excite another person to seek Hashem. More than anything, our personal prayers have the power to arouse our own hearts.

Amazing power

Rebbe Nachman of Breslev says (*Likutei Moharan* II:98) that when a person prays with tenacity, even if at first his mouth and his heart are far away from each other, if he persists and repeats his prayers, then eventually his words will filter down to his heart. These words of personal prayer have an amazing power to work wonders in addition to arousing the heart. With such prayers, "even a broomstick can shoot" (ibid, 96).

Rebbe Nachman of Breslev also writes (ibid, 99) that when Hashem helps a person in his personal prayer, then he actually feels the warmth of a loving close friend in his midst, and sincere heartfelt words flow forth from his mouth.

The best advice

Continuing, Rebbe Nachman of Breslev emphasizes (ibid, 101) that the very best advice for a person who seeks spiritual growth and proximity to Hashem is to devote as much time and effort as he can to personal prayer and speaking with Hashem, for this is the only strategy that enables a person to win the battle with his evil inclination. As in any war, one must persevere and be brave. Personal prayer is no exception, for dedication and conviction to personal prayer guarantees one's victory over the evil inclination.

Why is personal prayer the very best advice for a person who seeks spiritual growth and proximity to Hashem? Rebbe Nachman explains that although there are other good methods of getting close to Hashem, not every person is able to implement those methods. For example, intensive Talmudic study is extremely conducive in bringing a person close to Hashem, but not everyone is at the level where he is capable of intensive Talmudic study. Personal prayer is so special in that it not only brings a person close to Hashem, but it invokes Divine assistance in implementing the other ways of getting close to Hashem.

Rebbe Nachman promises that if a person perseveres in personal prayer, Hashem will answer him **without a doubt**.

Individually tailored

Personal prayer is the only mode of Divine service that's completely tailor-made to the individual. As such, personal prayer helps a person determine and successfully perform his individual mission in the world and live a truly satisfying life.

Your new path

Rebbe Natan of Breslev writes (ibid, 97), "I heard what he [Rebbe Nachman] said about the value of one's dialogue with his Creator, that all the accusing angels lie in ambush to obstruct one's prescribed prayers, for they all know the lanes that prescribed prayers ascend. For example, thieves and robbers lie in wait to pounce on the travelers along the well-travelled roads."

"But," continues Rebbe Natan, "when a person walks along his own new path that no one knows about, there are no "thieves and robbers" – in other words, the accusing angels aren't familiar with a person's new and individual path, so the prayers ascend intact and unobstructed. Even so, he [Rebbe Nachman] warned us not to underestimate the power of the prescribed prayers as well."

We learn from Rebbe Nachman's teachings that each prayer has its own path whereby it ascends, but only personal prayer blazes a bold new path upward to the Heavenly throne.

Personal prayer comes from the heart. The text of one's sincere impromptu prayers doesn't appear in any book. Personal prayers are neither rote nor routine. Like a kaleidoscope, they change with a person's mood, not only every single day but every single hour and minute. Even if the accusing angels could discover the path of a person's personal prayer on a certain day, by the time they could do any harm, a person who devotes daily time to personal prayer would already be on a new path with a new prayer.

Even more so, prescribed prayers require a person to connect his heart to the printed words in the prayer book. Few people are able to exercise such inner discipline to the extent that their minds don't wander from the prayer book and the words they're reciting. Yet, with personal prayer, one's heart is immediately bound with the personal words that are flowing forth from the heart. A person attains the level of *kavanna*, or sincere intent, with much less effort when praying in his own words, especially when spilling his heart out to Hashem about his individual difficulties, aspirations, and needs in life.

Prescribed prayer consequently requires much more effort and discipline than personal prayer. Most people don't reach a stage of "outpouring of the soul" with prescribed prayers and therefore have trouble praying with fervency. They therefore either pray either perfunctorily or with impatience, or scorn praying altogether. Their hearts and their mouths fail to focus on the same thing.

On the other hand, everyone can be successful in personal prayer. Even a person on a low spiritual level can speak to Hashem with sincerity and intent about whatever hurts him at the moment. The type of personal prayer said in your own words at your own convenience whenever you feel the need is the type of prayer that ascends straight up to the Heavenly throne. Such prayers emerge from the depth of the heart and are therefore supercharged with intent. These are the prayers that anyone can say. By way of personal prayer, anyone can connect with Hashem.

Rebbe Nachman therefore concludes (ibid, 100) that one can only become a "kosher person" by way of personal prayer, since without personal prayer, a person lacks a connection with Hashem.

Your personal path

In "The Tale of the Lost Princess," Rebbe Nachman writes (*for a complete explanation of Rebbe Nachman's "The Lost Princess", see "The Garden of Yearning", by the author*):

"And he saw a path to the side, and he **composed himself**: I've been walking so long in the desert, and I'm unable to find her. I'll take this path to the side and maybe I'll reach a settlement…"

Frequently, the hero or main character in Rebbe Nachman's stories stops and "composes himself" when faced with a major decision. This is indicative of personal prayer, when he appeals to Hashem for guidance. As such, the hero acts out of total self-composure, completely opposite to the type of instinctive reaction that leads to mistakes.

After years of searching for the lost princess, the viceroy decides to leave the beaten path and to take a side path. The path to the side is a metaphor for personal prayer, or *hitbodedut*.

A path is usually narrow, where one walks alone. The untrodden path to the side is therefore symbolizes one's individual and personal mode of intimate prayer.

Let's not underestimate for a single moment the power of the prescribed prayers, Psalms, and supplications, which are all vital for our spiritual health and well-being. But, without personal prayer, one cannot find "the lost princess," a metaphor for *emuna*, the full and complete belief in Hashem.

The viceroy evaluated himself and his lengthy trek along the beaten path, in other words, the viceroy realized that despite his years of praying from prayer books with prescribed prayers, he hadn't yet developed a full and complete faith in Hashem. But, once he pursued his personal path, he found *emuna*!

Realizing that no prescribed prayer could express his current mood, his process of soul-searching, and his deepest aspirations and thoughts, the viceroy had to turn to personal prayer. He also longed to thank and praise Hashem in his own words. Such a prayer cannot possibly be written anywhere, for it changes from day to day and from hour to hour. This is surely the path that will take him out of the "desert," indicative of a spiritual wasteland, to a "settlement," which symbolizes a state when one's emotions are "settled," in other words, tranquility and self-composure. With tranquility and self-composure, one attains one's soul correction and fulfills his or her true mission in life.

Always Fresh

Even though we have general obligations, each person has a specific job to do on earth according to his needed soul correction. Our individual task requires a personal and individual path in life. One cannot possibly find his or her specific individual path successfully without personal prayer. Just as each individual is different, so are personal prayers different from one another. Not only do Susan's prayers differ from Michael's prayers, but Michael's prayers differ from day to day and from hour to hour.

The events in the world around us are Hashem's way of communicating with us. These stimuli hint to us what we should pray for and how we should talk to Hashem on a particular day.

Since every day is different, and we grow and change from day to day, it's natural that our prayers from the heart change from day to day. Though many commandments are the same for all of us, such as Sabbath observance or wearing tefillin, personal prayer is our personal and creative spiritual expressiveness that is just as individual as our fingerprints. Personal prayer is always fresh, just like a new day's sunrise.

Shouting in Silence

No one should ever hear your personal prayers. Some people like to shout, scream, or sing, but they should do so out of earshot of anyone else. Yet, when it's not possible to find a totally isolated place for one's personal prayer session, one can rely of Rebbe Nachman's advice – the silent shout. A person can be sitting in the subway on the way to work surrounded by hundreds of other people, elbow to elbow. Yet, he or she can close their eyes and silently shout to Hashem from deep down in the heart. Such a cry will split the Heavens, yet the person in the adjacent seat won't hear a thing.

Since personal prayer should be intimate, we would no sooner expose our personal prayers than we would any other intimate act. No one should be privy to our private conversations with Hashem, for as soon as anyone hears us, the prayer is no longer personal.

Every step of the way

By speaking to Hashem for an hour a day every single day, we earn another benefit – we become accustomed to speaking to Hashem about everything! When we seek Hashem's advice about everything we do, when we thank Him, and when we share our innermost thoughts with Him, then we are living our lives with Hashem.

Five words summarize one's situation in the world: **Without prayer is without Hashem.** Let's be positive, for the opposite is also true: **With prayer is with Hashem.** Anything a person does with prayer means being together with Hashem. When you pray, Hashem is with you. When you don't, you're stuck with yourself, including your subjectivity, your ego, and your habits – all of which cloud the truth and prevent you from making the right decisions. But, when you do everything with Hashem – including prayer in every step of life's way – life becomes so much sweeter and easier. Why rely on our sorely limited resources when we can take advantage of Hashem's limitless knowledge and power? When we put our trust in Hashem, Hashem mobilizes all of creation to come to our aid.

It's so simple to speak to Hashem. All we have to do is open our mouths in our own words before everything we do. The way to succeed is to speak to Hashem before everything we do, every step of the way.

For example, before one eats, he or she can speak to Hashem in the following manner: "Master of the World, thank You for the food you give me. Please help me eat with holiness and with moderation. Help me say the blessings before and after the meal with proper intent. May the food I eat be beneficial to my body and conducive to good health. Help me avoid overeating. May the spiritual essence of this meal revitalize my soul, and give me the energy to seek You more and more…" You'll be amazed at how a few short sentences of personal prayer dramatically alter the dimension of whatever you do. In the example at hand, a short personal prayer uplifts a mundane meal to the level of an act of Divine service.

Short personal prayers do wonders for marital bliss. Imagine that you're just now coming home from a trying day at work. Stop for a moment, and before you walk in the front door, say a few words to Hashem, like this: "Master of the World, help me have a peaceful relationship with my wife. Open my heart so I'll understand her, and grant me the patience to listen intently to whatever she has to say and to give her the attention she needs. May there always be love and understanding between us. Please help me have a home of peace, Hashem…"

When a person comes home without Hashem, he might need to come home with a policeman instead. Those who rely on their own abilities and aptitudes stand few chances of success, especially in marriage. But, when one comes home with prayer on his lips, he's bringing Hashem into his household. The result is a home of peace and understanding.

Apply this ploy of a brief personal prayer to everything you do. Personal prayer that precedes any act is a guarantee of enhanced success. Whether you have a meeting at the bank, or you're getting in the car to drive home at rush hour, or helping one of the children with his homework, personal prayer invokes the type of constant Divine Providence that will accompany you and pave the way for whatever you're doing.

Speaking to Hashem is an expression of our *emuna*. One who truly believes, speaks to Hashem. Weak *emuna* is manifest by a low motivation for prayer, especially personal prayer.

King David said (Psalm 121:5), "Hashem is the shadow by your right side," in other words, Hashem is always with us. Just as one's shadow never leaves him, Hashem never leaves us. With every breath we take, Hashem is there with us. But, just as Hashem is with us, we should be with Hashem, speaking to Him constantly, thanking Him, and taking His advice.

Lofty perfection

Many of our sages and spiritual leaders - Chassidic, Sephardi, and Lithuanian - write about the concept of personal prayer. The Chazon Ish writes, "How wonderful it is when a person can tell his worries to his Creator as one speaks to a best friend. The Holy One blessed be He calls such a person His gratifying child."

Rabbi Yosef Chaim Zonnenfeld of blessed memory, one of the previous century's great spiritual leaders in Jerusalem, would say: "When a person accustoms himself to talking to Hashem always, he reaches the highest level of lofty perfection that he could possibly attain."

The Chofetz Chaim of blessed memory would spend at least an hour or more every day in personal prayer and asking for the full redemption of our people.

Personal prayer insures that we will successfully fulfill our intended mission in life with success.

Secret of the Good Life

Rebbe Natan of Breslev said, "Wherever I see deficiency, I see a lack of prayer." Within this statement is the secret of the good life.

If a person prays every day of his life for each of his needs – both material and spiritual – he'll certainly attain all those needs. People that fail to pray on the grounds that they have no time are like the dirty and disheveled prince that sleeps on the park bench. When a pitying bystander recognizes the prince, and asks him why he's walking around hungry and in rags, and why he doesn't ask his father the king for a hot meal, a bath, and a room in the palace, the slovenly prince answers, "I don't have time to…"

One who realizes the power of prayer will pray for all his needs, spiritual and material. On a higher spiritual level, he realizes that once he prays for spirituality, his material needs will be fulfilled automatically. For example, a benevolent king understands that his servants won't be efficient if they lack the basics of food, shelter, and clothing. Once our orientation is to serve Hashem the King as loyal servants, we see how easily our needs are fulfilled as well. Therefore, we should pray for every little detail of spirituality and take nothing for granted. We should ask Hashem to help us pray with intent, to help us learn Torah, and to successfully observe all the mitzvoth with joy. We should constantly ask Hashem to help us strengthen our *emuna* and to properly do *teshuva*. Leaving no stones unturned, we should beg Hashem to give us the right words of personal prayer every day, until we no longer have deficiencies.

Seek Hashem always

It's so important to devote a portion of one's daily personal prayer session to asking Hashem for *emuna*, as follows:

"Please Hashem, give me full and complete *emuna*. Help me believe that there's no such thing as "bad" in the world, for everything is in Your hands and everything You do is for the very best. Help me believe that You love me and that You derive gratification from me."

"Instill in me the complete *emuna* that there is no one but You. In other words, help me internalize the knowledge that no one can help me or harm me against Your will. Help me realize that anyone who brings troubles in my life is only a stick in Your loving hands to bring me closer to You. Let me fully realize that it's not my boss, my wife, or my mother-in-law that's upsetting me, but only a hint from You to arouse me to prayer and to *teshuva* ."

"Give me the *emuna* that everything is in Your hands, Hashem. Don't let me make the mistake of thinking that my talents and abilities are the cause of my successes. Help me invest my primary efforts in prayer. Let me believe that my deficiencies all stem from a deficiency of prayer…"

My prayer

Personal prayers are the necessary complement to the thrice-daily prescribed prayers. Personal prayers touch on all the intimate personal points that prescribed prayers don't. For that reason, the great *tzaddikim* throughout the generations invested extensive time and effort into personal prayer in addition to the prescribed prayers that they said slowly and soulfully, word for word. If the great *tzaddikim* devoted so much to correcting their "deficiencies" with personal prayer, then we with all we need to correct should certainly devote all we can to personal prayer.

Rabbi Yisrael Meir of Radin, the "Chofetz Chaim" of saintly and blessed memory, writes (*Likutei Amarim* 10:47):

"… If we would have prayed and spilled our hearts out to Hashem, our requests would have been fulfilled. Therefore, let one not be content with the thrice-daily prescribed *Shemona-Esrei* prayer, but throughout the day, let him pour out his prayers and supplications between himself and his Creator from his own home and from the bottom of his heart.

Torah and Divine service

Let's make no mistake and think that we can now put Torah learning aside in favor of prayer – Heaven forbid. One must totally immerse oneself in Torah – day and night – to the very best of one's abilities. Indeed, Torah strengthens our prayers, as Rebbe Nachman says (see *Abridged Likutei Moharan*, I:2), "Torah and prayer maintain one another and strengthen one another. Therefore, we must occupy ourselves with both. When a person learns Torah in order to observe and practice, then the holy letters of the Torah - which are sparks of souls - envelope themselves in that person's prayers and magnify the light of those prayers extremely."

Prayer without Torah is weak and empty, so we certainly must learn Torah. On the other hand, it's impossible to gain true Torah understanding without praying for it. Rabbi Akiva spilled rivers of tears in order to uplift himself from a simple peasant to one of history's hallmark Torah scholars. The famed "Ben Ish Chai" - Rabbi Yosef Chaim of Baghdad - devoted hours upon hours to personal prayer. The Chofetz Chaim set aside two hours a day for secluded personal prayer and soul searching, in addition to his exhaustive daily schedule of Torah learning and prescribed prayers.

Our holy Book of Psalms is the exalted remnant of King David's many personal prayers and the river of tears he shed every single day. The common denominator of the great *tzaddikim* is the time and effort that they invested in personal prayer.

If those great righteous men who clung to Hashem and to His Torah with all their being and all their might invested so much effort in personal prayer and asking Hashem to bring them close to Him, then one who is far away from Hashem should certainly pray continually in seeking Hashem's proximity. One should ask Hashem to bring him closer, to help him do *teshuva*, and to help him learn, observe, and teach Torah. We all must beg Hashem to protect us from sin and from the influences of the evil inclination, both external and the one within us. Overcoming a single bad habit or bodily appetite in itself requires tenacity in prayer and repeated daily requests for compassion and Divine assistance in overcoming and correcting lusts and negative traits that separate between us and between Hashem's light, Heaven forbid. A person must know that his or her personal salvation depends on prayer!

If one merits, it becomes an elixir of life

Frequently, people who have been learning Torah their entire lives come to me with their problems. I ask myself, what could be better than total absorption in Torah since three years old? Nevertheless, many of them are confused and stressed, often despairing and worrying about their respective tribulations and difficulties in life. They seem unable to escape the darkness that envelops them. Why? What are they lacking? They're light years away from their personal salvation and redemption because they're light years away from genuine prayer. Without prayer from the heart – and lots of it – they can't possibly implement on a practical basis what they learn.

The best way to implement what we learn is to pray for it. One who learns day and night, even with the lofty intent that he will practice everything he learns, must nonetheless pray to do so. Furthermore, our sages tell us that if a person has no intention of implementing on a daily basis the Torah he learns, then he'd be better off not learning Torah at all. Since implementing the Torah depends on prayer, then one who doesn't pray shows that he has no intention of putting what he learns into practice. Also, without prayer, one has no connection with Hashem, for prayer is the means whereby we connect to Hashem. Why learn Torah if one has no desire to connect with Hashem?

According to Rebbe Nachman's teachings (see *Likutei Moharan* I:22), the expression of sincere Torah learning is when the light of Torah stimulates a person to prayer. When prayer is combined with Torah, a person steadily ascends the spiritual ladder, and comprehends today what was beyond his comprehension yesterday.

Rebbe Nachman adds (ibid, 25) that a person who prays for Hashem's assistance in fulfilling the Torah he learns not only merits to find the truth and to attain a full understanding of what he has learned, but Hashem personally directs him on the path of truth and righteousness. More than anything, Hashem derives enormous gratification from a person who brings his Torah learning into his prayers.

Prayer builds receptacles for Divine abundance. Without prayer, a person can't absorb the light of the Torah that he learns. Without Torah, a person remains an ignoramus; there is no way that he can properly observe Hashem's commandments, for he doesn't know what's permissible and what's forbidden. But, learning alone is not sufficient. It's no simple task for the heart to internalize what the brain has learned. That's why we need extensive prayer, especially personal prayer. Prayer is an important part of observing the Torah.

Rebbe Nachman also teaches (ibid, 101) that acceptance of the yoke of Torah and intensive learning of Torah is conducive to overcoming negative character traits. Apparently, it would seem that learning - especially intensive learning - is enough for character improvement. Yet, without prayer, the power of Torah could be misused to enhance and strengthen one's negative traits rather than uproot them. Torah resembles atomic power: one can use it to illuminate a city or to destroy a city. Prayer assures that the power of Torah will be channeled into self-perfection rather than self-destruction, when a person uses the Torah to further inflate his ego or to disagree with truly righteous people.

A person needs extensive personal prayer to derive Torah's true benefits. One must ask for Hashem's help in learning Torah for the right reasons. There's a gigantic difference between a person that learns Torah for prestige and for ego enhancement and a person that learns Torah for the sake of acquiring the love of Hashem, a pure heart, and a perfection of character. Therefore, we must all ask for Divine mercy in helping us use the fire of Torah in the proper way. We can't leave this up to "luck", for our sages said that Torah properly learned is the elixir of life, but if improperly learned, it's a deadly poison, Heaven forbid.

Our prayers to learn Torah properly and to apply in our daily lives the laws and lessons that we learn should also be complemented with prayers of gratitude for whatever Torah we have been privileged to learn that particular day, no matter how much or little.

Vessels of abundance

One person told me that he doesn't ask Hashem for anything in his personal prayer, but only thanks Hashem for his blessings. I told him that by refraining to ask for anything from Hashem, he's denying limitless gratification from Hashem. A Hebrew folk expression says that the cow wants to give milk even more than the calf wants to drink. Hashem created the world in order to bestow His loving-kindness on mankind. Even more than man yearns for Divine abundance, Hashem desires to bestow His Divine abundance on man. Rebbe Nachman of Breslev therefore says (ibid, 102) that a person should therefore pray to invoke Divine abundance for himself and for the entire world.

The success of Israel and the Jews is a special sanctification of Hashem's name. Israel is a tiny country that according to natural phenomena and logic should have ceased to exist long ago. The Jews are a miniscule people on a quantitative basis. The fact that Israel and the Jewish people not only exist but flourish is a clear indication of Divine abundance. The nations of the world recognize that such success can only be attributed to Divine intervention, providence, and abundance.

Prayer is the means whereby we bring Divine abundance from the upper spiritual worlds to our low material world. The words of prayer are vessels of abundance. Imagine that a person is a wheat field at the time of harvest: the owner of the field invites him to take home as much wheat as he can carry. An unprepared person tries to stuff as many wheat grains as he can in his pockets, and carries whatever he can in his fists. Maybe he'll walk away with a pound or two of wheat. But, if the same person comes prepared for a burlap sack, he'll be able to walk away with fifty pounds of wheat. Even more so, if a person comes to the field with a pack mule and four burlap sacks, he'll walk away with two hundred pounds of wheat. In like manner, the more we pray, the more we create receptacles for Divine abundance.

The abundance we receive through prayer is so much more blessed that what we receive automatically, without prayer. Indeed, when a person lacks adequate vessels for Divine abundance, Hashem will refrain from sending the Divine abundance. No person in his right mind would pour a fine wine all over the table and on the floor if he couldn't find a proper wine goblet. Hashem too will not send down

Divine abundance if a person lacks an adequate receptacle. This causes untold anguish to Hashem, for He wants to give us all types of abundance in both spiritual and material forms as well.

If prayer is an adequate vessel of Divine abundance, then prayer that includes *teshuva,* or atonement for wrongdoing, is an especially superb vessel for Divine abundance.

We can conclude that one cannot receive Divine abundance without prayer, for two reasons: First, prayer stimulates *teshuva,* and *teshuva* invokes Divine abundance. Second, prayer creates a vessel for Divine abundance. One who doesn't pray inhibits the Divine desire to bestow abundance on the world.

The Master of Prayer's people

The words of prayer that become the spiritual vessels for Divine abundance are not necessarily the words of personal prayer only. Even the prescribed prayers, the recitation of Psalms, and any other prayer creates vessels for Divine abundance. Remember, that whenever you pray, you are bringing gratification to Hashem and stimulating the flow of Divine abundance. Such knowledge will help us all pray with more incentive and intent.

It's not enough to open our mouths and pray. In effect, we have to pray for the privilege of prayer. There are so many internal and external hindrances to prayer that we must ask Hashem's help in succeeding to pray in an earnest, sincere, and directed manner. Even more, we should pray to Hashem to help us feel happiness and spiritual stimulation, and enable us to sing our prayers and praises in the way that the Master of Prayer's people did. This should be our role model – we should strive to be one of the Master of Prayer's people.

Prayer in effect is a person's personal redemption. When a person succeeds in getting close to Hashem by way of prayer, for all practical purposes he is a redeemed person since his soul is no longer in exile. So, when we pray for Hashem's assistance in helping us pray, we are actually praying for our personal redemption.

Here's an example of how we should pray for Hashem's assistance in helping us pray: "Master of the World, please grant me the privilege to pray properly. Help me take my prescribed prayers seriously. In Your loving grace, help me say all my prayers – *Shacharit*, *Mincha*, Maariv, Psalms, *Tikkun Klali*, *Tikkun Chatzot* or whatever else I'm praying – with proper intent and with all my heart. Let me understand that my prime mode of connection to You is by way of prayer. Help me say my prayers in moderation, word for word, without rushing. Let me feel that I'm standing before You, my magnificent, loving, and all-powerful Father and King. Enable me to cling to You. Help me overcome the evil inclination that does everything in its power to obstruct my prayers and distract me from praying. Save me from foreign and extraneous thoughts, grant me pure thoughts, and help me think only of You when I'm praying. Help me believe in prayer and that my prayers reach the Heavenly throne. Give me complete *emuna*, so that I'll have the incentive to pray with all my heart and with all my might."

The evil inclination's hindrance to our prayers is tangibly apparent. Everyone knows that there's nothing better than Hashem and nothing sweeter than clinging to Hashem. The Jewish soul yearns to cling to Divine light, and seeks it always. Then – all of a sudden – when a person has the opportunity to pray and to cling to Hashem, he rushes through his prayers, mumbling them in a perfunctory manner. What could be more ridiculous or illogical? In such a manner, the evil inclination ruins the prayers of the entire world.

Once a person believes in the power of prayer and is convinced that prayer is the key to his personal redemption, he'll have the incentive to strive for pure and sincere prayer. Once a person becomes accustomed to prayer, he won't be able to live without it. We can now understand what Rebbe Natan of Breslev meant when he said, "My *Moshiach* has already come," since he invested so much time and effort into prayer. Any person that does likewise will ultimately feel that his or her personal *Moshiach* has arrived too.

Straight from the heart

The only way to overcome the evil inclination is by prayer. The *Gemara* (tractate *Succa*, 52b) says, "A person's evil inclination overcomes him every single day, and unless The Holy One blessed be He helps him, he cannot prevail." Therefore, our prayers requesting Divine assistance are crucial to the success of our prayers. We therefore must "pray to pray."

Rabbi Joseph Caro (*Shulchan Oruch, Orach Chaim*, Ch. 98) cites the Talmud (tractate *Berachot*, Ch. 5, *Mishna* 1), that the pious of former generations would meditate for an hour before praying so that their prayers would be properly intent. One might ask, why does Rabbi Caro, author and compiler of the classic *Shulchan Oruch* Code of Jewish Law, tell an anecdote from the *Mishna* in the middle of his extrapolation on the laws of the morning prayers? Since when is the Code of Jewish Law a place for the tales of *tzaddikim*?

Rabbi Caro isn't merely telling tales of yesteryear – he is showing how a person must conduct himself to attain a level of sincere prayer. Since the evil inclination vehemently obstructs our efforts to pray, we must make the proper preparations in reinforcing our prayers. Therefore, before we pray, we should take a few moments to contemplate what we're about to do and before Whom we will be standing – Hashem, the King of Kings. We should ask Hashem to help us pray in moderation, with love, and from the heart, not emptily repeating the words like a parrot. And, if the righteous men of former generations invested an entire hour of meditation in preparation of each prayer, then we certainly need to prepare our weak and materially-oriented minds if we want to pray with intent and enthusiasm.

The fact that Rabbi Caro included the above anecdote in the Code of Jewish Law shows that even the great Mishnaic sages needed to compose themselves, collect their thoughts, and prepare for an entire hour in order to properly pray. Without proper preparation, a person comes into prayer "cold," and his prayer is liable be sorely lacking in intent and concentration.

Imagine how much you'd prepare yourself before an important meeting with the head of your company or with a head of state. We have to stop and contemplate what we're about to do before we pray. In other words, we're about to speak to the Master of the World, the King of Kings. It goes without saying that the more we believe that we are standing before our awesome, great and mighty Creator, the more we feel the need to prepare ourselves.

Our daily commitments and pressure for time don't always leave us with adequate pre-prayer preparation time. Nevertheless, we should at least try to say a short personal preparation prayer, like this: "Master of the World, here I am standing before You, about to pray. You know how strong the evil inclination's resistance is to my prayers. This evil inclination makes me feel like the prayer is a heavy burden on my back, something I want to be quickly over and done with. Please have mercy on me and help me defeat the evil inclination so that I won't take my prayers lightly. Instead, help me say each word deliberately while connecting my heart and my mouth together so that my prayers will be sincere and worthy. Help me attain the spiritual and material abundance that prayer is capable of invoking, and grant me what I need in material and spiritual blessings – peace, good health, a good income, food, clothing, etc. and above all *emuna*, so that I can serve You properly."

The above prayer, or something similar in your own words and thoughts, is a wonderful preface to any prayer, whether prescribed prayer, Psalms, *Likutei Tefillot*, or personal prayer. Personal prayer is always stronger when we begin by asking Hashem for help in giving us the write words in expressing our innermost feelings. The evil inclination's distractions are especially strong when it come to the three daily prayers of *Shacharit*, *Mincha*, and *Maariv*. People are so used to thrice-daily prayers that they sometimes fall into a complete spiritual slumber during these prayers. This is especially true when it comes to the "*Shemona Esrei*" prayer, also known as the "*Amida*." Anytime a person feels that prayer is becoming rote, routine, or a burden, then he must stop and immediately pray for urgent Divine assistance. One must also be careful not to let daily personal prayer become rote, routine, or a burden.

The only way to insure that our prayers are sincere and heartfelt is to pray for Hashem's assistance in praying. Prayer is not only a person's main weapon; the entire redemption of our people depends on prayer.

Don't be smug

Some people are smug when it comes to prayer. They claim that the prescribed prayers are all they need. But, from what we've discussed up until now, effective prayer is virtually impossible without preparatory personal prayer. The *Gemara* itself testifies that a person cannot overcome the evil inclination unless Hashem comes to his aid. Hashem wants us to arouse ourselves and seek His help. In that respect, the evil inclination actually does us a favor in forcing us to seek Hashem.

Let's suppose that a person does succeed in praying the *Shemona Esrei* prayer with proper intent even without initial preparation. Even so, the *Shemona Esrei* prayer is no replacement for personal prayer. The *Shemona Esrei* prayer doesn't exempt a person from personal prayer either. One cannot possibly do extensive soul-searching and self evaluation during the *Shemona Esrei* prayer, nor can one thank Hashem for all the previous day's wonderful blessings. The intimate and extensive prayers that constitute the outpouring of our soul are best said during personal prayer.

One of the topics that we should include in our daily personal prayer session is the request that Hashem should put the right words in our mouth, help us enjoy and love praying, and to help us concentrate on our prayers. The evil inclination is very strong in dispersing a person's thoughts, like an unruly horse that carries its rider off the main path and into a thicket that goes nowhere. We need Hashem's help in keeping our prayers directed, just like a rider needs strength in handling a wily steed. For that, we need to pray for our success in prayer.

The four sons – substitute for suffering

There's a way to mitigate or to altogether neutralize our suffering and tribulations in this world, as we'll see in the following example:

A father punishes his son. If the son is stupid, he bears malice in his heart toward his father and hates him.

If this son has some sense, he understands that he was punished for a reason, even though he doesn't like the punishment. When he realizes what he did wrong, he admits his wrongdoing, expresses his remorse, apologizes, and promises to improve his ways. Even if he doesn't understand exactly what he did wrong, he asks his father's forgiveness in a general manner and says, "I'm sorry for upsetting you, Dad – help me to avoid making the same mistakes in the future."

A truly intelligent son realizes that his father loves him and that the punishment was for his ultimate benefit. He therefore willfully accepts the punishment, turns to his father and says: "Dad, I know that your intent was to wake me up and to bring me closer to you.

Thanks so much for paying such close attention to me – that really means a lot to me. Dad, please explain to me what I did wrong and help me improve…" Once the father shows the son his mistake, the son expresses remorse, admits the mistake, asks his father's forgiveness, and makes a firm resolution to do better in the future.

The third son is on a lofty level of spiritual awareness. He appreciates tribulations since he recognizes that he has deficiencies that need correcting.

Then again, there's a fourth son who surpasses all of his three brothers. He doesn't wait to be punished in order to improve his ways. Every day, he does a thorough process of self-evaluation where he weighs everything he did that day and asks himself if his deeds are really upright in light of his father's requests and standards. He then speaks to his father every single day and says, "Dad, by virtue of the wonderful education you gave me, I was fortunate in doing such-and-such good deeds. Thanks so much. On the other hand, I don't think my speech or behavior in a certain situation today was the way you would have wanted. I'm really sorry and I'll try my best to strengthen this weakness…"

The father of such a son glows with satisfaction and gratification. "What a beautiful human being! What a sensitive, considerate, and humble son! He doesn't wait for me to punish him – he's always trying to improve. Even if he were to do something seriously wrong, how could I punish him? He's constantly evaluating himself; he's always striving to fulfill my wishes. So, even if he does make a mistake, I'll just give him a gentle hint. With his sensitivity, he'll surely understand." The father will want nothing more than to fulfill this wonderful son's wishes.

Continuing to ponder his sons, the father says, "I wish my other three boys would come and speak to me on their own initiative every day. If they only realized how much I loved them, they'd ask for whatever they want and I'd be happy to give it to them. Even my son that bears malice toward me would realize how much I love him if he would only speak with me every day."

The loving son

Imagine a loving son or daughter that thanks a parent profusely every single day for every little amenity that he or she received. Imagine that the same son or daughter always confesses wrongdoing without having to be reprimanded. If that's not enough, the son or daughter always seeks more and more of the parent's love. If this were your child, how in the world could you ever punish him?

We can now understand how to be Hashem's beloved sons and daughters. All we have to do is to set aside an hour a day for prayer in solitude, whether out in the field, in the office or in the kitchen at home, and speak to Hashem – our beloved Father in Heaven – in our own words. We take stock of everything we did in the previous twenty-four hours since our last session of *hitbodedut*, or personal prayer in solitude. We judge ourselves on three levels – thoughts, speech, and deeds. We rectify our wrongdoings and resolve to improve. We ask Hashem to bring us closer to Him. Such a process of personal prayer frees a person from stress, worry, sadness, and all other negative emotions. Even better, when we judge ourselves, Hashem doesn't let the Heavenly court judge us, and we save ourselves untold anguish and severe judgments.

Pay attention

One who devotes an hour a day to personal prayer is on an even higher spiritual level than a person who accepts his tribulations with joy, for the former doesn't wait to be aroused by tribulations; he seeks to serve Hashem more and more on his own accord.

The *Gemara* says (tractate *Berachot* 7), that one measure of self-discipline is more effective than a hundred lashes. As such, the self-disciplined person saves himself limitless troubles in life.

Dear reader, stop and think about the wonderful gift that Hashem has given us by enabling us to speak to Him whenever we want to, any time day or night. We can now begin to understand what Rebbe Nachman of Breslev meant when he said that *hitbodedut* is more virtuous than literally anything else!

Start walking!

A group of friends once made a trip together. On the way to their destination, they saw someone standing with a backpack on a desert crossroads. Seven days later, on their way home, they encountered the same person with the backpack standing on the same desert crossroads in the hot sun. The group of friends asked the backpacker, "Why are you standing here?"

"I want to go to Jerusalem," responded the backpacker. "I'm waiting for a ride."

"How long have you been waiting?" they asked.

"More than a week," he answered.

They laughed. "Jerusalem's only a two-day walk from here. If you'd have started walking, you could have been there and back four times already!"

Many of us want to change, yet we expect it to happen automatically, with no effort on our part. Life doesn't work that way. An old Hebrew expression says, "Even a journey of a thousand kilometers begins with a first step."

The first step toward *teshuva,* self-correction, and character perfection is establishing a daily 60-minute session of personal prayer and self-evaluation. Nothing is so conducive to self-improvement as an hour a day of judging oneself, thanking Hashem, expressing hopes and aspirations, and praying for them.

A person that wants to improve, yet doesn't set aside a daily hour of personal prayer, resembles a person that wants to go somewhere yet doesn't take the first step in the proper direction. The only effective and practical means that we have at our disposal for improving character, overcoming lusts and bad habits, and avoiding transgression – even for correcting all of our previous reincarnations – is daily personal prayer and self evaluation.

What are you afraid of?

There's a catchy and cogent expression in Hebrew: **He who fears One, fears no one.**

Daily personal prayer than includes self-evaluation and *teshuva* is a clear sign that a person fears Hashem. *Teshuva* includes confessing our wrongdoing, expressing remorse, asking Hashem's forgiveness, and resolving to do our best to improve our ways in the future.

Repeated transgression without daily personal prayer and *teshuva* is a clear sign that a person has no fear of Hashem. So, with no fear of Hashem, he ends up deathly afraid of everybody else in the world – his employer, his neighbors, his competitors, the IRS – everyone! Therefore, fear, worries and anxiety can often be traced to a lack of daily personal prayer, which means that one doesn't truly fear Hashem.

The fear of Hashem (*Yir'at Shamayim*)

A man of truth knows that he commits serious transgressions on a daily basis. Here covets another man's wife and there he looks at a woman other than his wife. He deviates from the truth in business or says something derogative about his neighbor or colleague. His mind may have been far away from the prayer book that morning, or he said his blessings with no intent at all. In one instance, he completely forgets to say a blessing yet in another instance, he made a blessing that was superfluous. He's oftentimes disappointed with his lot in life and walks around depressed, which in itself is a transgression of Torah.

In short, a person commits a number of serious sins every single day. When he doesn't evaluate himself and ask Hashem's forgiveness on a daily basis, he neither fears Hashem or the consequences of his misdeeds. The lower-level fear of Hashem is a fear of retribution; one who fails to do *teshuva* on a daily basis doesn't even have that. The higher level fear of Hashem is the fear that we've done something to sadden Hashem, our loving and compassionate Father in Heaven, instead of bringing Him gratification. This is an exalted form of fearing Hashem, for it is rooted in the love of Hashem. *Teshuva* on this level is called "*teshuva* from love," and it has the power not only of cleansing all wrongdoing, but it can convert a person's transgressions into merits.

A person that seeks a sweet and satisfying life of *emuna, teshuva,* and joy – a life devoid of worry, anxiety, or fear of anything – must set aside an hour a day for personal prayer, self-evaluation, and simply to share his innermost thoughts with Hashem. It's impossible to overestimate the benefit one's soul derives from this daily hour of being completely together with Hashem.

Here's an example of *teshuva* in a typical daily personal prayer session"

"Hashem, please forgive me, for I unwittingly slipped up and (*describe whatever you did wrong*). Please don't be angry with me, and help me atone for my sins. Please be patient with me and don't punish me, because I'm sincerely trying my best to do better. I know that I still have a long way to go in overcoming my bodily appetites and bad habits that cause me to sin repeatedly. But believe me, Hashem, I didn't do this intentionally, and the last thing in the world I want to do is to sadden or disappoint you. I'm truly ashamed of what I did, and I beg your forgiveness. Please give me the inner strength and courage to do what's right, and to avoid making the same mistakes in the future. Hashem, please don't hide Your Divine Presence from me."

"Hashem, I'm only flesh-and-blood. My evil inclination always seems to know when to hone in on my weaknesses. I feel like a glassmaker that works for days on a fine crystal goblet – with one thoughtless nudge of the elbow, the goblet is smashed into smithereens on the floor. Hashem, I have such a tremendous desire to do Your will, but I repeatedly crash on the floor like broken glass. Please pick me up and help me start anew. Bring me close to You. Please help me overcome my evil inclination and to do Your will so I won't transgress anymore."

"Master of the world, my body aches (*state your sickness – physical or emotional - and what part of your body hurts or fails to function properly*). You are surely just in everything You do. If I hadn't sinned, I most likely wouldn't be suffering such anguish now. But please, Hashem, show me what I did wrong and why I'm suffering. Help me correct the root cause and guide me on the path of true and complete *teshuva*. My beloved Father in Heaven, please forgive me for my wrongdoing, for the pain of knowing how much I've gone against Your will is even more severe than my bodily pain. Please be patient and compassionate with me, and help me return to You with a pure and loving heart..."

Such daily personal prayer saves the wear and tear of fearing the police, the criminals, terrorists, stray dogs, the government, income tax or anyone else. Fearing Hashem is therefore like one-stop shopping: **He who fears One, fears no one.** The fear of Hashem is the gate to spiritual awareness, Torah comprehension, and humility. One who fears Hashem also merits the gift of dedication in prayer, where he is able to cast aside his ego and to completely subjugate himself to Hashem.

One of the finest benefits of a daily hour of personal prayer is *emuna*. A person that attains *emuna* is a person that lives a good life of joy and satisfaction.

A person that speaks to Hashem daily is capable of bouncing back on his feet after every setback. He's not heartbroken or depressed about his failures, because He knows that Hashem will not only pick him up, but help him to reach new heights, for in spirituality, rebounding from a descent leads to an even greater ascent. Such an individual never despairs, for he always has Hashem to turn to. In the most trying of times, he maintains his self composure for he knows that Hashem is always there to protect him and rescue him from all peril. To paraphrase a popular song from several decades ago, he just calls Hashem's name and no matter wherever he is, Hashem is there for him.

A respite from the rat race

In Hebrew, self-evaluation is called *cheshbon hanefesh*, or "accounting of the soul." We could write an entire separate volume listing the virtues and the praises that our sages said about daily self-evaluation, particularly the daily self-evaluation that's a part of one's daily hour-long personal prayer session. The greatest benefit of such a session is self-composure. For an hour a day, we take a respite from the rat race and take stock in ourselves – what we've done, where we are, and where we're heading.

A person with no purpose in life doesn't particularly care where he is or where he's going. But, once we have a goal in life, we owe it to ourselves to evaluate ourselves on a regular basis. Are we proud of our actions? Are we doing the right thing to realize our goals? A pilot for example always has one eye glued to his avionics – he doesn't deviate from the vector that guides him to his destination. In like manner, our daily self evaluation is our spiritual navigation tool. Without it, a person is virtually lost in the world.

How silly it would be for a pilot to say that he doesn't have time to check his headings. Yet, we allow the rat race to consume all of our time to the extent that some of us claim that there's no time in the day's hectic schedule for an hour of personal prayer! No wonder so many people are confused and lost. For that reason, our sages instructed us to get off the crazy rate-race carousel that spins endlessly round and round – at least for an hour a day – and to find ourselves a quiet place where we can spend a soothing hour in personal prayer and self-evaluation. Unfortunately, many people fail to do so, missing a golden opportunity to attain self-composure, emotional stability, a correction of the soul and their own personal redemption – four of the many wonderful benefits of daily personal prayer and self-evaluation.

Each new day

Imagine a family that buys a loaf of bread, a quart of milk, and a dozen eggs at the grocery store every day. Had they paid cash, their daily bill would have been approximately $5.50. Yet, every day, they charged the purchase. With thirty such purchases a month, they ran up a monthly bill of $165.00. Ten months later, the bill was yet unpaid, and the grocer demanded the immediate sum of $1, 650 for the accumulated debts. The head of the household was devastated; where would he get the money to pay such a massive bill when he barely had enough to pay the rent? If he would have paid his bills daily, he would have only been called upon to lay out an insignificant five and a half dollars a day.

People who don't devote a daily hour to introspection and personal prayer are called upon from time to time to pay the consequences of their uncorrected character traits or bad habits. Overcoming a negative trait or bad habit is like climbing a mountain peak. Who's capable of leaping over a mountain in one fell swoop? Yet, any mountain can be climbed step by step.

With daily personal prayer, we correct ourselves little by little, slowly but surely. We gradually climb the difficult peaks and pay our emotional and spiritual debts day by day, so we're not hit with tremendous spiritual bills at the end of the year. With no outstanding debts, we save ourselves untold severe judgments. Therefore, it's so very important that personal prayer and self-evaluation be done on a daily basis. With daily *teshuva*, a person maintains a constantly clean spiritual slate, which is conducive to emotional health and a sensation of happiness and well-being.

Now we can understand why some people have tried personal prayer but where disheartened almost immediately. Their *hitbodedut* left them with a feeling of sadness and melancholy. In light of the above, this is clear! As soon as such people took a serious look at themselves, they were overwhelmed with the revelation of what they saw. Rather than committing to fulfill our sages' directive that each person set aside a daily hour for self-evaluation, and thereby making the first important step to climbing their own personal mountain of challenges, they give up altogether. Nothing strengthens a person so much as daily "accounting of the soul" and outpouring one's heart to Hashem. In time, daily personal prayer brings dramatic results.

The power of perseverance

Gratitude is also an important part of one's daily personal prayer agenda. A person who fails to thank Hashem for his myriad of blessings every day both fails to recognize those blessings and takes them for granted. But, with daily thanks to Hashem, we observe the wonderful favors that Hashem does for us every day and we don't fall into the pitfalls of ingratitude.

No one likes an ingrate. Yet, if we're not perseverant about designating daily time for thanking Hashem, we either fail to recognize all the gifts that Hashem gave us that day (every heartbeat, every breath, shelter, clothing – think about it, the list is endless!) or we forget to thank Him altogether.

The barometer of *emuna* is satisfaction with one's lot in life. When we ponder our blessings, we appreciate them much more and express our gratitude. In that respect, perseverant personal prayer enhances one's satisfaction with his lot in life, and is therefore conducive to *emuna*. Reinforced *emuna* enables us to be closer to Hashem.

The three elements of daily gratitude, self-evaluation, and *teshuva* that are all incorporated in our personal prayer are marvelous for emotional and spiritual health.

A daily requirement

Rebbe Nachman of Breslev regards daily personal prayer as an absolute requirement for every person. He says (*Likutei Moharan*, I:100), "From young to old [literally, from "small to big"], one cannot be a truly upright [literally, a kosher] person without *hitbodedut*."

Why an hour a day? Many of our sages instructed the general populace to do at least an hour or more every day of personal prayer and soul-searching. Rebbe Nachman writes (ibid, II:25), "*Hitbodedut* is a lofty virtue and greater than anything, in other words, to designate **an hour or more** for secluded personal prayer in a room or out in the field and to converse with his Creator…this form of praying and speaking should be in his own spoken jargon." This daily hour is not only the key to a person's self composure, but a key to his emotional health and spiritual success. Without it, a person is liable to forget what he's really supposed to be doing in this world.

Self Evaluation

At the end of each day, a person has to ask himself what he's gained by transgressing the Torah, G-d forbid, and compare that with what he stands to lose by going against Hashem's will. On the other hand, he should ask himself what he's lost by doing a mitzvah, and compare that with what he stands to gain by doing Hashem's will (see *Pirkei Avot*, 2:1).

Anyone that engages in self evaluation is guaranteed to see the benefits of doing Hashem's will. He doesn't even have to wait until the world to come to reap his rewards, for in this world, he will already experience a sense of gratification, joy, and satisfaction. As for the next world, unfathomable rewards await him. Compare this to material amenities; we all know that they never satisfy us. Even when we dream of some material goal, once we reach it, we're not satisfied, especially since the neighbor has something better than we do. The jealousy and competition of this world leave us with a terrible bitter taste in our mouths.

Rebbe Nachman described the evil inclination as someone running in the marketplace with a closed fist. Everybody runs after him, because they think he has some rare treasure in his hand. After they've spent an entire day chasing him, he opens his hand and waves his empty palm at them, laughing at their gullibility. They wasted an entire day for nothing.

The same goes for bodily lusts. One would think that a person would be happy once he attains whatever he desires, but the opposite is true. Take for example the meal that a glutton eats in a fancy restaurant; after the meal, he has a guilty conscience about over-eating and breaking his diet. What's worse, he has to pay an exorbitant price for food that he now regrets eating. His body suffers, his conscience suffers, and his wallet suffers. Such is the outcome of bodily lusts.

On the other hand, mitzvahs impart a glowing illumination on the soul. Sure, maybe he didn't have the money to help a person in need, but once he strengthens himself and performs the mitzvah, his soul glows with gratification. With true self evaluation, when a person takes inventory of his day's deeds, he'll discover that a ten-dollar mitzvah is worth more to him than millions, for more than anything, the mitzvah brings a person closer to Hashem. Proximity to Hashem is a priceless commodity for the soul.

Daily self-evaluation helps us to keep our lives and goals in proper perspective. We can therefore conclude that a person who is close to self-evaluation is close to Hashem. By the same token, one who is far from self-evaluation is far from Hashem.

The way of the Torah is the way to a good life, marital bliss, successful children, adequate income and a myriad of other blessings. A Torah lifestyle is interesting, for one who learns Torah on a daily basis always his fresh challenges and intellectual stimulation. Compare this to a life of lust, bodily appetites, and pursuit of material amenities. They are all a mirage, a fantasy bubble that bursts and leaves a person with nothing. In fact, at the time of this writing, the world has entered a major financial recession, characterized by a crash of the stock exchange, bankruptcy of financial institutions and major corporations, and widespread unemployment. Millions who have devoted their lives to monetary goals are now left with nothing.

Without daily self-evaluation, a person will lack the inner strength and conviction that he needs to avoid the lies and pitfalls of this lowly material world. With daily self-evaluation, one will taste the sweetness of a life of truth and purpose.

What's the point of all the bodily lusts?

Rebbe Nachman calls self-evaluation. "self-composure." He says (*Likutei Moharan* II:10), "People are distant from Hashem because they lack self-composure… (they should ask themselves) what's the point of all the bodily lusts and the extra-bodily lusts such as prestige; then, they would surely return to Hashem."

Once we learn the teaching of our sages, we see that Rebbe Nachman's above thoughts are no nuance. Rebbe Nachman is therefore very firm in requiring us to devote an hour a day to personal prayer and self-evaluation.

The path through the maze

Our daily self-evaluation session is a golden opportunity to look objectively at what we've done during the previous 24 hours on the three levels of thoughts, speech, and deed. Then we can reexamine our priorities and make a plan of action to implement the changes that we'd like to make.

The temptations of transgressions and bodily appetites are like chocolate-covered poison: they're sweet, tasty and aromatic in the mouth, but once they're swallowed – look out! A life without daily self-evaluation is like a life of chocolate-covered poison. People stuff it in their mouths and gobble it down, then suffer the bitter consequences for years. With daily self-evaluation, we stop and ask ourselves, "Hey, what am I doing? Is this good for me? What did I benefit from 30 minutes of overeating (*or fill in any other bodily appetite or transgression that caught you off guard*)?" Such daily self-evaluation gives a person the strength and composure to overcome the evil inclination.

In his classic book "The Path of the Just," Rabbi Moshe Chaim Luzzato describes this world as a maze of paths, and whoever has no control over his evil inclination is trapped within the maze without knowing which path to take to reach his destination. If he doesn't know the way out, he certainly can't lead others out. But, the select few who rule over their evil inclinations know the way out of the maze and are therefore capable of leading others. We can trust their advice.

Rabbi Moshe Chaim Luzzato is one of the lofty *tzaddikim* who totally controlled his evil inclination. His "The Path of the Just" has been a leading handbook for those who seek Hashem for over three centuries already. Rabbi Luzzato calls upon the reader to set aside time for secluded personal prayer, observation, self-evaluation, and implementation of ways to purify his deeds and his character. In order to correct ourselves, we must first take a good look at ourselves.

The advice of all the great *tzaddikim* – and not just Rebbe Nachman – is to implement daily personal prayer and self evaluation in our lives. This is the time-tested path to character perfection and realization of personal potential.

The Rambam teaches that we need not expose our faults and misdeeds to others. The way to deal with them, though, is through our daily personal prayer session with Hashem.

The truly straight path

Rebbe Nachman lists another virtue of personal prayer that includes self evaluation and confession of sin (see *Likutei Moharan* I:4), namely, that when a person confesses his misdeeds every day, then Hashem leads that person on the path of a true soul correction according to the his individual spiritual needs. Consequently, such a person succeeds in fulfilling his mission here on earth, which was the reason his soul was sent here in the first place.

On the other hand, a person who neglects personal prayer, self-evaluation, confession and the consequent self-improvement and soul correction that result, has no idea where he's going in life. He doesn't know what his mission is at all. Lacking a clear destination, a person certainly has no idea which path to choose. The result is wasted potential, wasted time, and an unfulfilling life.

As long as a person fails to understand what he's doing here in this world and why he came here, he won't be able to correct himself, much less correct his previous reincarnations. If he fails to incorporate daily soul-searching and *teshuva* into his life, he'll simply accumulate more and more uncorrected misdeeds. Imagine that a small misdeed is only a tiny blemish on the soul; but, if uncorrected, the many accumulated blemishes soon become a thick dark cloud that totally blocks Divine light from reaching the soul. Cut off from Hashem's light, a person becomes arrogant and drifts away from true Torah observance. He deviates from the truly straight path that would have been his path to greatness, and walks a crooked path to personal and spiritual oblivion.

Daily personal prayer and self-evaluation enable a person to "fine-tune" and correct himself every single day. Hashem readily forgives him of his misdeeds, and leads him by the hand to his individual *tikkun*, or soul correction. Such a person is humble, spiritually aware, optimistic, and gratified. He lives a life of true *emuna*, for he maintains a strong connection with Hashem.

Baal teshuva

A person can't be called a *baal teshuva* unless he does *teshuva* every single day, and real *teshuva* means an hour of personal prayer that includes the confessing one's misdeeds, asking Hashem's forgiveness, and resolving to improve. Personal prayer not only hastens one's individual redemption, but the overall *Geula*, or full redemption of our people as well. Rebbe Nachman implores us (*Likutei Moharan*, I:79) to avoid being an obstacle that delays the *Geula*. So, when we invest an hour a day to personal prayer, we actually hasten the *Geula*. The more people that speak to Hashem in personal prayer every day, the faster we'll see the *Geula*. Not only that; the angels that are created from one's personal prayer implant a desire within other people to seek Hashem.

Eternal promise

A person once asked me for advice how to be happy. I gave him a one-word answer – *teshuva*! Do an hour of personal prayer every day, and you'll be happy. As long as a person fails to do *teshuva* – to return to Hashem with all his heart – he can't be truly happy. The reason is simple; uncorrected transgressions are like lead curtains on the soul. They block Hashem's light and make a person feel heavy, dark, and therefore worried and depressed. An hour a day of *teshuva* and personal prayer makes the lead curtains disappear, taking a tremendous weight off a person's heart and soul and enabling his soul to enjoy the exquisite and sublime illumination of Hashem's Divine light.

There are no shortcuts to an hour of personal prayer every day. One who hasn't yet tasted the sweetness of an hour of personal prayer doesn't yet know what real *teshuva* is. True *teshuva* means speaking with Hashem, for the Prophet said (Hoshea 14:3), "Take words with you and return to Hashem." Rebbe Nachman of Breslev gave those fortunate people who practice daily personal prayer wonderful promises for posterity, as he wrote in a famous letter:

To my close and dear pupil,

I request that you stop for a moment and listen carefully to my words. I am speaking for you eternal benefit. Know that I had much work to do before I brought you close to me. You can understand a bit and feel the miracles that stimulated your coming close to me. And so, one of the conditions that I stipulate with those whom I draw close to me is that they don't allow others to fool them, and that they don't fool themselves. You've heard frequently and have understood that my main method and advice for attaining one's complete soul correction and achieving what's possible to achieve is none other than *hitbodedut*, that a person designate a place for himself where he can speak his heart to Hashem, and ask for all his material and spiritual needs, to confess all his misdeeds whether intentional or accidental, under duress or by free will. He should thank Hashem for all His favors, material and spiritual. I have succeeded in arranging with Hashem that any person who implements this advice with complete simplicity, stands before Hashem for an hour a day of [personal] prayer – even if at this particular point in time he experiences no spiritual arousal – even if he can't say a single word, only that he should force himself to yearn to speak to Hashem, he shall merit everything good! There will be no severe judgment on him from Above, for with this [advice] he shall correct all three parts of his soul – *nefesh*, *ruach*, and *neshama* and all the [spiritual] worlds that depend on him from the time of Adam the first human until the coming of our Savior. This is solid valid truth, and I guarantee it. Signed, Rebbe Nachman of Breslev

Rebbe Nachman also promised that he arranged with Hashem that whoever does an hour a day of *hitbodedut* will also enjoy longevity until he succeeds in attaining the correction of his soul. Therefore, anyone who wants to enjoy length of days and the promise that he'll enter the Garden of Eden straight away without having to be cleansed in Purgatory – as well as the other promises that we mentioned in this chapter – should do an hour of personal prayer every day with no excuses.

The power of simple prayer

A person's hour of personal prayer and self-evaluation is so strong that it has the power to protect the entire world, as Rebbe Nachman asks (Discourses, 70):

"How do we allow Hashem to ponder and implement harsh decrees in the world? We must call Hashem away from all His other tasks. We must distract Him from sending harsh decrees to the world, Heaven forbid. We must tell Him to put everything else aside and listen to us, for we want to ask Him to draw us close. For when a person wishes to speak to Hashem, He casts aside everything else and all the harsh decrees that He wants to decree, and turns His attention to the person that wants to speak to Him and ask for assistance in getting close to Him."

Rebbe Nachman's above discourse has far-reaching implications: no matter how small, insignificant, or simple a person might be, no matter if he's an ex-convict or a person who's made every mistake in life – as soon as he or she calls Hashem's name, Hashem drops everything and listens! Not only does *everyone* have the right to turn to Hashem at any given moment – 24/7 – but by virtue of the person that seeks Hashem, the world is spared from calamity and harsh decrees. So, if there were people speaking to Hashem around the clock, there wouldn't be any harsh decrees.

Breslever tradition tells that the Breslever *Chassid* im of Poland had a round-the-clock personal prayer vigil where someone was always speaking to Hashem. The day that the vigil was interrupted, the terrible Holocaust began...

What could be better than having the personal attention of The King? Imagine that a bachelor that's looking for his soul-mate; someone arranges an hour-long audience for him with the country's leading matchmaker. Do you think he wouldn't bother showing up for such a meeting? He'd fly like a rocket to such a meeting! Or imagine that a needy person is granted a meeting with a millionaire philanthropist who with the snap of a finger could solve all the poor man's money problems. Would the poor man hesitate or be too lazy to keep the appointment? No way! Whoever we perceive can help us – the world's greatest physician, the number-one marriage counselor, the District bank manager, our representative in Parliament, or even the President or the Prime Minister – is futile and powerless compared to Hashem.

Hashem is the world's greatest Physician, Psychologist, Matchmaker, and Philanthropist. Like King David says (Psalm 145:9), "Hashem is good for everything," good for income, good for curing, good for matchmaking, good for advice, good to confide in, and good for whatever our needs are.

Our readers who are not yet familiar with the concept of an hour of *hitbodedut* should know that they may implement this hour at any time, any place, and in any form. Personal prayer is fine in any language, jargon, or dialect, preferably in simple sincere words from the heart. A person is not only allowed but encouraged to feel comfortable during personal prayer. You can sit in front of the fireplace in winter or with your feet in the lake in the summer. You can speak to Hashem on your flight from New York to London or while walking in the woods in rural Virginia. With *hitbodedut*, a lone sentry never feels alone and a young mother always has someone to speak to on a sleepless night. An office during lunch break and a wooded trail are both suitable places for personal prayer.

Put everything aside

If *hitbodedut* is so pleasant, convenient, and easy, why isn't everyone speaking to Hashem for an hour a day? What's stopping people from doing what they know is right and beneficial, from talking to Hashem in personal prayer?

The answer is that the *Yetzer Hara* – the Evil Inclination – knows full well the virtues of *hitbodedut*. He knows that by way of personal prayer, a person will realize his potential to the maximum and see blessings of success in all of his endeavors. Most of all, personal prayer is the vehicle that brings a person close to Hashem, to his true mission in life, and to his soul correction. For these reasons, the *Yetzer Hara* will fight tooth and nail against *hitbodedut* and do everything to convince and discourage a person from doing personal prayer.

Just knowing how badly the Evil Inclination wants to stop us from speaking to Hashem in personal prayer should be all the incentive we need to put everything aside and pursue it more and more. Those who regularly practice personal prayer enjoy a loving, gratifying, and intimately satisfying relationship with Hashem that defies adequate description. One cannot imagine how patiently, gently, and lovingly Hashem treats those who turn to Him in personal prayer. Man was created to live a life of *emuna* and proximity to Hashem; personal prayer enables a person to attain both.

The Book of Life

My esteemed teacher and spiritual guide Rabbi Levi Yitzchak Binder of saintly and blessed memory once told me that after a person finishes his 120 years on this earth, he is called upon to stand before the Heavenly Court. The judges open a thick book, where each page describes down to the tiniest details that person's thoughts, deeds, and speech for a given day, for this is the book of his life. Every single thought, deed, and utterance undergoes uncompromising scrutiny. But, when a given pages says, "Sixty minutes of *hitbodedut* – he spent sixty minutes in personal prayer and self-assessment, etc.," then the judges turn the page with no scrutiny whatsoever. Such is the power of personal prayer: Heavenly law forbids double jeopardy, so whenever a person judges himself, the Heavenly Court is not allowed to judge him for the same offense.

We can now begin to understand why the Evil Inclination tries so hard to obstruct our daily personal prayer session. Hashem is the epitome of mercy and lovingkindness; when we judge ourselves and confess to Him, He always forgives. When we don't, we are held responsible and accountable for every tiny thought, utterance, and deed. When we fail to devote an hour to personal prayer on a given day, we are judged according to the fine print of exacting justice. Who could be so senseless to forfeit the opportunity of judging oneself rather than having uncompromising stern judges preside over the trial?

Not only does a person's life have its overall *tikkun*, or soul correction, but each individual day has its *tikkun*. That's why each individual day has its renewed obstacles that we must overcome in order to devote our cherished hour to personal prayer. The desire and yearning that we activate in overcoming the hurdles that stand in our way only serve to elevate our personal prayers and make them ever so dear to Hashem. Things that come easy never have the power or the intrinsic value of accomplishments that we must work hard for.

Personal prayer is a golden daily opportunity to get close to Hashem, to solve our problems, to improve our character, and to realize our potential to the hilt. No wonder Rebbe Nachman declared that *Hitbodedut* surpasses everything!

Chapter Two:
For I Am Compassionate

Before we learn the practical side of personal prayer, we need to equip ourselves with one of the basic foundations of *emuna*, namely, Hashem's mercy.

The Aramaic word for prayer, *rachmei*, is derived from the Hebrew word for mercy, *rachamim*. This indicates that prayer is an extension of Hashem's mercy.

The purpose of creation

The Zohar teaches that Hashem created the world as an expression of His infinite mercy. Rebbe Nachman of Breslev writes (*Likutei Moharan* I:64): "Hashem created the world as an expression of mercy, since He desired to reveal His mercy, for if there were no world, to whom could He show His mercy? He therefore created all of creation from the loftiest spiritual worlds to the lowliest physical realm simply to show His mercy."

A main aspect of *emuna* is consequently the belief in Hashem's mercy and compassion. Any belief system that lacks the complete belief in Hashem's mercy is lacking, and it won't have the power to help a person in the time of need. The complete belief in Hashem's mercy and compassion is an intrinsic part in genuine *emuna* – the pure, simple and complete belief in Hashem – that stands by us and gives us strength during life's most difficult and trying circumstances. Such *emuna* leads to happiness, fulfillment, and recognition of truth.

A simple belief in God is laudable, but it's not always cogent enough to weather severe trials and tribulations. When enhanced with belief in Hashem's mercy – His love for every one of us,

His readiness to help us at all times, and His unfathomable, unconditional compassion – we attain the type of pure *emuna* that gives us phenomenal resolve and strength.

And I listen, for I am compassionate

The Torah teaches us in *Parshat Mishpatim* (Exodus 22:26) about a poor person that needs an urgent loan. The lender – rightfully so – asks the poor person for collateral. The poor person has nothing to offer, but the shirt on his back. The lender says, "Do you sleep in that shirt?" The poor person says no. The lender says, "Give me your night garment as collateral."

The Torah allows the lender to take the night garment, or pajama (they used to sleep in nightgowns, like a men's nightgown) as collateral, but then commands the lender to return the nightgown to the poor person every day at sundown, so the poor person will have something to sleep in. The poor person, in turn must return the collateral to the lender the next morning at dawn.

The Torah tells the lender, "OK, you want to demand collateral from this poor guy? Fine – take his one and only possession – his night clothing. But, I'm warning you," says Hashem, "return it to him every evening, because if you don't, and the poor person cries out to me in desperation, **I will listen, for I am compassionate.**"

The Torah is revealing to us one of the most powerful foundations in *emuna* – the pure and complete faith in Hashem. Whenever a desperate person cries out to Hashem from the bottom of his or her broken heart, Hashem listens. Hashem Himself promises: **"I will listen, for I am compassionate."**

The great 12th century Kabbalist and Torah commentator, the "Ramban", Nachmanides, explains that Hashem answers the cry of every single person who sincerely calls out to Him, even if that person isn't an upright person, for Hashem answers our prayers as a gift. He further elaborates that a person might say, "OK, I'll return the night garment to a poor *tzaddik* – a poor righteous person – but I won't bother with a poor scoundrel – let him suffer!" Hashem says, No! **Even if the suffering person is not righteous, I will still heed his or her cry to me! I will listen, for I am compassionate…"**

Gate of Salvation

Hashem hears the voice of *everyone* who calls out to Him, whether deserving or not. This is an intrinsic part of creation, for Hashem created the world to reveal His mercy and compassion.

The Torah teaches us about Hashem's compassion when mentioning the poor person, to teach us a remarkable lesson. Do you have any idea why the person is poor in the first place? Because he or she lacks *emuna*! People are poor because they don't call out to Hashem! The Torah testifies that Hashem is compassionate – if they would have called out Hashem's name, Hashem would have answered a long time ago and they wouldn't have fallen into such a destitute state.

Hashem gives us a wallet full of spiritual credit cards – Visa, Diners, Cart Blanche – and says, "Call My name and receive whatever you need." Yet, we all walk around like spiritual beggars, when in essence, we have carte blanche, an unlimited account to use and to draw from. Why don't we use it? Why don't we call out to Hashem?

The answer is simple – the Evil Inclination – the *Yetzer Hara* – will do anything in the world to keep a person from attaining *emuna*. Go right ahead and do whatever you want, just so long as you don't believe in Hashem. Since prayer, especially personal prayer, is the basis of *emuna*, the Evil Inclination does everything in his power to prevent a person from speaking to Hashem. He has 270 different arguments for every person, tailor made to clamp that person's heart and mouth air tight: For example –

* I'm full of bad deeds – Hashem won't listen to me. *(Wrong! Hashem listens to everyone that calls Him.)*

* If Hashem really cared about me, He wouldn't have let me be poor in the first place. (*Wrong! That's the only way Hashem could teach you emuna and correct your soul, for if you were rich, you'd have never sought Hashem.*)

* Hashem has bigger and better things to do; does he really care about me? (*He sure does! His phenomenal Divine providence extends from the greatest creation to the minutest creation. He certainly listens to every one of His beloved sons and daughters.*)

* Look at all the suffering in the world – is there really God in the world? (*The Evil Inclination is really begging the question, because the reason of the world's suffering is the fact that people transgress Hashem's will.*)

* I feel ridiculous talking to the wall... (*Do you feel ridiculous about spending your time and money chasing after people who can't guarantee a solution to your problems? With emuna, you're not talking to the wall, but to your merciful Father in Heaven!*)

The list goes on and on...

The Evil Inclination wants to close the very Gate of Salvation that Hashem promises us. Therefore, we must always remind ourselves of Hashem's explicit promise straight out of the Torah: **"I will listen, for I am compassionate."** When we pray, we should appeal to Hashem's mercy, cling to it, and believe in it with all our hearts.

Here's an example of how to speak to Hashem while appealing to His mercy: "Master of the World! The Torah testifies that You are compassionate and merciful and that You listen to the cries of everyone that calls Your name with no preconditions at all, whether a person's righteous or not, deserving or not. Hashem, I therefore beg You to give me the free gift of Your limitless mercy and to listen to my prayers. Hashem, I believe with all my heart in Your attributes of mercy and Compassion just as I believe in You, so please let me pour my heart out to You. Please grant me the salvation I need, for no one can help me but You. You created the world to show Your mercy, so please give me Your merciful help. Help me return to You with all my heart. Please help me to strengthen my *emuna* and correct whatever I did wrong that caused me the current problems I have. Hashem, please accept my prayers and fulfill my wishes even though I deserve nothing…"

Anytime we turn to Hashem for anything, we should appeal to His infinite mercy and compassion.

When a person strengthens himself in *emuna*, clinging to the steadfast belief in Hashem's mercy, he begins to see big miracles. Nothing can obstruct a humble and heartfelt appeal to Hashem's mercy! Hashem is honor-bound to answer the cries of all who turn to Him. One should not allow anyone to weaken his resolve to pray and pray until those prayers are answered.

Willfully poor

Three times a day, we say in our prescribed prayers (the "*Modim*" prayer), "The Good One, for Your mercy is never-ending, and The Merciful, for Your compassion has not terminated." Since Hashem is infinitely merciful and compassionate, it's ridiculous not to seek His help.

When people ask me to help solve their problems, I frequently suggest an hour a day of personal prayer. They often protest, saying that they don't have the time. Let's take an objective look at this excuse with the following parable:

The son of the wealthiest man in town was sleeping on a park bench, barefoot, hungry, disheveled, and sick. Some passersby recognized him, and asked, "Aren't you the rich man's son?" The young man looked up and nodded in the affirmative. They asked, "Then why don't you ask your father for some shoes, clean clothes, a meal, a bath, and some medical care? Why are you lying here like a bum on the park bench?" The son answers that he doesn't have time to talk to his father. After hearing such an inane answer, the passersby walk away in disgust mumbling that the senseless young man deserves what he gets...

In light of the above parable, any person that fails to turn to Hashem for whatever he needs is just as senseless as the son of the rich man on the park bench. Indeed, our beloved Father in Heaven has the unlimited resources to give us whatever we need whenever we need it. In His ultimate mercy, He is more than happy to fulfill all of our needs.

A person who strengthens himself in *emuna* while internalizing the belief in Hashem's infinite mercy and developing the confidence that Hashem listens unconditionally to all his prayers sees dramatic improvements in life. This is the type of *emuna* that we should all strive for.

A beggar's language

The Code of Jewish Law stipulates how a person should approach Hashem in prayer (see *Kitzur Shulchan Aruch*, ch. 18:5): "Like a beggar in the doorway." In other words, we should appeal to Hashem in the humility remindful of a beggar's language and not with the arrogance of a rich man who thinks he deserves everything.

One should avoid praying as if the prayer is a tiresome bother, like a heavy backpack that he can't wait to throw off his shoulders. Indeed, when one contemplates the value of prayer and realizes that this is one of Hashem's greatest gifts to mankind, one prays with joy and intent, savoring each word.

Our focus in prayer should be exclusively on Hashem, for no angel or celestial influence can fulfill our wishes; only Hashem can.

Rabbi Joseph Caro warns (*Shulchan Aruch, Orach Chaim* 98:5) that we shouldn't think that we deserve whatever we're asking for, for such an attitude triggers a full investigation of our debits and credits in the Heavenly Court to see if we really are deserving. Then, things become known that otherwise would have remained unopened files until Yom Kippur when Hashem would forgive us with the rest of the public that prays together. Since we don't want our files opened, it's much better to ask for whatever we want as a free gift that we don't deserve.

Anytime we make a request from Hashem, it's also a good idea to appeal to His infinite mercy and lovingkindness. When our prayers are built on Hashem's mercy and our request for a free gift that we don't deserve, they attain a special charm of humility. It's hard to refuse a humble beggar's request on the front doorstep. Not only should our daily prayers be in this tone, but our Psalms, supplementary prayers, and personal prayers should be the same way. We should stand before Hashem like humble beggars and never lose hope and faith until our prayers are ultimately answered.

We should always remind ourselves: Why be ragged derelicts on a park bench when we can be princes and princesses in the palace? As children of The King, all we have to do is to ask our all-powerful and ever-loving Father in Heaven for what we need.

On a spiritual level, the mouth builds the spiritual vessel that is a fitting container for the blessing of Divine abundance. The mouth initiates the flow of Divine abundance and opens the spiritual channels through which both material and spiritual abundance flows. Consequently, a lack of abundance – or deficiency in any particular area – can often be traced to a closed mouth. We should therefore always remember the passage, **And when he cries out to Me, I will listen, for I am compassionate** (Exodus 22:26). One should certainly not lose heart if his prayers aren't answered right away. Just like the humble beggar, keep knocking on Hashem's door until He opens the gate of salvation for us.

Bring us back to You

A spiritual rule of thumb says simply that the more something is difficult to attain or accomplish, the more we must pray for it. That's quite understandable, for everything has a spiritual price tag. A pair of socks costs much less than a holiday suit.

Here's an example: suppose a woman understands just how important modest dress is, but she's embarrassed to change her wardrobe because of social pressure, fear of ridicule, and the like. She should appeal to Hashem in the following manner: "Master of the World, I understand how important modest dress is and I want to do Your will but it's really difficult for me. Please grant me the inner strength to do what's right. Give me the backbone to stand firm, so that neither social pressure nor ridicule will make me waiver from the path that I know is right. Only You can help me, Hashem. Have mercy, and be by my side…"

Such prayers move mountains.

At this opportunity, we shall now expose one of the biggest lies of the century that fools people right and left: Before a person returns to Hashem with all his heart, he struts around the world with an outstretched chest like an arrogant peacock and declares that he's riding the four winds in complete freedom and that no one can tell him what to do. As soon as he wants to return to Hashem and do *teshuva,* his arrogance and self-confidence fly out the nearest window. All of a sudden his knees are knocking. He shudders at what people might say if he puts a kippa on his head. He sees donning *tzitzit* as something more ominous than a commando mission in Gaza. Where did the bravado of the free spirit and easy rider go? In retrospect, the pre-*teshuva* "self-confidence and savvy" weren't the real deal; they were only illusions of the Evil inclination.

One of the questions that the Heavenly Court asks a person when his cadence in this world terminates is, "Why were you embarrassed to do *teshuva* and you weren't embarrassed to transgress the Torah? Why did you say that you didn't have the strength to change your lifestyle but you had plenty of strength to commit transgressions?" Will we have answers to these questions?

Let's assume that we really don't have the strength to do what we're supposed to do. Or, assume that we've been looking for a soul mate, hoping for children, or yearning for a better and more fulfilling job for years but we've only become more frustrated and drained in the process. When we lack strength, it's the perfect time to appeal to Hashem and to plug in to His unlimited mercy and strength. We might be having trouble in finding a soul mate or a better job, but Hashem can do whatever He wants whenever He wants. Hashem can help us rid ourselves of a bad habit or something so difficult to overcome as substance abuse. No request is too big or small for Hashem. All we have to do is open our mouths in prayer. If *teshuva* is difficult, all we have to say is, "Hashem, bring us back to You." We have Hashem's eternal promise, **And when he cries out to Me, I will listen, for I am compassionate.** Who could ask for more?

No matter what how difficult your life is at the present, remind yourself that Hashem is merciful and compassionate. Don't let the evil inclination weaken your resolve, for Hashem answers our prayers whether we are deserving or not.

Even Moses, the greatest prophet of all times, appealed to Hashem as a beggar looking for a free gift. If Moses appealed to Hashem's mercy rather than relying on his own credit, then our prayers should certainly appeal to Hashem's mercy.

He gives us speech

Rebbe Natan of Breslev discusses an apparent paradox in spirituality (see *Likutei Halachot, Yura Dea, Hilchot Mezuza*, 5): From one standpoint, a person should realize how far he is from Hashem. On the other hand, he should realize that Hashem is everywhere, and in His magnificent mercy, He gives us the power of speech. All we have to do is call His name, and all of a sudden, He's right there with us, as King David said (Psalm 145: 18), "Hashem is near to all those who call Him, to those who call Him in truth."

Isaiah the Prophet said (57:19), "He gives us speech – peace to the far and the near." This passage means that by way of speech, even an unrighteous person that's far away from Hashem can come close to Hashem and attain the blessing of true inner peace and peace of mind by speaking to Him.

Let's be honest – when a person first comes close to Hashem after years of being far away, speaking to Hashem is not the easy in most cases. Even so, Rebbe Nachman warned us to strengthen ourselves and not to give up. Sometimes a person sets aside an hour for personal prayer only to open his mouth and nothing comes out! He shouldn't lose heart, for the mere desire to talk to Hashem invokes phenomenal Divine compassion and gratification. Ultimately, He who gives us the power of speech will also give us the words to speak to Him. As such, the words we speak to Hashem are cherished gems that are Divinely influenced. If we realized the true value of personal prayer, we'd spend every available moment speaking to Hashem.

Moses described himself as "heavy of tongue" (Exodus 4:10), that he found speech most difficult. Hashem dismissed that claim and said (ibid, 11), "Who gives a person the power of speech...I do! I am Hashem!" Hashem opens the mouths of those who seek him with strong and unswerving desire, giving them the words to speak to Him.

Hashem is near me

So really, as Rebbe Natan teaches, there's no paradox at all. Even though we deserve nothing by virtue of our own merit, Hashem is always near to us by virtue of His mercy. Hashem's proximity is an important benefit of *emuna* that enables us to turn to Him at any time, at any place, in any circumstance, seven days a week, twenty four hours a day, whether we're deserving or not. By virtue of Hashem's mercy, there's no room for despair ever.

Rebbe Natan promises that even though we're far away from Hashem, by way of speech and prayer, Hashem is suddenly near. As such, the power of speech and the words of one's prayers are superb receptacles of Divine abundance.

We can now understand what King David says (Psalm 20:10),

"Hashem will save us, The King will answer on the day that we call Him." When will Hashem save us? On the day that we call Him!

So, even if you have trouble finding the words to speak to Hashem, set aside an hour a day just to be alone with Him. With perseverance, desire, and a strong yearning, Hashem will soon give you a wealth of words that flow from your heart. Anyone who has experienced a true outpouring of the soul in personal prayer won't want to forfeit a single daily personal prayer session his entire life. Even more so, Rebbe Nachman of Breslev promised that anyone who spends an hour a day in personal prayer will certainly attain his soul correction. Eventually, one who is steadfast about devoting an hour a day to personal prayer will be able to speak to Hashem in an uninhibited manner.

Encouragement from father to son

In the following letter, Rebbe Natan encourages his son to devote an hour a day to personal prayer:

"…what weakens a person is the feeling that the prayers are of no use, until he drifts away from Hashem and loses faith in his power of calling out to Hashem. Happy is the person who verbalizes his desires, aspirations, and inner thoughts to Hashem every single day. It doesn't matter whether his speech is refined or not, or whether he's capable of speaking at all. No matter what, however it turns out, we should strengthen ourselves to call out to Hashem and to speak to Him any way we can, for not a single utterance is lost; not even a desire to utter a word is lost!"

Rebbe Natan writes in *Likutei Halachot* (*Choshen Mishpat, Oseh Shalich* 3) that, "There is no wisdom, advice, or ploy more effective than speaking to Hashem in an hour a day of personal prayer… The loftiness of individual personal prayer is beyond comprehension… Such prayers ascend unobstructed straight to the Heavenly throne…"

Infinite Mercy

Many people don't pray because they either believe that they're not worthy of prayer or they harbor the misconception that Hashem only listens to the prayers of the very pious. Neither one of these thoughts, or any other, should discourage a person from prayer.

Prayer is a gift to mankind from Hashem's infinite mercy. Therefore, anyone is welcome to pray, for Hashem's mercy is infinite and for everyone, not only for the righteous.

There's one prayer in Jewish liturgy that we say thrice daily every day of the year, including Shabbat, High Holidays, and Fast Days. It's known as the "*Modim*" prayer, where we say, "We thank You, Hashem," for a number of his magnificent blessings. One of our praises of Hashem within the Modim prayer says, "The Good One, for His mercy hasn't ended; and The Merciful One, for His acts of loving-kindness haven't terminated…" Once we internalize the concepts of Hashem's never-ending goodness and mercy, nothing can weaken our resolve to turn to Hashem in prayer anytime and anywhere.

The Checklist

There's a surefire way to destroy the Evil Inclination's lying propaganda that tries to weaken our resolve and discourage us from praying. We simply make a checklist with all the possible reasons we can think of for not praying. Let's make a sample checklist together:

* I'm not a righteous person.

* I haven't yet made *teshuva*.

* Who am I that Hashem should listen to my prayers, much less answer them?

* I don't deserve anything.

* I'm a nothing.

* I never seem to succeed at anything.

* I'm embarrassed to talk to Hashem, especially with the skeletons in my closet.

* I have no idea how to pray.

* I don't believe in the whole prayer deal.

* (fill in your own reason…)

Now, let's take our entire checklist of all the reasons that we think we can't pray (or the reasons that the *Yetzer* tells us that our prayers aren't worth anything), and convert them into a prayer! Look what we do with the above checklist:

Master of the World! I know full well that I'm not a righteous person and that I haven't yet made *teshuva*. I look at myself and ask myself who am I that You should listen to my prayers? I don't have any way to convince You that I deserve anything, because I feel like a nothing. I never seem to succeed at anything, and I'm embarrassed to talk to You, especially with the skeletons in my closet. Basically, I have no idea how to pray and I don't even know if I believe in this whole prayer deal. Despite all these shortcomings and more, I appeal to Your infinite mercy because I'm one of your creations like everyone else. King David said that You are good to everyone and that Your mercy is upon all Your creations – that includes me too! So despite everything, please hear my prayers and answer them, for Your mercy is infinite!

The above prayer is unbelievably cogent. We come to Hashem with all of our shortcomings, in humility, and without expecting a thing. Hashem created the world to demonstrate His mercy, and we appeal to that mercy. As such, we are no longer praying for ourselves, but we are helping Hashem fulfill the very purpose that He created the world, to show his mercy! Such prayer is very powerful. For example, a person with a terminal illness, Heaven forbid, can appeal to Hashem's mercy when all the doctors have given up hope. Here's how:

Hashem, the doctors say there's no cure for me. But, they don't decide who lives or dies – You do! Hashem, if You cure me, everyone that knows about my dire predicament will recognize Your infinite mercy and Your name will be sanctified. So please Hashem, for the sake of Your Holy Name, I appeal to Your infinite mercy that You should cure my ailments...

The poor man's prayer

The Zohar in its elaboration of Psalm 102 says that the poor man's prayer, calling out to Hashem with a broken heart from the tribulations of poverty, takes precedent even before the prayers of Moses and King David. The Zohar in *Parshat Balak* states:

"Rebbe Abba opened, 'A prayer of the poor man when he swoons...' (Psalm 102). The word 'prayer' talked about three people – Moses, David, and the poor man... Which of the three prayers is most important? The poor man's prayer! It takes precedence over Moses' and David's prayer, and is accepted before all other prayers in the world. Why? The poor man has a broken heart. Hashem is close to anyone with a broken heart (Psalm 34)... The poor man's prayers open the windows of the firmament... The Holy One blessed be He says: 'All other prayers shall move aside and the poor man's prayer shall enter unto Me first. The Heavenly Tribunal shall not judge whether the poor man's prayer is worthy or not. The poor man's supplications and I shall be alone!' Then, all the Heavenly Legions ask, 'Who is receiving The Holy One blessed be He's individual attention?' An answer came down from above, 'He is in solitude with His cherished vessels – the broken-hearted poor.'"

"The poor man has no greater yearning than to pour out his tears before The Holy One blessed be He; The Holy One blessed be He has no greater yearning than to receive those tears that are poured out before Him... King David saw how the windows of the firmament were open to the prayers of the poor man, so he took off his royal garb and sat on the floor like a poor man, and prayed his prayer."

"Rabbi Elazar says... every person should lower himself and pray like a poor person, so that his prayers will ascend with those of the other poor people. The Heavenly sentries don't easily allow other prayers to enter the upper thresholds like they allow the prayers of the poor people. The prayers of a poor person with a broken heart and a humble spirit need no permission to enter..." (*Zohar, Balak*, 195).

Moses, David, and the poor man

Now that we've seen the abovementioned passage from the Zohar, let's take a closer look. Moses, as the greatest of prophets, prayed on the highest level of spiritual awareness that a mortal ever attained. King David, Hashem's anointed, attained a complete level of self-nullification that enabled him to cling completely to Hashem. Now, we have the prayer of a poor man or women crying to Hashem with a broken heart.

Which prayer would we say is most important? Which would we think Hashem would accept first? The prayer of Moses? King David's prayer? No, the prayer of the broken-hearted pauper is heard before the prayers of history's greatest prophet, before the prayers of the king of Israel, and before the prayers of the entire world! This is an awesome concept, and if it wasn't written outright in the Zohar, we couldn't utter such a notion.

Imagine, Moses, King David, and a plain and simple poor man are standing in prayer. Moses is undoubtedly praying for the entire world. King David is reciting magnificent praises of Hashem's name. Poor Morris Levy from Brooklyn is complaining to Hashem that his meager income as a cab driver is barely enough for food and rent, but not enough to pay for the tuition of five children that must have Torah educations. If that's not enough, he doesn't have a single cent to make a wedding for his oldest daughter; to add insult to injury, he had two flat tires today, and they're radials, slit and beyond repair! If he doesn't come up with a fast $300, he won't be able to replace them, and then what? Just this morning, he paid the electric bill, and all he has is $65 in his pocket. Morris, standing on the side of the road by Ocean Parkway looks at the sky with tear-filled eyes and pleads with a choked voice, "Hashem, I can't stand this any longer? What do I do? I've got no one to help me! There's nothing in the bank and my credit's exhausted. What am I asking for, a palace, a Bermuda vacation? Are two radial tires and tuition so my kids can learn Torah too much to ask?" Morris breaks down and sobs uncontrollably.

Hashem gently pushes the prayers of Moses, David and the rest of the world aside. The tears of Morris the Cabbie have split the firmaments and have reached the Heavenly Throne unchallenged and unobstructed.

How do the prayers of Morris the poor Cabbie from Brooklyn take precedence over those of Moses and King David? So what if Morris has a broken heart? The Torah testifies that Moses was the humblest of any man that ever walked the face of the earth. Humble people also have broken hearts. And what about King David? The Psalms testify that he too was extremely humble and broken-hearted despite the fact that he was King of Israel!

The Zohar answers that the poor person has no greater solace than being able to pour out his heart to Hashem. Hashem therefore has no greater desire than accepting the heartfelt and teary-eyed supplications of the poor person.

Revelation of mercy

We now see a clear manifestation of what Rebbe Nachman wrote (see *Likutei Moharan* I:64, which we referred to at the beginning of this chapter), namely, that the purpose of creation was to reveal Hashem's mercy. Since the poor man has no one to turn to other than Hashem and so badly needs Hashem's mercy, his prayers become first in line!

It doesn't matter than Morris the Cabbie isn't a great scholar like Moses or a *tzaddik* like King David. The Zohar teaches us that Hashem's mercy is best revealed by way of the poor man, for no one but Hashem can help him. Even though Moses and David are perfectly righteous, deserving, and amazingly humble, they're not really poor people. Morris is – he needs Hashem's help right now. Hashem personally attends to the needs of the poor person and listens to his prayers.

Protecting the entire world

Now we can fully appreciate what Rebbe Nachman told his followers in Discourse 70:

"How do we allow Hashem to ponder and implement harsh decrees in the world? We must call Hashem away from all His other tasks. We must distract Him from sending harsh decrees to the world, Heaven forbid. We must tell Him to put everything else aside and listen to us, for we want to ask Him to draw us close. For when a person wishes to speak to Hashem, He casts aside everything else and all the harsh decrees that He wants to decree, and turns His attention to the person that wants to speak to Him and ask for assistance in getting close to Him."

When we combine Rebbe Nachman's teaching with the aforementioned Zohar, we can conclude that the poor man's prayer protects the entire world. Here's how: when the poor man appeals to Hashem, Hashem sends everyone away including the Heavenly Tribunal and the administering archangels. With no one else around but the poor man's prayer, there cannot be any accusation, stern judgments or harsh decrees.

We also learn that the prayers of our great *tzaddikim* – as humble and as pious as they might be – still lack the cogency of the poor and needy person. Even though Moses and David acted like poor people, they were spiritual multimillionaires. So, even if we're not collecting welfare, thank G-d, we can still appeal to Hashem as poor people, because on a spiritual level, our generation is starving. So in effect, when each one of us stands in prayer before Hashem, he or she protects the entire world.

An opportunity to get closer

Our sages said that if there's no flour, then there's no Torah. The deeper inner dimension of this ever-so-wise saying is that a person cannot serve Hashem if he lacks such basics as food, clothing, and shelter. Inasmuch as our material possessions enable us to serve Hashem, then our material requests actually become spiritual requests.

Going a step further, there's a lofty level in spirituality whereby a person prays exclusively for his spiritual needs. Once he succeeds in fulfilling his spiritual aspirations, then his material needs are met automatically, since once again, "if there's no flour, then there's no Torah." Yet in all fairness and practicality, a person is hard-pressed to seek spirituality when the landlord is threatening to evict him from his apartment or when creditors are banging on his front door all day long. A person in dire straits must appeal to Hashem for immediate help. Hashem puts people in high-pressure situations in order that they'll have to turn to Him.

Stress situations are really gifts from Hashem. Hashem puts people in such situations so that they can learn the power of prayer. When a person sees that no one can help him, he therefore turns to Hashem with all his broken heart in prayer. Hashem will oftentimes save that person from all calamity to reinforce that person's belief in Hashem and in the power of prayer.

The more we pray, the more we see the fantastic results of prayer, and the more we gain incentive to increase our prayers, both in quality and in quantity.

Hashem, the Master Creator, wants the very best for each of His creations. Ask yourself a question: Is it logical that Hashem would deliberately create a creation with deficiencies? Think about the things you do and create – you try your best to do a perfect and unblemished job. If we mortal and limited people strive for perfection in whatever we do, then it's obvious that Hashem certainly desires that His creations attain perfection as well. As such, when we pray to Hashem to help us correct our misdeeds, character blemishes, and whatever else in our spiritual and physical lives that needs correcting, we are actually doing Hashem's will. Such prayer that is in perfect congruence with Hashem's will is readily accepted.

I cried out from the depths

If a person in trouble clings to the lifesaver of prayer, he will undoubtedly be rescued. After having been saved from the whale, Yonah the Prophet exclaimed (Yonah 2:3), "I cried out from the depths; You heard my voice!" We learn from this passage that whenever a person cries out from the depths of his or her soul, then Hashem hears his voice. Such prayer is amazingly effective.

People have the mistaken opposite impression that when they're down in the dumps, their prayers are futile and ineffective. Why? A person with a broken heart sees himself as small and ineffective. The spiritual reality is that the opposite is true. A person in trouble or with a broken heart is humble – Hashem loves humility and the prayers of the humble. Hashem also cherishes those who put their trust exclusively in Him. As such, when a broken-hearted person realizes that no one can help him but Hashem, his prayers take on a powerful dimension and are readily answered.

The belief in Hashem and in the power of prayer is therefore a lifeline that a person can always count on, no matter what. With prayer, a person can overcome any predicament.

Your prayer

People chase after leading rabbis and *tzaddikim* in search of blessings. They don't realize that all the blessings of all the generation's *tzaddikim* are not as effective as a person's heartfelt prayers for himself. Once a person begins to pray for himself, he opens the gate of salvation.

People ask, "How can my prayers be stronger than the prayers of the great *tzaddikim* in this generation?" The answer is surprisingly simple: the prayers of the *tzaddikim* don't bring a person close to Hashem as his or her own prayers do. Getting to know Hashem and coming close to Him are our task on earth. By doing what we're supposed to do, we see blessings in whatever we do.

Getting to know Hashem means becoming familiar with Hashem's indescribable mercy. Only those who pray attain this priceless familiarity with Hashem's mercy.

What's going on with me?

We all have ups and downs. During "down" periods, people have a tendency to persecute themselves when they see the emotional and spiritual darkness that seems to envelop them. They lose faith in themselves and gradually lose faith in prayer and in Hashem, G-d forbid, until they completely fall by the wayside.

A lack of spiritual arousal means that some type of severe judgment is hovering over a person and is blocking the Divine illumination from reaching that person. That's where the feeling of darkness comes from.

If a person is weak in *emuna* and weak in the cognizance that there is no one but Hashem, then he attributes his lack of spiritual arousal to himself rather than to Hashem. If he'd only open his mouth and cry out to Hashem, he could pierce the darkness. Hashem is more than ready to help a person make *teshuva*, mitigate harsh judgments, and escape from the darkness.

In light of the above concepts, it's readily understandable how many people returned to Hashem after a difficult challenge or tribulation. People's suffering served to atone for their sins, mitigated harsh judgments, and brought them to subjugate their ego to Hashem to the point where Hashem's Divine light illuminated their souls giving them a prodigious desire to come home to Hashem and to their roots. Once a soul becomes a suitable receptacle for Divine light, the person tastes the sublime sweetness of Hashem's presence and returns to Hashem with all his heart.

Each of us should therefore do our utmost to invoke Divine mercy, and to mitigate the collective stern judgments against our people as a whole in addition to our personal stern judgments. The collective stern judgments block Divine illumination from the soul of the nation and thereby delay the *Geula*, the full redemption of our people. Apathy toward the prospects of *Geula* and the coming of

Moshiach can also be traced to outstanding stern judgments that block Divine light. Without Divine light, people are cold and dark; they lack a yearning for Hashem and therefore make no progress in accomplishing the very mission that their souls were sent here for in the first place.

Many fool themselves and think that they don't make *teshuva* because of their desire to live a "free" lifestyle; they're mistaken. They don't make *teshuva* because they don't have the merit. A cloud of stern judgment hovers above them like an iron curtain that blocks Divine light. One needs Divine light to declare a fresh start and to make *teshuva* **daily** as the Torah requires. A person that doesn't yearn for Hashem won't have the necessary spiritual visa that will enable him to enter the portals of *teshuva*.

True freedom

A lack of desire for *teshuva* is therefore not the sign of a blessing or of a person's free choice – the opposite holds true. Any person – nonreligious, religious, Chassidic, or whatever – that lacks a yearning for Hashem, for *teshuva*, and for prayer won't feel any spiritual arousal unless he first mitigates whatever stern judgments there might be against him.

We now begin to grasp the significance of *hitbodedut*, personal prayer. Nothing mitigates stern judgments like personal prayer. During personal prayer, we express our desires and yearning to get close to Hashem – this in itself pierces the spiritual darkness and invokes Divine compassion that serves to mitigate stern judgments.

Some people make the mistake of persecuting themselves and blaming themselves for their troubles even during personal prayer sessions; that's not being with Hashem. Talking to Hashem means that we cast ourselves on Hashem's infinite mercy. We ask Hashem to illuminate our lives and our souls, and to bring us close to Him. Our appeal to Hashem should be like the appeal of a baby or toddler to a loving parent. Prayers that invoke Divine mercy are the same prayers that trigger spiritual arousal and enthusiasm for the service of Hashem.

Don't be discouraged if you feel far away from Hashem or if you feel like a dried-up log on a spiritual level. Nothing's inherently wrong with you. We all make mistakes from time to time that invoke stern judgments. So, rather than persecuting ourselves, we simply have to turn to Hashem and seek His assistance in helping us do *teshuva* and to remove whatever obstacles that are obstructing Hashem's Divine light from reaching our souls. With such simple, sincere, and straightforward personal prayer that purely and innocently appeals to Hashem's infinite mercy, there's no such thing as despair in the world. Ultimately, Hashem will send us an opening in the darkness and illuminate our lives.

A Free Gift

Moses never felt that he deserved a thing. He appealed to Hashem for a free gift. Even so, he prayed at length, for forty days and forty nights for one request! At no time did he feel any sense of entitlement. He simply asked for Hashem's mercy.

We must be careful not to feel like we deserve anything when we pray at length. Let's remember that the privilege of praying is a gift from Hashem. When we've succeeded in praying with heartfelt intent, it's because Hashem has come to our aid and has opened our hearts for a few precious moments. Rather than feeling smug about ourselves, we should thank Hashem for helping us and continue to pray like poor beggars asking for a handout. The important thing is to never stop praying; eventually, our prayers will be answered.

The Language of a beggar

Moses prayed like a beggar that doesn't deserve a thing. He appealed to Hashem's infinite compassion. We should do the same. No matter how righteous a person is, he's not yet a Moses. Moses knew that the feeling of entitlement prevents a person's prayers from being accepted. No matter how great a person's merits are, they're microscopic in comparison to Hashem's mercy and compassion, which know no bounds. We should therefore use the language of a beggar - just like Moses did – in our prayers.

Hashem's infinite compassion enables a person with virtually no merit at all (theoretically, for there is no person with no merit) to pray. When anyone approaches Hashem with the humility of a poor person asking for alms at the front door, Hashem answers those prayers as a free gift to whoever sought His help. Both Moses and King David, despite their unfathomable merits and righteousness, prayed to Hashem in the language of beggars (Psalm 102 is a classic example).

The odor of the material world

An hour a day of personal prayer is certainly laudable. But, when a person speaks to Hashem for an hour a day out of obligation, he's still far away from Hashem. We should be thirsting to be with Hashem while asking Him for *emuna* and to help us overcome our shortcomings so that we can truly get close to Him.

One's goal should be to speak to Hashem more and more until his soul no longer bears the odor of the physical world. Breslever tradition tells about Rebbe Shimshon, a pious servant of Hashem and a Breslever *Chassid*; after his passing, Rebbe Shimshon's soul ascended to the Heavenly Court. Rebbe Nachman scolded him: "Shimshon, you can't come inside here with the odor of the material world sticking to you. Go dunk in the Dinor River!"

The Dinor River is the river of fire that separates this world from the next world (see Zohar III, 32b). A soul must pass through the River of Dinor to cleanse itself of any residue of the material world before it is allowed to enter the world to come. For a person that hasn't purified himself in this world, every microsecond of immersion in the Dinor River exceeds all the anguish and tribulations of an entire lifetime. But, for a person that perfected and purified himself in this world, like Rebbe Natan of Breslev, immersion in the Dinor River is a sublime pleasure.

We should therefore beg Hashem to instill in us the yearning to pray, to speak to Him constantly, and to cleanse our souls from the odor of this lowly material world. Once again, we should appeal to Hashem's mercy. Once we accustom ourselves to speaking to Hashem daily, our hour of personal prayer becomes the focal point of our day. Life then becomes easy and beautiful.

Most importantly, never forget what the Torah teaches us: And when he cries out to Me, I will listen, for I am compassionate.

Chapter Three:
Learning Hitbodedut

This chapter teaches the easiest method to implement the wonderful gift of *hitbodedut* – secluded personal prayer – in one's daily routine. First of all, it's critically important that we set aside an hour a day for *hitbodedut*.

We all know that the tennis court, swimming pool, and golf course are not limited to world-champions tennis players, swimmers, or golfers. Anyone can enjoy himself in these types of recreational sports. By the same token, *hitbodedut* is not limited to the great *tzaddikim*. Anyone is welcome to take advantage of a private audience with Hashem any time of the day, any day of the week.

Every person can speak to Hashem on his or her own level. As parents, we know that we are just as receptive to conversing with our two-year old as we are with our married son or daughter. Hashem, whose love for each of us transcends a compassionate mother's love for her baby a million times over, is certainly no less receptive to each of us, no matter whether we're the Talmudic scholar of the generation or an inmate in prison. Irrespective of a person's age, spiritual level, IQ, social station or any other factor, Hashem listens to whoever approaches Him in personal prayer.

Hitbodedut should be done in your own jargon, namely, in the language you're most comfortable with. The better you express yourself, the more your heart is aroused. Don't stifle yourself with any rigid format. Use your mother tongue and your local slang as well. Rebbe Nachman teaches that one's simple and natural speech makes the best *hitbodedut*.

Find a place where you feel comfortable. Any place where you can have a bit of privacy and peace of mind is suitable, whether it's a park bench, a wooded path, the beach, or your bedroom. The important thing is to speak your heart out.

Every man, woman, and child should speak to Hashem daily in personal prayer. A sixty-minute session that includes soul-searching, confession, and resolve to improve is tantamount to a mini Yom Kippur that atones for the entire day. That's why our daily *hitbodedut* should carry us from yesterday's mini Yom Kippur to today's mini Yom Kippur. That way, we are constantly living in complete atonement and free from sin.

Anytime is opportune

Hitbodedut is like any other new venture in life that requires initial instruction and subsequent practice. The key to success is perseverance. Prayer is not a one-shot deal.

With every personal prayer session, a person gains a better understanding of how to pray. Personal prayer is a golden opportunity to get to know yourself, your true aspirations, your strengths and weaknesses, and most important – your mission in life. Every successive personal-prayer session brings a person closer to self-awareness. Self-awareness is the key to character improvement, for if a person doesn't know where he is, he can't know where he's going. *Hitbodedut* gives a person the level of self-awareness where he or she knows where they are at present and where they want to go in the future. The benefits of *hitbodedut* are so great that one cannot expect the gates of personal prayer to be wide open at the beginning, before a person invests concerted effort.

Anytime is an opportune time to talk to Hashem. Simply designating the hour for personal prayer is an accomplishment in itself. Therefore, a person shouldn't be discouraged if he or she didn't know what to say or lacked what to say on a particular day. No matter what, a person can always conclude his hour of personal prayer with a simple expression of gratitude: "Thank You, Hashem, for the privilege of being able to talk to You today. Please enable me to set aside an hour for *hitbodedut* tomorrow as well." Eventually, the steadfast practice of personal prayer will lead to greater proficiency, to the point where a person derives so much gratification that he'll never want to miss a day of personal prayer.

Setting aside an hour for personal prayer is in itself a major achievement. The outcome of a personal prayer session is less important than the session itself. Here's why: many people become discouraged. They entertain fantasies that right away they'll reach the plateau of prophecy in their personal prayer. Others don't feel "moved" or inspired enough when the reality of their personal prayers fails to meet up to their expectations. Still others feel that no one hears their prayers and they succumb to anger, despair, or both. These people fall by the wayside before they've achieved proficiency in personal prayer.

Probably the biggest obstacle people have in their minds against personal prayer is the claim that they don't have a free hour in a day. This is simply because they don't believe in the power of prayer or in the fact that Hashem hears their prayers. How does the very same person succeed in finding much more than an hour to watch the Super Bowl game or to go to the hairdresser? What a person truly desires, he'll do.

A person that believes in the truth of our Torah and in the words of our holy sages will do everything to speak to Hashem for at least an hour a day in personal prayer. The Zohar says that a person who devotes an hour a day to *hitbodedut* will never see purgatory.

Most important, a person shouldn't persecute himself if his personal prayer session failed to meet his expectations. The important thing is to set aside the hour and try one's best to speak to Hashem regardless of the outcome. Don't give up! Eventually, with perseverance, the personal prayer practitioner will attain an especially close relationship with Hashem. There's no loftier mitzvah than spending an intimate hour speaking with Hashem.

Every day Shabbat

Everyone knows the importance of a breather every once in a while. During the week, people dream of Shabbat, the day of rest. Probably more important than the physical aspect of Shabbat, when the body is at leisure, is the mental aspect, when the mind simply has a chance to unwind from the weekdays' constant pressures.

A walk in the park, a late-afternoon stroll along the river, or a short drive to the countryside is also very conducive to mental relaxation. As soon as a person removes himself from the environment of tensions and high pressure, he is able to view life in a completely different perspective. All of a sudden, he sees things that previously eluded his attention. Other confusing matters all of a sudden become clear, as if his thought process had improved in some way.

Such is the power of *hitbodedut*. The hour a day of tranquility and mental relaxation is probably the biggest gift a person could bestow on himself. It's a mini Shabbat every single day of the week. It's a break from the rat race and from the crazy carousel of constant pressures. An hour a day of personal prayer is a gift of emotional rejuvenation, physical and mental health, and self-composure.

No money in the world could convince a Sabbath-observant person to give up his weekly day of rest. By the same token, those fortunate people who become accustomed to spending an hour a day in secluded personal prayer wouldn't relinquish this daily gift for anything. Personal prayer is a little taste of Heaven in this world. It's something we all owe ourselves every single day.

Feel at home

Prescribed prayers are regimented. They must be said within given time frames. A person should not eat before the morning prayers. One is required to stand during certain segments, and even remain stationary in one place during other segments. Personal prayer is not like that at all. The unregimented atmosphere of personal prayer helps a person attain tranquility of the soul and a relaxed mindset. One may walk, stand, sit, or even lie in bed under the covers during personal prayer. The important thing is to feel comfortable.

Feeling good in the surroundings is a vital aspect of personal prayer. There should be no pressure or fear. There should be no one around to bother or interrupt you. Turn your cell phone off. Relax. Breathe deeply. Imagine that a feeling of freedom is flowing in your veins. Tranquility and composure are the key words.

A field or the woods are a wonderful setting for personal prayer, because a person's heart readily opens in an environment of calm and natural beauty. Spiritually, midnight is the perfect time. But, if a person is afraid, uncomfortable, or pressured for time, he or she won't attain the desired self composure and the attributes of the time and place will become drawbacks that defeat the purpose of personal prayer.

With the above in mind, pick a time that's convenient for you and a place where you feel comfortable. Once again, the key word is tranquility.

Speaking in the field

Rebbe Nachman of Breslev writes (*Likutei Moharan* I:52), "Mostly, *hitbodedut* is at night when the world relaxes from its daily pressures. Since during the day, people are chasing after the amenities of this world, it's difficult to cling to Hashem and to attain a state of self-nullification."

Preferably, *hitbodedut* should be in a place where there's no "spiritual static" to interfere with one's communication with Hashem. Ideally, it should be in a place where there are no other people around. On the other hand, Rebbe Nachman writes in several places that when a person prays among the grasses, trees, and plants, they all join his prayers. Such personal prayer takes on the spiritual dimension of a magnificent symphony.

Let's not fool ourselves: not everyone lives near a field or secluded woods. Even if they did, it's not advisable for a woman to be out alone, especially at night. In that respect, any place where you can feel comfortable is good enough to reap the wonderful benefits of personal prayer.

Praying for hitbodedut

Hitbodedut dramatically improves the quality of a person's life. If so, then why doesn't everyone engage in *hitbodedut*? And even more so, why do many people try *hitbodedut* and then give up?

The answer is simple. Nothing in life – especially in spirituality – is worth much without prayer. Therefore, one must pray for the privilege of *hitbodedut*. We need to ask Hashem to help us set aside our daily hour for *hitbodedut*, to help us find a proper setting to pray from, and to open our hearts and give us the ability to express our innermost thoughts.

Probably the best way to begin a session of *hitbodedut* is with five minutes of prayer for the *hitbodedut* itself. We should ask Hashem to give us the right words, to help us evaluate ourselves, and to help us thank Him for all our blessings. We ask Hashem to help us see our shortcomings and to guide us in self-improvement. Finally, we should ask Hashem to help us pray for all of our needs - material and spiritual – the most important of which is *emuna*. "Hashem, help me believe in the power of prayer. Help me reinforce my *emuna* so that I can feel that You are right here with me, listening to all my prayers. Hashem, grant me the humility to ask for all my needs as a free gift, without any sense of entitlement at all."

Prayer should precede any venture, especially something as lofty as a session of personal prayer. The prayers that preface *hitbodedut* have a special capability of mitigating stern judgments and invoking Divine compassion. There's no comparison between success with prayer and success without prayer. Whereas the latter gives a person a smug feeling of arrogance that severs himself from Hashem, the former enhances *emuna* and brings a person even closer to Hashem.

Hashem doesn't like to grant us successes if He knows they'll be detrimental to us, such as causing us to be arrogant or egotistic. Conversely, Hashem is happy to grant us success after extensive prayer. Why? When a person attains his heart's desire after extensive prayer, he knows that he has received a gift from Above, and neither arrogance nor egotism gets in his way. This is true success, the result of *emuna*, prayer, and knowing there is no one but Hashem.

The order of hitbodedut

In essence, *hitbodedut* is personal prayer, for as you see, we use these two terms interchangeably throughout this book. In that *hitbodedut* is personal prayer, it's very personal in nature, tailor-made for each person, and with no set rules or rigid framework. You speak to Hashem like you would to a best friend or a loving grandparent. Even so, there are certain useful guidelines that prevent us from making mistakes and help use utilize our personal prayer session for optimal results. These guidelines were set forth by Rebbe Nachman of Breslev and further developed by subsequent generations of his pupils and followers. As such, the advice in this chapter is both time- and field-tested.

The advice in this chapter is not meant to stifle or limit a person in any way, but to facilitate one's navigation through personal prayer and utilization of his time for the best. Let's discuss the general topics that should be included in our *hitbodedut*. The time and effort we devote to each of these topics will vary from day to day and from person to person. Once again, they are a guideline but not a rigid framework. Emuna

In order to speak to Hashem, a person needs *emuna*. Therefore, the first component we need for effective *hitbodedut* is *emuna*. One should believe that everything in life comes from Hashem and is for the very best. Every individual should be able to tell himself, "Hashem loves me; He loves my prayers and wants to help me. He is unlimited and His mercy knows no bounds. He has compassion on me, regardless of my deeds. Everything is under His care."

Most importantly, one should internalize the *emuna* that everything is for the very best. Even if things look askew and problematic, with repeated personal prayer, a person will gradually realize how Hashem has done everything for our ultimate benefit and soul correction.

In this respect, *emuna* and the resulting joy of *emuna* are a good opener for our *hitbodedut* session. This is an opportune time to pray for *emuna* and joy. While in the initial stages of spiritual self-development, our main prayers should be for *emuna* and happiness. Both are gateways to true Divine service and an escalator for spiritual growth. Whenever things don't go the way we want them to, when suffering or challenged, or when we feel more down that up, our *emuna* will enable us to continue on with a smile on our face. Since *emuna* and joy are the main tools that a person needs to traverse this world, we should beg Hashem to help reinforce our *emuna* and to be happy with our lot in life no matter what.

A. Giving thanks

Giving thanks is one of the most important segments of *hitbodedut*. Gratitude mitigates stern judgments and strengthens *emuna*. It brings a person to the point of truth, where he sees the myriad of Hashem's blessings that he would otherwise taken for granted or failed to acknowledge, had he failed to devote time to personal prayer and to giving thanks. Gratitude leads to happiness. Without happiness, a person can barely open his mouth. What's more, thanking Hashem for our blessings prevents a person from falling into the pitfalls of complaint, pessimism, grievances, the type of negativity that arouses and invokes harsh judgments, G-d forbid. Giving thanks has a marvelous effect on our souls, for it's like a sieve that sifts the good from the bad within us.

Maybe you don't feel sincere in giving thanks at this particular point in time, and you just want to cry or to yell about whatever hurts you, you should still force yourself to thank Hashem for your basic blessings in life (heart, lungs, clothing on your back, the food you ate earlier in the day) remembering that plenty of folks are less fortunate. Gratitude for life's basics illuminates truth and enables a person to avoid the type of bitterness that destroys personal prayer.

The advice of giving thanks is time-tested and proven. In my own personal experience, many are the times when I arrived at my *hitbodedut* session confused, upset, bitter, and tormented inside and out.

There were times when the whole world looked like one dismal black pit. I started to thank Hashem for all the difficult things in my life. Once I started thanking Hashem for the seemingly bad, my *emuna* was strengthened to the extent that I started seeing how everything was really for the best. Once I internalized that, I began to thank Hashem with all my heart. The sadness left me and I began to see the world in its proper perspective, realizing that everything is for the best, Divinely arranged and guided, created by Hashem and under His personal supervision. I discovered the wonderful feeling of standing before Hashem, being able to say whatever I want, and knowing that Hashem can solve all my problems.

If I would have skipped giving thanks to Hashem on the pretense that I wasn't sincere, because during difficult times I felt like venting emotions, crying and shouting, then I would have forfeited the blessings of reinforced *emuna*, happiness, and enhanced spiritual awareness. Also, I could have easily slid into a rut of bitterness and self-pity, thereby making my situation even worse by arousing stern judgments. By thanking Hashem, we solidify our *emuna* that everything is for the very best.

In light of the above, even if you want to flow with personal prayer according to the way you feel at a given time, don't neglect giving thanks for the basic blessings in life that you enjoy. People protest that their crying and shouting is real, whereas their gratitude is not. Yet, crying and shouting can sink a person into a deeper depression and a fit of anger, while gratitude can save him from anger and depression.

Despite the importance of giving thanks, personal prayer is still personal prayer. We should realize the importance of giving thanks, but we don't need to plan a regimented *hitbodedut*. It's enough that the rest our daily agenda is regimented. Our *hitbodedut* should flow with no limitations or rigid rules. The goal of our discussion about giving thanks is to realize the benefits of incorporating our gratitude to Hashem within the framework of our *hitbodedut*. When we ponder the things we should be thankful for, we become aware of Hashem's blessings and stop taking things for granted. The more we realize "How good it is to thank Hashem (Psalm 92:2)," the more we'll naturally gravitate toward thanking Hashem in the beginning of our personal prayer session.

Here are a few of the blessings that a person can always be thankful for: the Torah, the mitzvas, the Sabbath and holidays, the gift of personal prayers, the privilege of having a connection with *tzaddikim*, one's rabbi and spiritual guide, and many more. These are the spiritual blessings that one can't sufficiently thank Hashem for in a million years of personal prayer. That's why it's important to thank Hashem for these blessings at least once a day.

Most of us have two eyes that see, a normal heart, all of our limbs, a functioning brain, and many more blessings. Some people don't appreciate their blessings until they lose them, G-d forbid. By thanking Hashem for our healthy organs one by one, we assure their continued health.

The important aspect is to count our blessings and to thank Hashem for them. This is ever so conducive to more and bigger blessings.

B. Praying for hitbodedut

As we mentioned earlier, everything in life requires prayer; *hitbodedut* is no exception. The opportune time to ask Hashem to help us make the most out of our personal prayer session, to open our hearts, and to put the right words in our mouths is at the beginning of the session. This helps us enter *hitbodedut* with *emuna* and humility.

We especially need to ask Hashem to remind us of all the things we need to atone for and everything we need to pray for. We also ask Hashem to enlighten us as to what we should concentrate on during today's session and to assist us in honestly and candidly evaluating ourselves. More than anything, we should beg Hashem to lead us in the path of truth.

C. A prayer for the People of Israel

Praying daily for our brothers and sisters around the world is critically important. We should pray that everyone should come close to the true *tzaddik* and make *teshuva*. We should pray that everyone should learn *emuna*, and that each person talk to Hashem for an hour a day in personal prayer. We should pray for an end to exile and assimilation, and that Hashem should send us *Moshiach* and our rebuilt Holy Temple in Jerusalem. It's also important to pray for the nations of the world, that they should all recognize that Hashem is King; when that day comes, there will be true peace on earth. Self-evaluation

Rebbe Nachman cites the many blessings of self evaluation, when a person judges himself and resolves to improve his ways. By judging himself, he attains the true fear of G-d and therefore fears no one else (*Likutei Moharan* I:15). Also, by virtue of self-evaluation and introspection, what we call in Hebrew *cheshbon nefesh*, he acquires a deeper insight of the way Hashem runs the world and understands how everything in his life is for the very best. As such, this life becomes heavenly, as sweet as life in the next world (ibid. I:4).

The Zohar teaches that there is no double jeopardy in Heavenly jurisprudence: if a person judges himself, then the Heavenly court is not allowed to touch the case. Not only that, but Hashem casts away the accusing angels that come to report the said person's misdeeds, for the person has already confessed to Hashem.

The two huge benefits of judging oneself are: one, a person is much more lenient toward himself than anyone else is; and two, Hashem is ever-so-patient and forgiving, happy to accept our sincere *teshuva* and to let us make a new beginning.

Rabbi Levi Yitzchak Binder of blessed memory said that a person's life is like a book and each day is a page. When a person devotes an hour to self-evaluation and personal prayer, Hashem turns that day's page without judging that person at all for any misdeeds that he might have done that day.

Our session of self-evaluation is also an opportune time to thank Hashem for all the previous day's blessings, both material and spiritual. One need not spare words – the more we talk to Hashem, the better, for our expressions of gratitude to Hashem open our heart and enable us to express ourselves even more.

Daily self-evaluation and expressions of gratitude should be an integral part of our daily agenda, including Sabbath and holidays. Although we don't ask for material blessings on the Sabbath such as a good livelihood or a new house, we nevertheless don't miss a day of personal prayer. Our personal prayer sessions on Shabbat should center on expressions of thanks and praise to Hashem. If a person doesn't engage himself in personal prayer every single day, then expressing his gratitude is preferable to self-evaluation and *teshuva* on the Sabbath day. But, if a person is used to cleansing his soul every single day by way of self-evaluation and *teshuva*, he may do so also on the Sabbath.

As a general rule, one may not cry on the Sabbath day. Yet the Ram"a writes (*Shulchan Oruch, Orach Chaim* 288:2), "Whoever takes pleasure in crying so that sorrow will leave his heart, he may cry on Shabbat." As such, one who delights in doing *teshuva* may do so on Shabbat. Even if he cries while confessing his misdeeds, he will purge his heart from sorrow and will attain the level of happiness and pleasure that honors the Sabbath.

Avot D'Rebbe Natan (Chapter 15) relates an anecdote about Rabbi Eliezer who said, "Return to Hashem the day before you die." His students asked him how a person knows when he's going to die. Rabbi Eliezer answered, "Therefore, you must return to Hashem every single day; that way, all your days are in *teshuva*!"

The above anecdote teaches us that a person must make daily *teshuva*, for he never knows which day on earth will be his last. *Hitbodedut*, self-evaluation and *teshuva* are therefore vital parts of our daily routine seven days a week, including Shabbat.

Spiritually, Shabbat is a time of elevation. Our sages said (see tractate *Berachot*, 31) that the Heavenly Court rescinds seventy years of harsh decrees against a person who fasts on the Sabbath. Even though our personal prayers on the Sabbath should center around praise and gratitude, we should nonetheless never forget about *teshuva* and self-evaluation so that all our days will be spent in *teshuva*.

D. Regular prayers

Our sages teach us that a person's evil inclination attempts to overcome him every single day. Therefore, we must seek Hashem's help in overcoming our evil inclination daily. Most importantly, we should ask Hashem to help us guard our eyes, for one who guards his eyes will be spared of a long list of transgressions including coveting, adultery, and lewd thoughts, just to name a few. One cannot possibly guard one's eyes without constant supplication to Hashem, every single day of a person's life, for guarding our eyes is a lifelong test.

Another vital need we must ask for every day is *shalom bayit*, or marital peace. As mentioned in The **Garden of Peace**, marital peace is a person's foremost obligation, since his entire mitzvah observance, Torah study, and service of Hashem depend on his *shalom bayit*. Like guarding one's eyes, one must never stop praying for marital peace. A person who loses focus on making every effort toward marital peace in thought, speech, deed, and especially prayer is liable to see an immediate decrease in *shalom bayit*. The evil inclination is more than ready to fill the void left by the lack of prayer and to wreak havoc on a person's marital peace, G-d forbid. As such, we must always be on guard with our prayers.

E. Self improvement

Rebbe Nachman explains (*Likutei Moharan* I:52) that in order to overcome a bad habit or a certain lust one must devote extensive personal prayer, at least 30 minutes per day. The more serious the habit and the more difficult it is to overcome, the more daily personal prayer is required. In this manner, a person should pray daily until he rids himself of the habit altogether; this is the road to self improvement.

Once a person overcomes one particular negative trait or habit, he can then move forward to work on the next bad habit or negative characteristic on his self-improvement priority list. For example, suppose a person suffers from a bad temper and easily succumbs to anger. He should devote a substantial portion of his daily personal prayer session in begging Hashem to help him overcome his anger until he uproots anger altogether from his life. Other problems that arise from time to time necessitate core treatment, such as debts, marital strife, and health problems, all of which indicate a deeper root cause that must be reckoned with. Our problems in life are normally wake-up calls designed to trigger our self-evaluation and self-improvement.

An important element of self-improvement is praying to implement and internalize what we learn. This is what Rebbe Nachman referred to when he said that we should convert our Torah learning into prayers (see Rebbe Nachman's Discourses, 145; *Likutei Halachot, Rosh Chodesh*, 5; Outpouring of the Soul, 11). For example, when we read a *tzaddik*'s essay on the importance of guarding our eyes, we should then pray that Hashem will help us to implement and internalize all the points that were mentioned in the essay.

In summary, our daily personal prayer sessions are not only a time for us to give thanks to Hashem, to take stock in ourselves and to do daily *teshuva*, but also a time for self improvement. In addition to overcoming bad habits and negative character traits, we must ask incessantly for the positive attributes in the service of Hashem such as *emuna*, joy, humility, and diligence.

If only one could pray all day long...

Now that we've learned some of the basics of personal prayer, it's much easier to understand why Rebbe Nachman instructed us to devote at least an hour a day to *hitbodedut*. There are so many subjects that we have to cover in *hitbodedut* that in reality an hour is not enough. Rebbe Nachman therefore said that the strong-hearted person that truly desires to cling to Hashem aspires to pray all day long, just as our sages said in the *Gemara* (see tractate *Berachot*, page 21). But, since praying all day long isn't feasible for anyone other than a few rare *tzaddikim*, Rebbe Nachman prescribed an hour a day of personal prayer for each of us; understandably, an hour a day is the barest minimum.

A person that's truly honest with himself knows how much he needs improvement in the areas of praying with intent and learning Torah with diligence. He knows how hard it is to break his stubborn bad habits and to overcome his negative character traits. He's fully aware that his shalom bayit needs improvement. With so much to talk about with Hashem and to pray for, he knows that an hour is not enough. Such an individual never asks. "What do I talk to Hashem about for a whole hour?" A person who's honest with himself, recognizes his shortcomings and desires to improve them grabs every opportunity to speak to Hashem for two or even three hours. At any rate, he uses every opportunity during the day to speak to Hashem.

Learning to do an hour a day of *hitbodedut*

First of all, a person must accustom himself to talking to Hashem for an hour a day. This becomes second nature as soon as a person gets the feeling that he can't let the day go by without pouring his heart out to Hashem. To facilitate making *hitbodedut* a part of one's daily routine, a person should search for the easiest and most accessible way to do *hitbodedut*. For example, the beach might be your favorite place for *hitbodedut*. But, if you can't get there with ease – in other words, if it takes you two or three hours travel time – you're better off planning your personal prayer session in a local park or a nearby meadow.

In your first steps in *hitbodedut*, don't regiment yourself too much. Pray for whatever you want and talk to Hashem about whatever comes to mind. Let your conversation with Hashem flow. Use the seven areas that we discussed earlier in this chapter (order of *hitbodedut*, A to G) as guidelines. With a mere nine minutes devoted to each area, you will already have spent more than an hour in personal prayer. In time, you'll find that self-evaluation alone takes much more than nine minutes a session. Oftentimes, a problem or crisis that comes up will dominate a particular day's personal prayer session.

Daily self evaluation, when we take a good hard look at our deeds – both positive and otherwise – is an easy way to fill our designated daily hour. People who are new to personal prayer have trouble recalling the events of the previous day; since transgressions weaken a person's memory, one's uncorrected misdeeds cause forgetfulness. Daily *teshuva* that results from daily self-evaluation therefore sharpens the memory and makes it easier for a person to judge himself as time goes on.

A good way to start one's self-evaluation is by assessing one's daily mitzvoth. How was my *Shacharit*? Did I pray with intent? Did my mind wander? Did I fly through the prayers with impatience? How was my *Mincha*? My *Maariv*? Did I say the Grace after Meals properly, or did I speed through that too?

Don't be upset if you can't remember everything. Just speak to Hashem with innocence, with sincerity, and with candor. Let your feeling flow forth.

True daily self-evaluation requires an hour in itself. But, as we said before, one's first steps in *hitbodedut* should be simple and easy until he feels that he can't get through a day without an hour of personal prayer. Therefore, structure is less important that a free flow of speaking with Hashem that includes whatever subject comes to mind, gratitude, self-evaluation, asking for our spiritual and material needs, and praying for others.

The self-evaluation and self-improvement segments of our personal prayer are chances of a lifetime to better our lives in every aspect. Here, we can identify, analyze, and pray to overcome our shortcomings, bad habits, and negative character traits. We focus on the most pressing issues in our lives. We accustom ourselves to turn to Hashem for all our needs and we establish a most intimate relationship with Him.

Important points

Each of us has his or her focal points in life which become important points for daily personal prayer. A Yeshiva student will naturally gravitate toward prayers for increased understanding and success in his Torah studies. A young man or woman that has come of age will be asking for a soul mate. People with health issues will spend extra time talking to Hashem about their health. A smart businessman will seek Hashem's advice in regards to his current investments and transactions. An overweight person with an uncontrollable appetite will devote time and effort in asking for Hashem's assistance in overcoming his lust for food. All of us should be asking for *emuna*, for no single attribute so dramatically improves the quality of our lives like *emuna* does.

To flow with the hour

To summarize, a person must persevere with his daily hour of personal prayer until it becomes second nature, for as Rebbe Nachman teaches us, *hitbodedut* is a virtue that surpasses all other virtues (*Likutei Moharan* II:25). The Zohar promises that those who do daily self-evaluation will never see a moment of purgatory.

No matter how successful or unsuccessful one's daily hour of personal prayer may be, it still has the power to mitigate stern judgments. Hashem sees that a person is facing the challenge of setting aside an hour for personal prayer in attempt to get closer to Him, and whether or not the person speaks fluently or convincingly – even if he's choked up and doesn't speak at all – the mere desire to speak to Hashem atones for all sins and mitigates stern judgments.

Once a person becomes used to a daily hour of personal prayer, the hour seems to flow naturally, be it a weekday, Shabbat, or holiday.

Chapter Four:
The Truest Connection

Gratitude is the truest and strongest connection that a person can have with Hashem. As long as a person lacks gratitude, his relationship with Hashem will be lacking. Gratitude is not only the result of intellectual honesty and personal integrity; it's the basis of *emuna*. A grateful person sees Hashem's many favors and acts of loving-kindness and is therefore on a higher level of spiritual awareness than other people, for he recognizes Hashem's Divine providence all around him. The grateful person more easily internalizes the principles of *emuna*, particularly that Hashem does everything for the best. People with gratitude are therefore happy and much better adjusted than those who lack gratitude.

Prayers of gratitude should be the opening segment of our personal prayer session, ahead of all other prayers including confession and *teshuva*.

Gratitude is a matter of common sense and basic decency. It's only proper that a person should express appreciation for a gift, especially for the gift of life and livelihood. Saying "thank you" is the barest minimum show of gratitude. As such, we should be thanking Hashem constantly, for He's doing favors for us constantly. It's therefore no surprise that we say in the "*Nishmat*" prayer, "If our mouths were as full of song as the sea, and our tongues exultation as its many waves, and our lips praise as the breadth of the horizon, we can't sufficiently thank You Hashem our G-d for even one of the thousand and thousands of thousands and tens of thousands of favors, miracles, and wonders that You did for our fathers and for us..."

In reality, no amount of thanks is sufficient payment for even one tiny favor that Hashem does for us. Nevertheless, we must try to show our gratitude the best way we can.

The Zohar teaches that expressions of gratitude unlock the upper portals to our prayers. A person's thanks are an entry ticket directly to the Heavenly Throne. Gratitude silences the negative spiritual forces that are always honing in on people's faults. Conversely, nothing invokes the negative spiritual forces – *mekatregim* – like ingratitude. Our sages say that a person with gratitude makes the world worthwhile.

Gratitude is the first step toward *emuna*. According to Jewish law (see *Shulchan Aruch, Orach Chaim* 222:3), a person must thank Hashem for the seemingly bad as well as for the good. One cannot possibly implement this obligation without internalizing the principle of *emuna* that teaches that everything Hashem does is for the very best. Once we know that everything Hashem does is for our ultimate welfare, we can thank Him for everything, good or otherwise. Rebbe Nachman of Breslev teaches us that when a person knows that everything in life is for the very best, it's like living in paradise (*Likutei Moharan* I:4).

Emuna and tranquility

A person that comes to Hashem in personal prayer brings all his emotional "dirty laundry" – the things that sadden and discourage him, his fears and worries, the points where he's disappointed in himself, his dislikes – everything! *Emuna* and personal prayer "whiten the laundry" and brighten his life by helping him to realize that everything Hashem does is for the very best. In the respect, the optimal mindset for *hitbodedut* is the desire to live our *emuna* and realize that everything is for the best. This is a level of spiritual awareness that enables us to truly thank Hashem for everything – our successes and setbacks, our blessings and our shortcomings.

Thanking Hashem for life's problems and deficiencies brings a person to pure *emuna*. *Emuna* – the pure and simple belief in Hashem – is a prerequisite to true personal prayer, for how can a person speak to Hashem if he doesn't believe that Hashem is with him and listening? In addition, nothing in the world brings a person to such tranquility of the soul as *emuna* – knowing that everything is from Hashem and for the best. This soothes the pain of life's most difficult challenges.

Emuna brings a person to *simcha*, a deep inner sense of true joy. Therefore, the expressions of gratitude that lead to *emuna* are the key to successful and satisfying personal prayer. Rebbe Nachman of Breslev teaches (*Likutei Moharan* I:10) that *simcha* is the key to self composure, for a person who is happy has control over his thought process. One who isn't happy is bewildered and therefore sorely limited in his ability to express himself to Hashem. For that reason, we should begin our personal prayers with expressions of gratitude to Hashem. In summary, gratitude leads to *emuna*, *emuna* leads to joy, and joy leads to inner peace.

Simcha prevails

Nachman of Breslev teaches (*Likutei Moharan* II:23) that a person must chase after despair and depression and drag them into the joy department.

People ask, "What if something is really bothering me? I just don't feel happy!"

A depressed person can't express gratitude for the things that he knows are good, much less for life's challenges and hardships. Sometimes he adopts a strategy of looking for a good point and thanking Hashem for it, rather than directly confronting whatever it is that's bothering him. That's not the best way to escape depression.

The old expression says to grab the bull by the horns. We should take the most difficult problem we face and deal with it, asking Hashem to show us the truth and help us understand how our problem is for our very best. Frequently, we'll need extensive prayer to *believe* that our biggest problem in life is for our ultimate good. Yet, in the meanwhile, we must cling to the belief that it certainly *is* for the best. Once we attain the *emuna* that whatever is upsetting us is for the best, we can now truly thank Hashem and do proper *teshuva* and self-evaluation.

Without feeling gratitude to Hashem and expressing it, a person cannot possibly pray sincerely or conduct effective self-evaluation, for with no gratitude there's no *emuna*. Once a person begins to thank Hashem, *simcha* prevails, and one is now capable of moving forward in his personal prayer session to effective self-evaluation. Effective self-evaluation enables a person to identify that transgression or misdeed that triggered the difficult tribulation in the first place. Now that the person has identified his misdeed, he can correct it. Once he has done *teshuva* and has corrected the misdeed, then Heavenly sanctions are rendered superfluous. At this stage, the person's problem simply vanishes. When we arouse ourselves to seek Hashem, He doesn't need harsh wake-up calls to keep us from straying.

An honest heart

The advice of thanking Hashem for our problems is critical before serious soul-searching. Without it, intensive introspection is liable to bring a person to self-persecution and self-disdain. Thanking Hashem for our problems brings us to proper personal prayer whereas improper personal prayer is liable to perpetuate sadness and depression.

The reason people have difficulty in speaking to Hashem is because they're not happy. Rabby Nachman of Breslev says (Rebbe Nachman's Discouses, 20), that a person who's happy for 23 hours a day can easily speak from a broken heart for an hour a day. But, a person who's entire day is spent in depression and anxiety can't speak to Hashem, for depression and *emuna* are mutually exclusive and without *emuna*, one cannot talk to Hashem. Therefore, we confront our most difficult problem and deal with it, asking Hashem to show us the truth and help us strengthen our *emuna* to the extent that we realize how our problem is for our very best. In essence, we are asking Hashem to help us truly believe in Him with an honest heart to open our door to sincere and effective personal prayer.

The ploy of thanking Hashem for our problems is not only for those on a high spiritual plateau – it's for all of us. Remember, the negative feelings of unhappiness and depression are the opposite of *emuna*; *emuna* means that everything is for the best.

Gratitude is the result of an honest heart, for ingratitude is dishonesty, when one denies the wonderful favors that someone has done for him. An honest heart acknowledges those wonderful favors – large and small – and is therefore happy. King David therefore said (Psalm 97:11), "Joy goes to the honest of heart."

Everyone must express gratitude

No matter where a person is situated on the spiritual scale, expressing his or her gratitude to Hashem is the gateway of personal prayer and connecting to Hashem. As long as he doesn't realize that Hashem does everything for the very best and fails to thank Him, he won't be able to reach the point where he can properly correct the root cause of whatever it is that's bothering him. Once he attains the joy that results from gratitude, he can properly proceed to the stages of self-evaluation and *teshuva*.

Good points

Nachman of Breslev teaches us (*Likutei Moharan* I:4) that by way of confessing one's misdeeds, one realizes that everything if for the best. Therefore, the true *emuna* that everything is for the best necessitates daily *teshuva*. For that reason, self-evaluation and *teshuva* should always follow the initial stage of expressions of gratitude in our personal prayer.

What if despite our best efforts we don't yet feel happy and we can't properly do *teshuva*? A person can take a shortcut to happiness by searching for his own good points and rejoicing in them to the point of singing and dancing, as Rebbe Nachman teaches (ibid., 282). If you care enough about your relationship with Hashem to be reading this book, then you can sing and dance already. Our sages say that the mere desire to be righteous elevates a person to the level of a tzaddik!

Rebbe Nachman says that when a person identifies his good points and thanks Hashem for them, he in effect sifts his inner good from the bad; in the Heavens, such sifting creates an exquisite melody that resounds within that person's soul and brings him joy. That joy once again enables him to do *teshuva* (*Likutei Moharan* II:23).

In light of everything we've said until now, it's so very important that we ask Hashem to help us understand how everything in our life is for the very best and to thank Him for it. Rebbe Nachman writes (ibid. I:178) most people have difficulty in admitting their sins. Some forget them because they don't do daily self-evaluation. Others have a spiritual heaviness – feelings of depression and unhappiness - that preclude confession. But, by searching for our good points, we overcome the problem and open the gate to *teshuva*. As long as we neglect *teshuva*, we won't properly acquire *emuna*.

Emuna is the bridge

At this stage, people frequently ask how they can feasibly thank Hashem for whatever is causing them extreme pain or anguish. "It's totally illogical!" they protest. That's the whole point – once we put our logic aside, we open our clogged hearts and brains to the light of *emuna*. Once we internalize the knowledge and feeling that Hashem does everything for the best, we neutralize all bitter feelings and negative emotions with one snap of the fingers.

Emuna is the bridge that enables us to traverse this world in peace with ourselves and with our environment. Simple *emuna* is an express spiritual elevator that carries us directly to the upper echelons of spirituality and spiritual awareness.

Rebbe Natan of Breslev teaches that even if we haven't yet internalized the feeling that everything Hashem does is for the very best, it's enough that we believe in the true tzaddikim that tell us that everything Hashem does is truly for the very best. This enables us to thank Hashem and to praise His name for everything He does. If we did, says Rebbe Natan, all our troubles would disappear!

There is no despair

Rebbe Nachman taught us that there is no despair in the world at all. How can that be? Aren't there serious transgressions that severely blemish a person's soul? The answer is yes, but every cloud has a silver lining: Although we do our best to avoid transgressing, a person that has transgressed but has now done *teshuva* attains a greater soul correction than a person who has never transgressed. We see this principle in the physical world as well – if a cracked or broken metal object is properly welded, then the weld will be stronger than the original metal.

We can now understand why there's no despair in the world at all. Let's take a worst-case scenario: you've done a whopping misdeed that you're really upset about. The *Yetzer Hara* tells you that you're finished, complicating your own feelings of inadequacy because you haven't yet internalized the *emuna* that Hashem does everything for the best.

Here's the ray of hope: if you believe Rebbe Nachman was telling the truth when he promised us that there's no despair in the world at all, and as long as we're alive we can rectify ourselves, then we'll have the incentive to confess our wrongdoing and ask Hashem's forgiveness which will in turn bring us to joy and *emuna*.

The above principle is straight out of the *Gemara* (see tractate *Yoma* 86a). When a person makes *teshuva* out of love rather than out of fear of punishment, then his spiritual debits actually become credits!

Who can claim that their *teshuva* is the result of love of Hashem and not fear of punishment? Any person that invests an hour in personal prayer on his own initiative certainly falls into the category of those whose *teshuva* stems from the love of Hashem.

The way of emuna

Even if a voice from Heaven or a prophet comes along and tells you that you're finished, there's no hope, Hashem doesn't want you or your *teshuva*, or whatever you do is worthless, don't believe any of it! In such a case, one must tell oneself, "Hashem loves me! Everything is for the best! Rebbe Nachman promised that there's never room for despair!" That's the way of *emuna*.

Let's say – for the sake of argument – that we've done something so terrible that despite our *teshuva*, we've lost our portion in the world to come, Heaven forbid. Even this is for the best! Rebbe Nachman emphasizes (*Likutei Moharan* II:37) that true service of Hashem is when a person has no expectation of any reward, physical or spiritual, in this world or in the world to come. So, when we do sincere *teshuva* and serve Hashem after we've been told that we won't be remunerated in any way, we've attained a very lofty spiritual level of serving Hashem completely altruistically with no ulterior motives. Few people reach this exalted level that actually invokes every imaginable blessing in this world and in the next.

The *Gemara* tells the story of a scholar with brilliant potential, Elisha ben Abuya (see tractate *Chagiga*, 16a). He suffered several spiritual setbacks until a voice from Heaven declared that all mischievous sons are invited to come back to Hashem except him. He became so discouraged that he completely left the world of Torah and holiness. If Elisha ben Abuya would have had Rebbe Nachman's advice telling him that there's no despair in the world, he could have made a heroic spiritual comeback.

It's ever so important for our generation to know that with *emuna*, there's never any despair and there's always hope. When we reinforce ourselves with the resolve to do *teshuva* no matter what, we not only get back on our feet but we become much stronger than we were before the misdeed. A person must remember three critical words that are an effective spiritual lifesaver under any circumstances – "Hashem loves me!"

The ultimate purpose

One of life's mysteries is that many G-d-fearing people somehow fail to sing songs of praise to Hashem and to thank Him. Rebbe Nachman writes (*Likutei Moharan* II:2) that a person's Torah learning should bring him to gratitude, for expressing one's gratitude to Hashem is the sublime pleasure of the world to come. The Midrash says (*Vayikra Raba* 9:7) that in the future, all the ritual sacrifices will be cancelled except for the thanks-offering.

The Torah lists 98 terrible curses that are liable to befall on the Jewish people, G-d forbid. We ask ourselves why; what could a person do that's so terrible to warrant such calamity that the Torah describes in Chapter 28 of Deuteronomy? Bloodshed? Idolatry? Illicit sex? None of the three; the Torah says (Deuteronomy 28:47), "For you didn't serve Hashem with joy and with a willing heart," which is chastisement for not thanking Hashem.

A Jew in Hebrew is *Yehudi*, which comes from the Hebrew root word for giving thanks, *lehodot*. A Jew is one who gives thanks, for without giving thanks, there can be no *emuna*.

Throughout our book "The Garden of *Emuna*," we mentioned that ingratitude invokes stern judgments. A person can be judged leniently on his setbacks to lust, temptation, and sin, for one doesn't always win the battle with his evil inclination. But, there's no excuse for ingratitude. A person's constant complaints awaken the wrath of the Heavenly Court, while gratitude mitigates the sternest of judgments.

Educating to say thank you

Our sages of blessed memory had one goal when they codified our daily blessings and liturgy – to heighten our sense of appreciation for our many blessings in life and therefore to educate us to say "thank You" to Hashem.

We should therefore pray with joy, say our blessings with intent, and to recite our prayers with joy and song. We can even recite our silent *Shemona Esrei* with a silent melody in our heart, which on a spiritual level adorns the Divine Presence and mitigates all severe judgments.

Niggun, a melody, is powerful in arousing a person's heart. Breslever tradition relates a beautiful story about Rebbe Natan, who would travel from place to place in a covered wagon. Once, he was accompanied by one of his students who noticed that Rebbe Natan began his prayers with a heaviness of heart. Gradually, Rebbe Natan become humming a melody which he later applied to his prayers. His praying became progressively more joyous until his face was on fire with enthusiasm. He was so absorbed in his prayer that he was impervious to everything going on around him. He was singing in such magnificient sweetness that the Ukrainian peasants began running after the wagon to hear.

By the time Rebbe Natan reached the *Shemona Esrei* prayer, he was so deep in prayer that he didn't feel the bitter cold of the Ukrainian winter or the fact that the wagon had now come to a halt in front of an inn. His student had to help him off the wagon and take him inside the inn so that he could pray his Shmona Esrei prayer indoors.

When Rebbe Natan completed his prayers, his student asked him how he was able to uplift himself from the heaviness that characterized the beginning of his prayers and to ultimately pray in such joy and holy fervor. Rebbe Natan answered, "I remembered what Rebbe Nachman taught me: A person has to revitalize himself with a melody of happiness and especially during prayer, for such a melody pulls the heart to Hashem (see Rebbe Nachman's Discourses, 273). So I implemented his advice and was therefore able to bring my heart to Hashem." Amazing

It's amazing that many of us fly through our prayers, especially in light of the fact that our prayers are based on King David's Psalms, which are none other than songs of praise and gratitude to Hashem. It seems rather odd – we begin our morning prayers ("*Hodu*") with a call to all of creation to thank Hashem, to sing His praise, and to tell of His wonders; yet, we ourselves are not doing what we're calling everyone else to do. We call the world to rejoice in Hashem, but we ourselves don't.

If only we'd sing to Hashem and thank Him sincerely, all our troubles would be null and void. Diaspora would give way to redemption, for all of life's difficulties are rooted in our lack of joy and gratitude in our service of Hashem.

Torah in song

For one to fully appreciate Hashem and to thank Him, one must learn Torah. Yet, Torah learners mustn't forget that the ultimate purpose of Torah learning is to bring a person to thank Hashem.

The Torah itself must be recited in melody. We should sing our blessings, our Psalms, our Torah learning and our prayers as well.

The virtue of a melody

Rebbe Natan spares no praise when describing the virtue of a melody: "The primary way to get close to Hashem and to cling to Him is by way of the holy sounds of songs of praise and melodies" (Likutei Halachot, even Haezer, Ishut, 4). Learning

Learning about *emuna* is a wonderful and effective way to bring a person to gratitude.

Daily learning of *halacha* (Jewish law) is an absolute necessity for the correction of one's soul. Since transgressions blemish the soul and thereby distance a person from Hashem, one who doesn't know what's permissible and what's not will ultimately have a soul that's extremely blemished. Such a soul is not a suitable receptacle for Divine light and therefore loses its proximity to Hashem. For that reason, a person should learn *halacha* every single day.

What's right and what's wrong is the outer dimension of *halacha*. The inner dimension of *halacha* tells us how to strengthen our *emuna*, how to do proper *teshuva*, and how to heal the blemishes of the soul. This inner dimension is best-learned in the writings of the tzaddik, who guides people on the proven path to Hashem. *Emuna* and the knowledge of Hashem are the principle lessons we learn from the tzaddik, as seen in the book, "The Garden of *Emuna*," which brings a person to a life of joy, purpose, meaning, and closeness to Hashem.

The perfect ploy

A childless woman came to me several years ago complaining that she had done everything in an effort to receive the blessing of children. She prayed incessantly, made daily *teshuva*, gave as much as she could to charity, visited Kabbalists and did all kinds of Kabbala ploys, ate health foods only, exercised, and visited the leading fertility specialists, but to no avail. She and her husband were at their wits' end. "Will I never hug my own baby?" she pleaded tearfully.

I told the woman to forget about the Kabbala incantations, the ploys, and even the prayers. All she has to do is to speak to Hashem for an hour a day and thank Him. I told her exactly what to say: "Thank You, Hashem, for not giving me children until now, for I'm sure that my being childless is for the very best, since everything You do is for the best and surely to help me correct my soul. Thank You, Hashem, for giving children to my girlfriends. Help me be magnanimous and wish the very best for other women, that I should never be jealous or resentful of other people's blessings. Let me thank You with a pure and true heart for each child that's born to one of my girlfriends." Then, I told her to conclude her daily hour of personal prayer with a humble appeal to Hashem: "Master of the World, beloved Father in Heaven, if the idea of my having children finds favor in Your eyes, please bless me with the free gift of my own children." I then promised her that with such personal prayer she will surely be blessed with children.

She asked me, "How are these prayers any different from all the other prayers I've been saying? I've been praying, pleading, and doing *teshuva* all along!"

I answered that the major difference is one word – gratitude. Gratitude is a marvelous expression of *emuna*, namely, that a person recognizes that everything Hashem does is for the very best and therefore thanks Hashem for everything, the good and the seemingly bad (as required by *Halacha*, see *Shulchan Aruch, Orach Chaim* 222:3). "You are showing Hashem with your words of gratitude that you know that the only reason you don't have children is because of His will only," I concluded.

Without expressing our gratitude to Hashem – which of course is one of the most cogent statements of *emuna* that can be – our prayers, *teshuva*, and mitzvah observance are limited in their effectiveness. When people fail to recognize Hashem's guiding hand behind all of life's events, they are liable to become very bitter, blaming themselves or other people for their problems. What's worse, when they haven't learned and internalized the principles of *emuna*, they blame Hashem for making their lives miserable and causing them to suffer.

We therefore see a shocking misinterpretation of events wherever people are blind to *emuna*: what should be gratitude – thanking Hashem for doing everything for our ultimate good – turns into blasphemy, where people feel bitter towards Hashem because they see no purpose to their tribulations in life. Such feelings not only obstruct the ascent of their prayers, but arouse even more stern judgments.

Thanking for everything

Giving thanks is our main purpose in this world and in the world to come, for it brings us to true *emuna*, brings us close to Hashem, and mitigates severe judgments. What's more, giving thanks hastens the *Geula*, the full redemption of our people.

A main tenet in our faith, as mentioned earlier, requires a person to thank Hashem for the seemingly bad as well as for the good. For example, a person must thank Hashem if he doesn't feel well or if he fails to close an important and potentially lucrative deal. Why? Ultimately, all the trials and tribulations of this world are actually enormously beneficial to the soul in the long run. Rebbe Nachman of Breslev teaches that if a person looks at the spiritual value of his suffering – its ability to atone for wrongdoing, its power to cleanse a soul, its intent of stimulating a person to do *teshuva* and to seek Hashem, and its value in strengthening a person's character – his heart fills with joy, for truly, there is nothing bad, and everything is good (*Likutei Moharan* I:65).

With the above teaching in mind, we can truly thank Hashem for life's setbacks, shortcomings, and tribulations, for everything is certainly for the very best. When we truly realize that the essence of the seemingly bad is to draw us closer to Hashem, our hearts fill with joy and the gates of prayer open wide for us.

The good measure – all the more so

To understand just how powerful expressions of gratitude are, let's examine the opposite – complaining for no reason. A person's lack of content in life – the shortcoming of most people – is the principle manifestation of heresy. As such, nothing so terribly separates a person from Hashem and invokes stern judgments as complaints and malcontent. Even worse, they prolong the exile and delay the full redemption of our people.

We learn how dangerous complaining is from the sin of the spies who slandered the land of Israel and thereby weakened the people's resolve to fulfill Hashem's commandment to enter the Land (see

Numbers, Chapters 13-14). The People of Israel cried and complained a whole night for no reason. Their blasphemy against Hashem was terrible, for they said (see Deuteronomy 1:27) that Hashem took them out of Egypt because He hates them, G-d forbid, and wants to deliver them into the hand of the Amorites in Canaan.

The Midrash and the Gemara both tell us that because of one night's crying (that happened to be on the 9th day of Av, what's known in Hebrew as *Tisha B'av*), this night will be a night of crying for posterity. From this decree came the destruction of both Holy Temples, the Spanish Inquisition, and the exile of our people to this very day. Not only that, but the entire generation was killed off and not allowed to enter the Land of Israel except for Yehoshua Bin Nun and Calev ben Yephune, the two spies who spoke favorably about Hashem and the Land of Israel.

One is dumbstruck: Why does Hashem punish the Children of Israel for posterity because of one night's crying? They didn't commit idolatry, spill a fellow man's blood, or engage in debauchery, the three worst sins in the Torah. They simply cried and complained for a night. Let's give them a break - the spies frightened them. Or, maybe they were just weary from traveling in the desert. Why were they punished so severely?

We learn here that crying and complaining that stems from a lack of *emuna* is by far the most heinous transgression in the Torah!

A principle of Torah states that the reward for a good deed is five-hundred times greater than the punishment for an equivalent misdeed. Therefore, if crying and complaining have the power of invoking the most severe judgments in the Torah, then expressing our gratitude to Hashem mitigates those very same severe judgments 500 times over and invoke limitless blessings.

On a practical level, if a person is undergoing harsh trials and tribulations, the very best thing he can do for himself is to begin thanking Hashem, and thanking, and thanking…

The best advice is to thank Hashem for the severe tribulation itself! An expression of gratitude is the greatest statement of *emuna* there can be. It shows that a person recognizes that everything comes from Hashem, Who does everything for one's ultimate good, including the current trials and tribulations. Since the tribulation is from Hashem, it's obviously for one's own benefit and therefore worthy of one's gratitude to Hashem. Hashem knows just how vital life's difficulties are for each person's individual soul correction. Therefore, complaining about those difficulties indicates a lack of *emuna*. Constant expressions of gratitude are therefore vital for a person's spiritual growth.

No troubles and no exile

Gratitude is the most important element of personal prayer. Gratitude determines the quality of a person's entire connection with Hashem as well as the quality of one's personal prayers. Consequently, many obstacles try to obstruct our expressions of gratitude. It seems so much easier – and more natural – to complain and cry about our deficiencies and to ask Hashem to provide us with whatever we lack.

Most people are unaware that gratitude more than anything else invokes Divine abundance. One should therefore begin every *hitbodedut* session with expressions of gratitude, beginning with the fixed blessings in our lives (those that don't change from day to day) such as our parents, our spouses, and our children. Take nothing for granted and don't forget to thank Hashem for our lungs and for the air we breathe. Afterward, we can thank Hashem for the particular blessings in the last 24 hours.

Gratitude redeems

The evil inclination incites a person to cut his expressions of gratitude short and to begin praying for salvation from his problems. People often feel a greater need to yell out to Hashem and plead for relief from their troubles than they do to say thank-you for their blessings in life. Yet, expressions of gratitude are much more conducive in arousing Divine compassion than tears, because the catalyst of a person's troubles in the first place is ingratitude.

Rebbe Natan writes (*Likutei Halachot, Prika V'tina* 4), that a person's difficulties in life stem from the fact that he doesn't believe that everything is for the best. He sees occurrences that he doesn't understand and he's suspicious that Hashem is guilty of injustice, Heaven forbid. This feeling invokes Divine concealment and a subsequent spiritual void that is soon filled with troubles of all kinds.

Conversely, expressions of gratitude to Hashem both for life's good and for its seemingly bad are an acknowledgment that we believe that Hashem does everything for the best. This combination of *emuna* and gratitude turns Divine concealment into Divine proximity. Under Hashem's wing, troubles end and a person sees Divine salvation eye to eye. As such, *emuna* and gratitude are the best way to overcome our problems.

The light of truth

Rebbe Nachman teaches us an additional principle (see *Likutei Moharan* II:2), namely, that a person can speak the truth only if he is accustomed to giving thanks to Hashem. Expressions of gratitude cause the light of truth to be revealed and to illuminate. As such, any speech – even prayer – that's devoid of gratitude is flawed with falsities. One might ask, what's false about it? The answer is simple – there's no greater falsity than thinking that Hashem doesn't do everything for the best. So, when a person fails to thank Hashem for everything, he's far from the truth and therefore falls into the darkness of Divine concealment.

Darkness and unholy influences (*kelipot*) surround a person when he begins to pray and do their best to prevent him from praying or at least to rob him of his intent during prayer (ibid. I:9). Rebbe Nachman says that the solution to this is to speak a few words with truth and intent, so that these few words will illuminate the darkness. Gratitude enables a person to utter those few truthful words, which create an opening to escape from the darkness.

Why did You make things worse?

Hashem sent Moses to demand that Pharaoh free the Children of Israel from bondage. The immediate result of Moses's confrontation with Pharaoh resulted in a worsening of conditions for the Israelite slaves. The two infamous troublemakers Dothan and Aviram insolently protested that Moses did more damage than good. (Exodus 5:21). Moses then turned to Hashem in an apparent bitter complaint, "Why have You made made things worse for this nation, why did you send me? (ibid. 22).

Could it be that Moses sided with the evil Dothan and Aviram by doubting that Hashem does everything for the best? Definitely not! Moses protested the fact that Dothan and Aviram were allowed to weaken the *emuna* of their brethren, and thereby delay their redemption from bondage. For, as Rebbe Natan teaches, a person's difficulties in life stem from the fact that he doesn't believe that everything is for the best. In retrospect, we know today that Moses's confrontations with Pharaoh played a big part in the redemption process. But, by Dothan and Aviram's denial that Hashem does everything for the best, Moses was worried that the entire redemption process would be delayed. In fact, Rebbe

Natan writes emphatically that the Dothan and Aviram of every generation prolong exile and Diaspora.

At any rate, Hashem chastised Moses for asking, "Why have You made made things worse?" Everything – with no exceptions – is for the ultimate and absolute benefit of every creation. Therefore, no matter how dire or difficult one's predicament or circumstance may seem, salvation lies in our expressions of gratitude and pure and simple *emuna* that everything is for the best. By thanking Hashem for the seemingly bad as well as for the good, He will surely redeem us and all of Israel in the nearest future.

The gates of joy

Most people entertain the misconception that tears and wailing are what constitutes good prayer. They're disappointed if they don't cry during the silent *Amida* or during *hitbodedut*, citing the *Gemara* that says the gates of tears are never closed. Yet, perfect prayer is the prayer that emerges from joy, for crying and tears are liable to be damaging.

Rebbe Natan of Breslev cites (see *Likutei Halachot, Kriat Shema*, 2) King David's directive in Psalm 100 to serve Hashem with joy, referring to prayer, which is called "service of the heart." Our sages conclude (*Gemara*, tractate *Berachot* 31a) that one should pray with the orientation of joy.

How then do we reconcile the apparent contradiction in the *Gemara* (ibid, 32b) that the gates of tears are never locked? These are not the tears of despair, but the tears of longing for Hashem. Even though tears have their value in stimulating deep emotion and intent, what we call "kavanna" in prayer, if not used properly, tears can cause many people to slip into self-pity and a mindset of complaint and discontent. As such, only the tears of joy and yearning for Hashem are effective in unlocking the gates of prayer. But, with joy and gratitude, there are no gates at all. The prayer that results from inner joy is an agent for healing and salvation for virtually everything.

Caution – crying for nothing!

Tears during prayer are not prerequisites for our prayers to be accepted, as many people seem to believe. In fact, they could be detrimental, especially if a person cries for no reason. As we mentioned previously, the Midrash and the Gemara both tell us that because of one night's crying for nothing (that happened to be on the 9th day of Av, what's known in Hebrew as *Tisha B'av*), the Jewish people would cry for posterity. From this decree came the destruction of both Holy Temples, the Spanish Inquisition, and the exile of our people to this very day…

There is no transgression in the Torah that has even one millionth of the punishment that crying, complaining, and ingratitude have, as we so blatantly see in the aftermath of the complainers, which the Torah calls '*nirganim*' – those who cry and complain for no reason. King Solomon, the wisest of all men says (Proverbs 16:28), *Nirgan mafrid aluph,* in other words, complaining creates a total breach with Hashem, Heaven forbid. In other words, as soon as a person cries for no reason, he severs himself from Hashem, Heaven forbid.

A wonderful benefit

"And Yeshurun waxed fat and kicked (Deuteronomy 32:15)" is the Torah's own testimony that when people are too successful, too affluent, and too comfortable, they not only drift away from Hashem, but they kick as well!

Imagine that you had a seven-figure annual income after taxes, career success, public recognition, prestige, a perfect marriage, perfect health, wonderful problem-free children, and all the amenities in life you dreamed of. Would you be calling Hashem's Name? Would you seek Him at all? The Torah says no. Because Hashem does everything for the best, He doesn't put us in a situation that's conducive to spiritual slumber.

Life's difficulties and challenges are wonderfully beneficial in that they stimulate us to seek Hashem constantly. Our deficiency prods us to pray with fervor. Our setbacks prevent us from becoming arrogant and trigger heartfelt pleas for Hashem's assistance and guidance. Knowing how our troubles in life are so spiritually beneficial – in this world and in the world to come - we must thank Hashem for them always!

A woman came to me with a terrible case of acne that scarred and marred her face. She desired to do a six-hour session of *hitbodedut* to invoke Divine compassion.

I told her that she could certainly do a lengthy personal prayer session, but to begin by thanking Hashem for her acne, for by virtue of her terrible complexion problem, she's making spiritual growth in leaps and bounds. If she were a magazine-cover model, she certainly wouldn't be seeking Hashem. Once she makes peace with Hashem and truly believes that her problem is indeed for her ultimate benefit, then she can contemplate in her *hitbodedut* why Hashem is using this particular problem as an attention-getter or wake-up call.

Pray with a smile

When a person is not grateful to Hashem for his problems, he doesn't understand and appreciate the true kindness and mercy that is instilled in this "problem". If he prays by crying and complaining, as if Hashem had, G-d forbid, wronged him - such a prayer does more harm than no prayer at all. Many people err in this way; all of their prayer sounds like complaint, lacking the faith that all is for the good.

On the other hand, if a person prays with joy, he doesn't risk being turned away. Hashem will smile with gratification. Tears that result from one's yearning for Hashem or a broken heart are no problem. But, crying should not be the central element of one's prayer, for he is then liable to fall into pointless crying, which is very detrimental.

We shouldn't begin any prayer that will be a weeping and grievance session. Rebbe Nachman teaches (*Likutei Moharan* II:24), that even from a truly broken heart, one can easily fall into sadness, and all the more so when at the outset, one intends to make a complaint. The transgression of sadness is much more severe than any other sin. For pointless crying, a terrible decree was brought down upon generations, which incurred a punishment more severe than that of any other wrongdoing in the Torah.

The next few pages show several examples of how to correctly cope with the challenges of life, and how one should approach each prayer in such a way that it will be accepted. Also, one will be able to reinforce *emuna* and to become close to Hashem in every situation, better or worse. Even from the very greatest sorrow, one can merit spiritual growth, recognize the merciful Creator, and be redeemed from his sorrows as well.

A wonderful gift

About thirty years ago, Hashem gave me a wonderful gift—debts.

Not small debts of thousands of dollars, but rather large debts which amounted to many tens of thousands. By natural law, these debts should have been impossible to return, because I would have had to work day and night just to pay off the monthly interest.

I did some soul-searching and understood that since there's no suffering without prior transgression, then surely I must need a *tikkun* ("soul correction" to repair some spiritual flaw), and due to this, I had become a debtor.

I said to myself: These debts are like a tree. Every solution I find, every effort I make, is only like cutting a branch off of the tree. In place of the severed branch, other branches will grow back. The only solution is to make a thorough treatment at the root of the problem. This is only possible by prayer and repentance.

My teacher and Rabbi, Rav Eliezer Berland, *Shlit"a*, who also went through a time in his life when he had heavy debts, encouraged me and said, "You should know! The way that the debts brought me close to Hashem - nothing else in the world ever brought me so close!"

I received additional encouragement from my friend, who owed a sum of money to a certain Rabbi. That Rabbi told him that according to the *halacha* (Jewish religious law), my friend was obligated to leave the Yeshiva and work, until he would have paid off his debt.

That friend was a very honest, upright person. He went out and did *hitbodedut*, relating to Hashem that the Rabbi had told him to leave the Yeshiva and go to work. Then, he made the following proposal to Hashem: instead of going to work to do odd jobs, forfeiting a great deal of Torah and prayer, he would instead indenture himself into the service of Hashem! How many hours are there in a typical workday? Eight hours? He promised to do eight daily hours of *hitbodedut*. So it was! Each day, my friend would go and do a full day of *hitbodedut* in the fields, and he quickly paid off the debt!

True, relative to the large debts that I had, my friend owed only a small amount of money. But his story still gave me great encouragement! I, too, decided to go to work in Hashem's service! And when people would tell me that I was obligated to go to work or to collect charity, I wouldn't argue. I would listen to their advice and go to work - for Hashem! I'd also collect charity, but from Hashem only!

It was clear to me that Hashem was, is, and will be the only One that can possibly solve the problem for me, especially with these enormous debts. If I would have attempted to cover them by working or by charity, I wouldn't have been able to pay them off.

Double Profit

I began to do *hitbodedut* daily, concentrating on the matter of the debts. At the beginning of my solitary personal prayer session, I would thank Hashem for the gift of debts. I clearly recognized the debts as a marvelous gift inspiring me to come closer to Hashem. From enduring these debts, I immediately benefited in two ways:

First, I was inspired to lengthen my prayers, since without the debts my prayers would have been much shorter. In such dire trouble, one has no difficulty praying from the depths of the heart and crying out to Hashem with all his might. I saw in this a great salvation. I had been stimulated to pray with power and with heartfelt intent as opposed to mechanically going through the motions of *hitbodedut*. I clearly recognized the enormous spiritual difference between the two types of *hitbodedut* that I had experienced, before I had the debts and after I had the debts.

Second, with every personal prayer regarding the debts, Hashem granted me another insight - additional spiritual elements in my life that I needed to correct. By virtue of the debts, I became closer and closer to Hashem, and this gave me great happiness.

In summary, I recognized that my spiritual state was improving every day by virtue of my prayers and repentance. This filled me with tremendous joy, for nothing is greater than getting close to

Hashem, as King David, of blessed memory, said, "But as for me, G-d's nearness is my good," (Psalm 73:28). For in truth, what brings happiness in this world? Even if a man has all the wealth on earth, this world's bitterness will not bring him satisfaction. If so, what joy is there on earth, except for coming close to Hashem? With this in mind, at the outset of each *hitbodedut*, I expressed sincere gratitude for the debts.

After I looked at my predicament with eyes of *emuna* and rejoiced in the debts, I danced with happiness at every opportunity. It reached a point that people who knew me and knew of my situation were amazed. They wondered, "What on earth is he dancing about? Such a terrible predicament, and he's dancing and happy! Has Shalom lost his wits, G-d forbid?

I'd answer them like the Simple one in Rebbe Nachman's tale of "The Simple and the Clever" (Tales, 13): "I live a good life, lacking nothing whatsoever. What constitutes my good life? I have debts!"

I never became at all disoriented from my debts. I believed with wholehearted faith that there is no error in Hashem's Divine Providence. The fact that I have debts is surely for the good. I used to encourage my wife that we'd soon emerge from debt. I reassured her that once we pass this test without losing our steadfast faith - serving Hashem with prayer and repentance - we'd be in the clear. Even better, we'll have attained marvelous tools of faith and security, tools that will accompany us throughout our lives.

He Who Knows Secrets

After I thanked Hashem profusely, I would pray for a long time that Hashem should enlighten me as to the wrongdoing I had been punished for by becoming a debtor, and that He should grant me the privilege to repent and to make a spiritual rectification. I prayed that I'd be able to repent daily for this wrongdoing until it was fully atoned for it. And since I still didn't know for which specific wrongdoing I had become a debtor, most of my prayer was general:

"Master of the World! The wrongdoing, for which I have been punished with debts, is clear and known only to You. For our sages have said that there is a wrongdoing for which a man becomes a debtor, but they did not reveal which wrongdoing. Master of the World, please have mercy upon me. Forgive me for my misdeeds. Grant me the opportunity to repent and to atone for them. Please be patient with me."

A New Proximity

And so, I prayed daily for a long time, at least an hour each time, and every time, I saw miracles, salvations, and Divine protection. Within a year from the time I began my intensive service of Hashem and daily *hitbodedut*, Hashem helped me to be free of all my debts!

My Rabbi and teacher encouraged me. I was privileged with a new proximity to Hashem, a closeness which I would not have possibly merited except by these very debts. I also received many wonderful gifts of faith and spiritual security, gifts which to this day accompany me personally and help me in the service of the entire Jewish people.

Throughout all the time that I had debts, I was not saddened by them. I was happy all the time. Even though we sometimes lacked a loaf of bread at home, I felt no sadness. We simply repented daily and prayed in regard to the debts; as such, we were spared from all stern judgments.

People must understand that when one feels sadness, it is the result of stern judgments from Above. The Heavenly Court asks, "Why doesn't he wake up and evaluate himself? Why doesn't he search for the root of his problem?" A person has debts, but instead of repenting, he foolishly attributes the debts to nature and happenstance. This lack of spiritual awareness triggers a stiff measure of harsh judgments upon a person, as the Torah says: "And if despite this you will not heed Me, and you behave towards Me with casualness, I will behave toward you with a fury of casualness; I will chastise you, even I, seven ways for your sins." (Leviticus 26:27-28).

Stern judgments manifest themselves in all sorts of ways to torment a person until he realizes that no tribulations come without prior transgression. The moment a person wakes up and tries to repent, the stern judgments come to a halt. Without them, one feels no sorrow. Therefore, one who repents daily never suffers, even though he has not yet completed the necessary spiritual correction, or *tikkun,* and is still in a difficult material situation. *Emuna* illuminates his soul, and he feels joy.

Even more so, if he does his best to prevent other people from suffering because of his debts, Hashem helps him and redeems him from the debts easily and quickly.

It could have been different

I would not have been able to return the debts so quickly, had I sunk down into a negative mental state, blaming myself or my wife or other people, becoming pressured, unhappy, despairing, tormenting myself or feeling pathetic, looking for pity, shaking off all responsibility and causing others anguish. Who knows if to this day, I would have ever emerged from debt? Who knows what sufferings could have come about if I would have angered and irritated those whom I owed money? And surely, had I sunk into depression, I wouldn't have received the wonderful gifts which I received. I wouldn't have written this book and other books, I would not have established Yeshivot and brought secular Jews closer to Torah, and I would not have rescued many debtors whom I have guided to emerge from debts for large monetary sums.

All these accomplishments were possible because I clung to my *emuna* in Hashem and was therefore able to come closer to Him, to believe that all is for the good, and to recognize that this is what He wills. I refused to sink into the quagmire of depression, but rather went happily to communicate with Hashem with the goal of becoming closer to Him from these very debts.

Hashem rescued me from my huge debts in the easiest of ways, through the wonderful path of prayer and repentance. This experience inspired me to teach Torah classes and write books in order to guide other Jews in this path of repentance and prayer so that they too will merit the main part of the salvation—getting closer to Hashem. Finding the practical solution to the difficulties at hand actually becomes secondary.

Using the problem as a lever

Approaching any challenge with *emuna* and remembering that everything in life comes from Hashem for the very best and for the purpose of bringing a person closer to Hashem, enables one to pray properly. With *emuna*, a person's problem becomes a stimulus that inspires long and heartfelt prayer. He doesn't allow the evil inclination to weaken his resolve or confuse him.

One with no challenges sleeps his life away. Nothing awakens him to the authentic Divine service of repentance, spiritual introspection, and lengthy prayer. A tribulation that causes pain or requires work triggers Divine service.

No one wants to suffer. But, when problems befall a person such as a delay in finding a soul mate or in having children, illness, debts, and so forth, one should address himself to the Infinite G-d, Who is all goodness. He should perceive that all the Creator's intentions are only for his ultimate benefit—to awaken him to repentance or to cleanse him of wrongdoing. When he focuses upon the Infinite G-d, that is, upon His intentions, he will no longer experience any suffering whatsoever. On the contrary, he will be filled with joy from the great benefit he derives from these very sufferings. He'll begin to express heartfelt gratitude. These very problems represent a golden opportunity to pray with great devotion and to come much closer to Hashem.

Suffering should not reduce a person to pettiness and sadness, G-d forbid, but rather evoke in him the realization that all Hashem's actions are for the good. Tribulations awaken him to pray more and to repent. In this way, by means of his problems, he gets closer to Hashem.

Waking Up

Anyone experiencing a problem of any sort should give abundant thanks for that very problem. Then, he can pray to Hashem about the problem, doing his best to decipher the Creator's message to him. If he fails to accept his situation with *emuna*, his prayer won't be received. Prayers of faith reach their destination.

Once, a young married man told me that he had a very difficult problem with getting up in the morning. It made no difference what he did and how many alarm clocks he put near his bed, or how much his wife tried to shake him awake. Nothing helped - he remained sound asleep and woke up only in the afternoon hours. Then, he'd begin the day on the wrong foot, unable to accomplish anything. Clearly, his inability to rise in the morning brought on many related difficulties.

Obviously, his wife couldn't stand seeing her husband snoring away throughout the morning. When she left for work, he'd roll over and continue sleeping. She already had threatened to leave him if this continued. He didn't know what to do. How could he rejoice in this dreadful situation? From every direction, he caught insults. He violated Jewish law in a number of ways, particularly by not praying in time. His wife could no longer endure this situation. How could he thank Hashem for this problem? Would it not be complete irresponsibility on his part to rejoice in such a difficulty?

I answered him: "If you use this problem as a lever to initiate heartfelt, extensive prayers, and you invest each day at least a half hour in asking Hashem to help you with this problem of your inability to rise in the morning, then there is no irresponsibility. I promise that if you do so, you will suffer no anguish from the late rising. Your wife will also not be upset. You won't incur any stern judgments regarding the transgressed religious laws.

"Rejoice in that you are fulfilling your role. Hashem doesn't hold grievances against His creatures. Prayer is the only solution to your problem. What else can you do? Persecute yourself? Sink into depression? Will that solve your problem?

"On the contrary, as long as you do not rejoice with your problem, you won't be able to solve it! The first thing you must do is to rejoice that Hashem has granted you the gift of this problem. It's a prime stimulus to inspire your prayer and repentance. Nothing is better than this. Only afterwards should you devote yourself to lengthy prayers regarding the particulars of this problem.

"Then, you'll surely find the solution to your difficulty. You'll attain wonderful gifts and come closer to Hashem. Even during the time during which you have not yet solved the problem, it will cause you no grief."

This helps us understand what Rebbe Nachman wrote (*Likutei Moharan* I:10), that through dancing and clapping, we can sweeten all the stern judgments. The explanation given there shows that according to mystical tradition and Kabbalah, a Jew's every movement affects the higher worlds. When a Jew dances and claps his hands, marvelous metaphysical *tikkunim* are achieved. One attains *emuna*, atheism is rendered null and void, and the Divine spirit is brought closer. In addition, when a Jew dances and claps his hands, he does so only to sing and thank Hashem. His expression of thanks and singing mitigates all stern judgments, as explained above.

We can now understand the words of our Sages, of blessed memory: "If someone utters *Amen yehei shemei rabbah mevorach* with all his might, he merits that even a seventy-year-long decree is torn up for him." The response of *Amen yehei shemei rabbah mevorach* in the Kaddish prayer is a marvelous expression of gratitude and praise to Hashem. Through this response, all stern judgments are sweetened.

Jewish law accordingly requires that when the members of the congregation are reciting the *Modim* prayer, one is obligated to bow down together with them, even if he is not up to that section of the prayers. Similarly, when the members of the congregation recite the *Aleinu Lishabe'ach* prayer, every person present must say it together with them, even if he had already concluded his prayers and is only passing by. Rabbinical authorities teach that if he does not do so, the ministering angels are liable to say accusingly: "Look at that man! When the congregation praises Hashem, he does not join in with them! "

The expression of thanks to Hashem is the ultimate goal, beyond all other goals. Creation was created for the ultimate purpose that man will recognize his Creator and thank Him. This is explained in the works of the Ramban (*Al HaTorah, Parashat Bo*). Thus, a man who expresses thanks to Hashem fulfills his ultimate goal and the goal of all Creation. Hashem performs miracles and wonders in his behalf, and he merits phenominal redemptions.

Thanking Hashem is a prime expression of *emuna* and of understanding Hashem's reign. A person who does not express gratitude for everything is far from *emuna*. True faith only begins when a person expresses gratitude to Hashem for everything.

The Evil Inclination—Very Good!

Emuna enables a person to taste the sweetness of this world. *Emuna* alone is the answer to all questions and the solution to the world's problems. Where there's *emuna*, everything is good. There is no concept of "bad" at all. With *emuna*, even the evil inclination is very good.

The moment a man begins to live with *emuna* and to request that Hashem should guide him and direct him in life, then everything is excellent. Life's difficulties, challenges, and problems all become part of a marvelous journey in coming closer to Hashem.

Hashem is omniscient. One must simply turn to Him and request: "Master of the Universe! You know everything. You know exactly what my soul correction and my mission are. Guide me, teach me, and show me what I have to do!"

Thanks for everything

One must know that the Creator is watching over him and hears his prayer. He must accept all that happens to him with love.

To achieve true happiness, one must have *emuna* that all is for the good. When a person believes that everything is for the good, the evil inclination is neutralized, for it has nothing to hold onto.

Why? The evil inclination has no way to attack a person other than injecting heretical thoughts into his mind. In other words, the evil inclination makes him think that something is evil. This is the essence of heresy. The evil inclination tells a person: "This matter is not good for you. See how you have fallen. What troubles you have! Look what faults you have. Despair! There's no hope for you!"

If someone is unfamiliar with the principles of *emuna*, he almost certainly falls prey to the evil inclination's attacks. If the evil inclination succeeds in injecting heretical thoughts in one's mind, that person almost immediately sinks into sadness, despair, anxiety, and confusion. This is most people's problem. If one would only begin to smile, thank Hashem, and rejoice, then all of his problems would be solved. *Emuna* means that everything is good. Even one's most difficulties in life are all for the good. The moment a person believes this, he rises above his problems.

Joy and gratitude to the rescue!

Let's speak with Hashem and thank Him for life's hardships: "Master of the Universe, I am grateful for the hardships that you have tailor-made for me. Surely, each tribulation is for the best, because everything is for the best and there is no such thing as bad in the world. I don't look for difficulties in life, but now that I have them, I believe they enable me to become closer to You. These very obstacles show me my shortcomings, what I need to rectify, what to learn, and what to pray for. Setbacks are growth opportunities and a gift from You. Our Sages of blessed memory said, "Only when someone makes a mistake does he truly learn.""

The prime benefit of self composure is that one no longer persecutes himself. One realizes that if Hashem wants him to experience hardships, then this is the very best thing for him, since Hashem does everything for the best.

With such *emuna*, one can begin to speak with Hashem and thus get close to Him. But, the moment a person thinks that something is not good, his bond with the Creator is immediately severed, for he has fallen into a heretical mindset. How can a heretic communicate with the Creator? Once a person separates himself from Hashem, Heaven forbid, he falls into the clutches of the evil inclination.

The *Gemara* says that a mortal can't overcome the evil inclination on his own. We therefore have to seek Hashem's perpetual assistance in our fight against the evil inclination, as the *Gemara* says, "Were it not for the help a man has from the Holy One, Blessed is He, he could not overcome him [the evil inclination]."

There are no complaints

I was once approached by a man who had already reached middle age but had never married. He began to complain and weep about this problem, saying, "Look, I am already middle-aged but I never married."

I told him, "First of all, express gratitude for the fact that you never married, and only afterwards can I help you."

He replied, "How can you tell me to do so? You tell me to express my gratitude for not having married. How can I give thanks for this problem, which causes me great pain?"

I answered, "If Hashem did not marry you off until now, then this situation is the best thing for you. So express your gratitude. As long as you live with the feeling that the present situation is no good for you, you can't live, much less smile. Say 'thank you' to Hashem, and understand that you were never married for your own good. Realize that all that Hashem does is for the very best. There are no mistakes here, for everything takes place exactly according to what you need for your specific *tikkun*.

Devoted to the ultimate goal

A person of faith can always express gratitude for everything. He believes that all is for his good, bringing him closer to his ultimate goal. If a person recognizes in himself an inability to express gratitude for everything, he should realize that this is only because his ultimate goal is not coming closer to Hashem. His goals are rather related to material and mundane success.

If one is unhappy, he'll have no desire to seek Hashem. He won't be concerned with his ultimate goal in the world. Rather, all that'll ever matter to him is his comfort zone.

On the other hand, if someone truly wants to accomplish his ultimate goal, he'll realize that he should express abundant gratitude about everything. He can easily be grateful for the fact that he never got married because he knows that this is the best thing possible for him. Hashem grants each person precisely what he needs to accomplish his mission on earth.

Hashem cares that you have exactly what you need to attain your soul correction!

Does a person really know what is best for him? If he had a million dollars, would that be good for him? Not necessarily; in fact, such a sum might be detrimental.

The first thing to do when coping with any problem, even before trying to figure out a solution, is to build *emuna*, to be grateful for the very problem that he wants to cry about. **The evil inclination says that the current challenge will destroy you when in fact it's the best thing in the universe for you.** Remembering this one point destroys the evil inclination, who like a pest buzzing in your ear tries to convince you there's no hope. "Things aren't going right for you," he says.

The man of faith responds, "So what if things aren't going right for me? Excellent! It's great that things aren't going right for me! That's what Hashem wants, that things shouldn't go right for me!" He then turns to Hashem and says, "Thank You very much, Hashem, that things aren't going right for me! I know that You do everything for my ultimate benefit. Thank You, Hashem!"

The evil inclination tries again and again to get his foot in the door. After a setback, he makes every effort to drag a person way down into a pit of depression and melancholy.

Instead of debating with the evil inclination, one should turn to Hashem again and say, "Thank you very much, Hashem, that I failed! I must have faith that this failure is very good for me; it's surely just what I need in order to come close to You!" Once we make a mistake and learn from it, we already become better people.

We're lucky that we all have an evil inclination. Our Sages, of blessed memory, when commenting about hashem's satisfaction in creating the world said, "Very good - this refers to the evil inclination." Do you possess a certain negative character trait? Very good! You need this undesirable trait in order to come closer to Hashem. Without an evil inclination, we wouldn't be fighting to get close to Hashem all the time. In this respect, the evil inclination does us a tremendous service.

Emuna and acceptance of prayers

A person's *emuna* determines whether his prayer are accepted or not. *Emuna* signifies that one must believe that everything is for the good, with no exceptions. Therefore, he must express gratitude for everything, each person according to his individual lot in life.

A person's evil inclination amplifies his feeling of egocentrism and power of choice. This is dangerous, for a person is liable to become very arrogant when successful and terribly depressed when not. Self-persecution and the blame game are direct results from setbacks with no *emuna* to cushion the fall. People often confuse their self-persecution – which stems directly from their evil inclination – and identify it as is their good inclination. They attribute their self-hating thoughts to their piety and "fear of Heaven".

This is not fear of Heaven at all. It's stupidity, as Job was told (Job 4:6),"Your so-called fear of heaven is your folly."

One must cast his ego aside. Instead of thinking "I don't want this situation," he should say, "This is the way Hashem wants it." One should focus on Hashem rather than on himself, thinking, "Hashem wanted me to fail. Now I will ask Hashem to help me, so that in the future, I won't fail."

One must take into account that it is possible that Hashem will not help him immediately, and that he will need more and more prayers. It is not at all certain that one's supplication is immediately accepted. Perhaps it will be accepted only after a great many prayers. If so, then this situation is also for the best, because everything is for the good, including the delay of his salvation in this matter.

Receiving a gift without prayer is detrimental to a person, as I learned from my teachers, Rabbi Levi Yitzchak Bender, of blessed memory, and, may he live long, Rav Eliezer Berland Shlit"a. Whatever a person receives without prayer harms him, both in this world and in the next world. As such, Hashem puts a person in a position where he'll need to pray. Thus when he receives what he has requested, the gift will truly be beneficial for him.

The light at the end of the tunnel

Hashem decides every person's tribulation and suffering, but Hashem also has prepared a solution. One should therefore strengthen himself to remember that there is no total sorrow. The salvation has already been prepared even before the trouble befell him.

Knowing that everything comes from Hashem, one can find encouragement and avoid falling into darkness or despair. Despair ruins hope, as if there were no way out of his problem and nothing to do, as if the stern judgment was irreversible.

There is no such thing as "nothing to do" about a problem or predicament. It only seems that way to man's limited vision, for in truth, one does not know where salvation will come from. Indeed, a person need not worry about where the solution to his problem or predicament will come from. Rather, he should thank Hashem for the problem itself, which is surely for his ultimate benefit, whether it has come in order to arouse him to repentance or in order to cleanse him from sin. One can derive strength in remembering what Rebbe Nachman taught us, that at any given time, **Hashem can take the worst situation and turn it completely around for the good**.

No matter what, there's never room for despair in our lexicon or in our lives. The most important principle in life that we must engrave on our hearts is that **Hashem does everything, and everything He does is for the best**. Hashem sees what we don't see. Hashem can, in one moment, transform everything to the good! If you have faith that it is possible to ruin things, have faith that it is possible to repair them! Hashem prepares the medication before the injury!

As long as a person fails to believe that everything is for the good, and as long as he doesn't express his thanks, then every time he approaches Hashem, he'll have the feeling that something in life is askew. His subsequent "prayer" is then worthless crying and complaining, and it only annoys Hashem.

When someone approaches Hashem with the feeling that things are bad for him, his prayers go unheeded. Sefer HaMidot says: "Through sadness, Hashem is not with a person." On the other hand, when a person expresses his abundant gratitude to Hashem, his prayers are readily accepted. In the language of the holy Zohar, the grateful person is immediately allowed to enter the King's palace. The King awaits him with great anticipation and asks, "Who has come to bring me a gift, to express his thanks to me? Come, my son…" The grateful person now merits an audience with the King – Hashem – and can now talk to Him about anything.

Here's an example: A person that hasn't ben able to find his or her soul mate should say, "Thank you very much, Hashem, that I haven't yet found my partner in life. Surely this is for the very best. Enable me to understand what wrongdoing I've committed, what I need to rectify, and how to pray for what I lack." All this should be said with a smile and with *emuna*, for as soon as he begins to complain, he severs himself from Hashem. Hashem didn't create the world so that His creatures will weep; instead, He wants us to smile and have faith in Him, realizing that all of His ways are for our ultimate good.

Once again, the fact that "the gateways of tears are never locked" doesn't refer to tears of complaint and sadness. This kind of crying not only locks all the gates but even provokes harsh judgments, Heaven forbid. In contrast, the holy Zohar states that the gates of gratitude are never locked. Gratitude enables prayers to be accepted and lays the foundation for salvation from any problem.

Many people pray profusely yet are stricken again and again with more and more difficulties in life because they cry and complain. Expressing gratitude is always better than complaining. Once a person feels joy and is certain that not even a tiny note of crying and complaining has crept, he is then free to ask for all his heart's wishes, especially for clarification of the truth, repentance, and *emuna*.

Chapter Five:
Self Composure

One of the definitions of correct *hitbodedut* is *yishuv hadaat,* self composure. We learn in *Likutei Moharan* II, Torah 10: "The reason people are distant from G-d and not seeking His proximity is only that they lack self composure. And so the main principle is to strive for self composure and ask ourselves, where do all the bodily amenities and appetites of this world lead to?"

Self composure can only be attained through the practice of *hitbodedut.* For during the hour of *hitbodedut* one has the time to settle one's mind "well" as Rebbe Nachman says, in regard to the purpose of all the physical desires of this world and so forth. Rabbi Levi Yitzchak Bender of blessed memory, one of the elders of Breslov, described the hour of *hitbodedut*: "An hour of self composure". Rabbi Levi Yitzchak rarely described the practice of *hitbodedut* in a different fashion. Rebbe Nachman promises that through this hour of "self composure" one will surely do *teshuva*!

Self composure is exceedingly essential for every prayer, and in particular for prayers incorporating self-evaluation.

Strong and decisive

The essence of self composure is for one to clarify the truth in his own mind until it becomes crystal clear what Hashem demands of him in every area of life. This self composure must be lucid and strong enough to dispel doubt and so decisive so that it won't change in time. As we find in Sichot Haran (Rebbe Nachman's Discourses), "... even if he enjoys occasional self composure, the certainty of thought does not remain with him. And even the minimal self composure he has achieved is neither strong nor decisive. Therefore he does not grasp the folly of this earthly world. Yet if a person attains the ability to think clearly in a strong and decisive manner, he understands the follies and vanities of this world."

To believe in oneself

One of the most essential factors in achieving strong and resolute self composure is the belief in oneself. In other words, one believes that what has become clear to him as the truth is indeed the truth. In this manner, nothing and no one can cause him to doubt the truth that he has realized. Furthermore, he must be so strong-willed in this, until his resolve to achieve his goal will not be shaken no matter how distant that goal may be or how difficult it will be in obtaining. Once he knows unwaveringly that he has found the truth, nothing can weaken his determination or budge him from reaching his goal. This is true self composure.

As long as a person still has doubts as to what is true and the correct path for him to follow, his evil inclination can easily bring him to err or fail. It may confuse him so that he chooses to act in an erroneous manner, or it may draw him into despair by convincing him that his goal is absolutely unattainable. This is why the word "doubt" is equivalent in Hebrew numerology to the word "Amalek", for doubts are one's inner "Amalek"' causing him to fall, to become weak and sinful. They prevent a person from being consistent in his labors and from accomplishing his ambitions.

The manifest flaw in lack of self composure is more a lack of faith in oneself than a lack of belief in G-d or in the holy Tzaddikim. Everyone must believe in himself; this includes believing that what he learns from the Torah and what he hears from the Tzaddik is true and worth fighting for. He must not give in to any person, but rather he must continue tenaciously until he achieves his goal.

If we observe the Torah in depth, we see that the instances of transgression described within all stem from a lack of self-belief.

For example, Eve was commanded not to eat from the Tree of Knowledge, yet the snake succeeded in enticing her. The snake succeeded because she lacked faith in herself, and therefore began to doubt whether she had indeed heard Adam's warning properly. If she had had total faith that she had heard correctly, she would have known exactly how to behave.

Our holy sages of blessed memory said: The words of a rabbi or the words of his pupils – to who should one believe? G-d (the rabbi) commanded not to eat the fruit of that tree, while the snake (the pupil) said to eat that forbidden fruit. Who should one listen to – the rabbi or the pupil? Surely one should listen to the rabbi. So why then did Eve listen instead to the snake?

Eve was shaky in her belief in herself; she wasn't certain that she knew the absolute truth. Had she been completely sure of what she had heard, no one could have convinced her to act otherwise! There would have been nothing to talk about and she would not have listened to any words of enticement! The fruit is forbidden – period. She would have told the snake that if he was interested he could talk to her about other things, but the subject of eating from that tree was closed! Yet, because she lacked that self composure and complete faith, her defenses were weak.

Adam heard from G-d Himself that it is forbidden to eat from the Tree of Knowledge. Had he believed in himself, he wouldn't have been tempted. He'd have proclaimed: The fruit is forbidden! That is the truth! What I heard from G-d is the one and absolute truth! Then and there, the story would have come to a close with no dialogue and no negotiation! It would have been utterly impossible for anyone to entice him, even if Eve had indeed become part of the enticement.

King Saul is another example of insufficient truth clarification and believing in oneself. He failed to entirely destroy the Amalekites as he had been commanded, for he did not believe in himself. "And

Samuel said, "Even if you are small in your own eyes, are you
not the head of the tribes of Israel? And the Lord anointed you as

king over Israel (Samuel II, Chapter 15)." In this passage, Samuel
rebukes Saul for the flaw of not having faith in himself that Hashem
had anointed him king so that **he** would choose what was good in
the eyes of G-d and not listen to the people. Hashem commanded
him to destroy Amalek in its entirety, including all their flocks and
possessions. If Hashem commanded him to destroy Amalek in its
entirety, why did Saul even listen to talk that was contrary to the
Word of G-d?

But he refused

Let's now see a positive example of complete truth clarification
and belief in oneself. Joseph the Tzaddik had perfect clarity as to
what the truth is. When he was tempted by Potipher's wife, the text
reads "[he] refused". The musical sign above that phrase denotes a
long note, what's called a *shalshelet*, when the Torah reader sings
up and down an octave three times, indicating that he refused and
refused and refused! Joseph's refusal was absolute. None of the
lady's charms and threats could make him budge from the truth
that she is forbidden to him. Joseph had complete faith in himself:
This is what I have been taught! This is the truth! This is how I
must behave!

To ascertain the absolute truth

A person generally strives to deal with a specific issue during
his *hitbodedut*, such as overcoming a certain physical desire or
bad character trait or to do *teshuva* for a particular transgression.
His first task - even prior to requesting Hashem's assistance in
overcoming his evil inclination and attaining his goals - should
be to clarify for himself what the truth of the matter in question is

according to Torah. Once this truth is well-established in his mind, he'll know how to act and what Hashem wants from him. Once he can confidently declare that "This is the truth," nothing in the world will be able to sway him in the wrong direction. This is what we define as having belief in oneself, to believe in each and every point of truth that we've clarified and recognized in regard to the issue at hand.

This first stage of clarifying the truth of the matter should be reinforced with a second stage of prayer. This is a daily prayer asking Hashem to help us live according to this point of truth and maintain a clear and strong conception of this truth no matter what tries to influence us otherwise. We therefore ask Hashem to help us resist all forms of temptation that try to make us deviate from the truth that we have clarified and verified for ourselves.

Caution: the evil inclination's opposition and resistance always tries to sidetrack a person from the truth. If the *Yetzer Hara* never gives up, we too should never give up, always asking for Hashem assistance and never letting a day go by without an hour of personal prayer.

To learn for the sake of doing

Let's examine a practical example: Suppose that a person has learned that he should guard his eyes – this is an absolute Torah commandment, codified in *Halacha* and elaborated on extensively in Chassidic and Jewish-ethics literature. Let's say that the person has also heard relevant lectures teaching him that he cannot guard his eyes without closing them, and that he won't be able to close his eyes without exhaustive prayer asking for Hashem's assistance.

Yet, regardless of what they learn, many people still walk the city streets with their eyes wide open. Why do they do this despite the Torah's teachings in this regard?

Simple. They lack self composure in this area. They have yet to sift through what they've learned, preparing themselves to fight tenaciously for the truth that must be recognized through proper truth clarification in *hitbodedut*. They've not yet made daily self-evaluation that includes every time they've failed to guard their eyes. Not only that, they've yet to seek Hashem's help in guarding their eyes. Without earnest daily prayers, they're bound to transgress in this area, for they don't yet see their failure to guard their eyes as a transgression. It's simply not yet truth in the minds of those who haven't clarified the truth for themselves.

Proper *hitbodedut* requires us to stand in front of the Creator and pray to live by what we've clarified for ourselves until we've removed all doubt from our heart.

Concluding the example at hand, one must know full heartedly that he must walk while confining his eyesight to the sidewalk immediately in front of him. He must clarify the truth in his *hitbodedut* until he knows that no situation allows him to look at woman outside the context of what is explicitly allowed in *halacha*, period.

Once we've clarified the truth, we should devote at least a half an hour of our daily personal prayer to internalizing it. We must judge ourselves daily – how did we behave in the last 24 hours? Where did we fail to act according to this truth that we've already recognized? We should also thank Hashem for helping us in the situations where we did succeed in acting according to this truth. Afterwards, we should prepare ourselves for the following day's challenges that are likely to confront us. Hashem surely assists us when we pray in this manner. This is a template for daily personal prayer in clarifying the truth and overcoming a character flaw or bad habit.

With consistent daily effort, anyone can succeed in guarding of his eyes, which means protection from a multitude of sins, transgressions and flaws. One who guards his eyes is deemed a tzaddik; he merits complete faith, success, an abundance of material and spiritual prosperity, and miraculous Divine Providence.

Why does a person lose all this? Two reasons: first, he does not fully believe in himself that he knows the absolute truth; and second, he does not fight for it! For if he believed in himself, he would pray daily to succeed; he would be absolutely certain that this is a transgression and would be absolutely unwilling to fail once more. And when he failed, he would not ignore this failure but rather he would make self-evaluation and do *teshuva* and continue to pray not to fail again.

Repetition becomes permission

The *Gemara* says, "If a person transgresses and repeats that transgression, then it becomes in his mind a permitted thing to do" (tractate *Yoma* 86b). This transgression seems like a permissible act whenever a person is not making a daily effort to rectify his deeds. As long as he's struggling to do *teshuva*, praying, and making a comprehensive daily self-evaluation of his actions, then even his failures become part of his personal and spiritual growth. The transgression doesn't become "a permitted thing to do" for he has not allowed the sin to become an accepted norm in his life.

On the other hand, if a person has not yet clarified the truth and is yet unaware that he is sinning, then he'll obviously perpetuate his errant ways because he does not even feel that he is transgressing. Such people are often indignant in the face of harsh judgments, for they don't realize that their own failure to clarify the truth and to improve their ways is the root cause of many – if not all – of their troubles in life.

Teshuva always saves a person from harsh judgments. If between the two sinful acts one does *teshuva*, then the second act would not be regarded as "repetition" for the *teshuva* would have cleansed him of the first act's sin. This is surely one of the most wondrous benefits of daily *teshuva* and *hitbodedut*.

Even if a person does not yet succeed in living according to the truth he knows, it is of great significance that he at least recognizes the truth and strives to live in according with it. This fact can be a major reinforcement to those who are trying their best but haven't yet fully rectified their ways. With daily effort in personal prayer that includes self-evaluation and *teshuva*, a setback is neither failing nor descending, but rather an integral part in one's battle to do true *teshuva* and correct his ways.

The above principles of truth clarification, self-evaluation, and daily *teshuva* are vital in implementing all of the commandments set forth in the Torah, improving our character traits, and ridding ourselves of bodily lust. If a person works on each matter in consistent daily *hitbodedut*, he'll make dramatic improvement in that given area. If he continues to do lengthy *hitbodedut* on each and every matter until the truth is crystal clear in his mind, and prays to act according to the truth, he'll become a true complete Tzaddik.

Rejoice, O righteous!

Let's see why a prayer that comes without preparatory self-composure isn't effective: A person came to me with a complaint. He had listened to a stimulating lesson about anger. He said that he had taken the lesson to heart and had been praying for a long time to overcome his anger. Yet, despite his prayers he finds himself angry all the time. He asked, "What should I do? What is lacking in my labor?" After all, he had listened to the lesson, had been attentive, and desired to improve. He had even prayed daily for salvation in this area. What else should he be doing? What else does Hashem require of him? Why is his salvation delayed in its coming?

Where is the setback here? What's missing, that even such a person who prays for salvation does not realize any change for the better in his bad character traits? Having learned the power of prayer, how is it possible that a person fails to do what he must? The abovementioned example is not extraordinary. Many people suffer similar difficulties. Despite learning, awareness, and prayer, they still feel that they have not experienced any significant change.

What's lacking in the above example is *yishuv hadaat*, of self composure. Rebbe Nachman teaches that this is the vital element in our spiritual endeavors. He states explicitly that the obstacle that keeps the world distant from Hashem is a lack in *yishuv hadaat*. As such, any person who feels that he is distant from Hashem must strive to achieve self composure and a complete clarification of the truth.

Rebbe Nachman describes (see *Sichot HaRan*, 47) the self composure one must aspire to attain: "One must find the time to contemplate everything he is doing in this world, and because he does not compose his thoughts, he lacks true spiritual cognizance. Even if he does have some measure of self composure, it doesn't last for an extended period of time but rather quickly escapes him, for the little self composure he has attained is not strong, decisive and unwavering. Therefore, he does not understand the folly of this world. But, if he'd clarify the truth, he'd realize the folly and vanities of this world…"

Rebbe Nachman says that he who doesn't compose and clarify his thoughts lacks *daat*, or spiritual cognizance. We can conclude from this that he who does not clarify his thoughts has no true knowledge, and that one who does achieve self composure attains the knowledge and insight that are gained from spiritual cognizance.

A person's confusion, his many conflicting and divisive thoughts, thinking once one thing and afterwards something quite to the contrary, surely signifies that he lacks true self composure.

"Knowledge" is in effect the verification and clarification of truth in our minds, which equip us to make the right decisions in any situation. One who has yet to compose his thoughts can't possibly be certain of the truth and therefore won't know how to act. The awareness that he must clarify the truth on certain points can also be considered self composure, for the desire to accomplish something is already half the goal.

Clarity of Knowledge

Let's now return to our previously mentioned difficulty and contemplate it from two directions: How is it possible that a person who prays for specific matters, such as a rectification of character flaws, does not merit any true improvement? And why is it that Rebbe Nachman teaches that the distance from Hashem that our world suffers is due to a lack of self composure rather than due to insufficient prayer?

Without a proper attainment of self composure and clarity of thought, even prayer cannot be of full assistance. Prayer should draw our knowledge into our hearts, for the Torah commands: "And

you shall know this day and consider it in your heart" (Deuteronomy, Chapter 4). In practical terms, if a person has failed to reach self composure and therefore remains confused and in doubt as to what the truth is, then he lacks knowledge! Without knowledge, what will he be able to draw into his heart through prayer? The best he will be able to do is to bring his confusion into his heart, and this surely will not help him to rid himself of anger or any other bad character trait, or to nullify any base desire. The person might be praying, but despite his prayer he perpetuates his uncertainty; this is exactly where the evil inclination strikes him.

On the other hand, if a person has achieved self composure and has clarified his understanding of things, then his prayers will facilitate the complete internalization of truth and clarity into his heart; this is absolute knowledge. When truth shines clear in his mind, clarity prevails in the heart. Subsequently, he'll be able to act according to the truth that he now knows so clearly, for a person acts according to the knowledge internalized in his heart. He'll be able to live according to this clarified truth and thereby immunize himself against the influence of the evil inclination.

A Fortified Wall

The *hitbodedut* that one devotes to self-correction resembles a wall that is erected for the purpose of protecting a city from enemies. Rebbe Nachman calls the mind a "wall", for it is a partition against base desires. Prayer too is called a wall in that it protects from trials and tribulations. When a person is certain of the truth of things, he brings this clarity into his heart and fortifies this clarity with prayer, then he too erects a protective wall.

A wall that has no openings or cracks protects best. Yet, if this wall is breached in any way, namely, if one's self composure is incomplete, then his prayers won't be effective. If he prays many prayers over an extended period of time, he may think that he has erected a thick and strong wall, but in essence he has in fact erected a wall full of cracks. These cracks represent all the unclarified points in his mind that he failed to internalize in the heart. Prayers aren't effective with cracks in one's wall of prayer. Through these cracks, the enemy invades his heart. Despite the apparent wall, he still fails again and again because of the breach, which is none other than lack of truth clarification, or self composure.

One who prays for something like overcoming anger, attaining marital joy, or guarding one's eyes and so forth must first be crystal clear about the importance and truth of what he's trying to achieve. Once he attains that clarity, nothing can divert him from the path.

Let's return to the original example we mentioned at the beginning of this chapter: A person can pray to overcome anger, and ask Hashem to protect him from feeling angry and acting out of anger. Yet, until he's not fully convinced that getting angry is just as bad as the worst of transgressions, then he'll still be prone to anger.

If he does sincere soul-searching and finds that he still justifies being angry in certain situations, then he hasn't yet fully clarified the truth. As a result, he doesn't pray to be cured of his anger in regard to all those situations that still appear make his anger justifiable. He will continue to pray only for those situations that he understands should not bring him to anger, and in those situations, he'll succeed in refraining from anger. Yet, in connection to those circumstances that in his understanding still justify anger, he won't feel that Hashem is helping him overcome his anger. In truth, he has not truly asked Hashem to help him overcome his anger in those particular situations because **in his mind, they are not categorized as situations where he must avoid being angry at all costs.**

If this person had already clarified the truth in his mind about what anger is, what the Torah teaches about anger, that **no** circumstance justifies an angry reaction, and that anger is an outright transgression, then he'll be well on the way of ridding himself from anger.

One must work at clarifying his thought until he is above any doubt. He must feel with deep conviction that nothing justifies anger. Once he has composed himself well enough, he'll have the clarity of thought that will enable him to act strongly and decisively. This is the strength that internalizes truth in his heart. In the case at hand, such a person will never be angry again!

One would be best advised to devote at least a half an hour daily praying for what he's trying to attain. "Master of the Universe, have mercy upon me, help me comprehend in my heart that there is no situation in the world that justifies or permits me to be angry and no circumstance that makes anger worthwhile. Have pity upon me and help me, that my heart will not be tempted to become angry, not in this situation or in any other… It must be perfectly clear to me that if I am angry, I am transgressing. Help me identify my weakness and the way the evil inclination succeeds in enticing me to anger. Help me mend the crack in my emotional and spiritual wall that gives the evil inclination access to my heart and brain. Help me attain a strong and decisive conviction that I must not be angry no matter what, so I'll resist any temptation to being angry."

Each day's *hitbodedut* must include a personal assessment of how he acted during the last 24 hours in regard to anger. Did the evil inclination succeed in tempting him? Did he discover an opening where the evil inclination could enter? If so, he must "close" that opening. In other words, he must make a firm decision to be more careful in similar situations in the future, and not be drawn into anger, praying daily for help and guidance in this area: "Master of the Universe, have mercy upon me and please help me avoid being angry in future test situations. Help me retain my self-composure and remember the truth, that anger is never allowed or justifiable."

Usually a person fails repeated tests of anger in recurring situations such as in educating his children, in marriage, or at the workplace. One must examine the circumstances where he is susceptible to anger, where the evil inclination usually succeeds in tempting him. He can then clarify his thoughts in regard to these specific situations. He'll subsequently be able to withstand the test the next time he is confronted with a similar situation. This is how one succeeds to attaining self-composure.

A person must acquire all four aspects of self-composure as Rebbe Nachman teaches: **objective thought, clarification of the truth, inner strength, and conviction**. If one of these four links is lacking, a person will not be able to pass the test of temptation and will inevitably fail. Rebbe Nachman describes self-composure as composed, strong, and forceful intelligence.

Here's why the four aspects of self-composure are so important:

Objective thought – a person has no chance of ascertaining what's right and wrong if he begins his self-assessment and personal pray subjectively.

Clarification of truth – once a person has obtained knowledge that results from learning about a particular subject and thinking about it objectively, he can apply it to day to day situations. For example, once a person learns about the damage of over-eating and eating what the body doesn't need, he clarify the truth in his mind about whether or not he should eat pizza and drink beer.

Inner strength – once the truth is clarified, a person gains inner strength. When he knows that over-eating is not what Hashem wants him to do, he'll regard overeating just like he regards eating a forbidden food.

Conviction – with inner strength, he won't be tempted under any circumstance.

The composed, strong, and forceful intelligence of self-composure is the only means whereby a person can attain true character improvement. Without the self composure that includes the knowledge that results from objective thought, clarification of truth and unyielding conviction, he won't fully succeed.

As shown in the abovementioned example of overeating, these principles are applicable not only in the rectification of all character traits, but in ridding ourselves of bodily appetites, bad habits, and lust as well. If one strives for self composure until he is clear and decisive about the matter at hand, if he prays frequently and practices self-evaluation, he will certainly attain a high level of *teshuva* and self-improvement.

Indeed, one of the most essential factors in reaching self composure is appreciating every time Hashem helps us succeed. For example, each time we successfully pass a test without failing, or improve in an area we've been working on, we should express our gratitude to Hashem. Gratitude invokes Divine assistance for further improvement.

Now we can understand why prayer is so ineffective when one lacks self composure. If he's not decisive and strong, all his prayer will erect nothing more than an incomplete wall, full of holes through which his anger (or any other character weakness) enters again and again. One's wall of self composure and truth clarification must be impenetrable to the evil inclination. Effective prayer depends on self composure.

Proper Hitbodedut

Another important principle for a person to achieve self composure is "equalizing". Proper *hitbodedut* requires a person to come before Hashem in faith. Faith is expressed through a person's nullifying his will to the Will of Hashem. That is to say, that whether or not Hashem fulfills one's request, the person will be equally satisfied with whatever Hashem does. In other words, all is "equal" in his eyes. From the following tale presented in the book *Kochavei Or* we learn that "equalizing" is a basis for attaining truth:

A person named Israel from Nemirov asked for Rebbe Nachman's blessing in traveling to a war zone for the sake of his livelihood. Rebbe Nachman did not want this man to travel, yet too he did not want to deny him free choice. So, the Rebbe advised him: "Equalize in your mind both the 'yes' and no' (in other words, be equally happy whether you go or not)." He then advised him to say five chapters of Psalms, and then he should do what comes to his mind. And so the man did.

Afterwards, Israel came to Rebbe Nachman and told him what had come to mind, that he decided to make the trip. Rebbe Nachman was not pleased with this, because he knew very clearly that the man had not truly equalized the 'yes' and 'no' in his heart as instructed. Rebbe Nachman knew that this man's craving for money had led him to a very strong desire to travel. Israel did in fact make the trip...

According to the principles of *emuna*, one must understand that only Hashem knows the individual path each person must take in this life. One who truly believes this knows that all things are equal – if he travels to a certain place, or not; if he does a certain business transaction, or not; if he meets with so-and-so, or not, and so on. With *emuna*, a person recognizes that Hashem knows best what is right for him no matter what. Everything is the will of Hashem and therefore the very best for him.

The Holy Baal Shem Tov elaborated on King David's expression (Psalms 16:8), "I have set Hashem before me always". How can one know that he has truly set Hashem before him? How can he know that he truly lives with *emuna* that there is "no one but Him"? The word in Hebrew *shiviti* - "I have set", can also be translated in conjunction with its root word *shivyon*, or equality, namely, that all is equal before him.

Only when the 'yes' and 'no' are truly equal in one's eyes can one truly know Hashem's Will. Hashem will illuminate the truth in the heart of an "equalizer" and show him what he should do in every situation. As such, a goal of self composure is to equalize one's thoughts and thereby rid oneself of the effects of lust or bad character traits.

To Act According to His Will

King David nullified his personal desires and prayed to recognize what Hashem's Will is in all matters, for he prayed (Psalms 25:5), "Guide me with Your truth and teach me" – guide me in Your truth Hashem, and not what I might misconstrue as the truth, because my perception could very well be influenced by lust and bodily appetites.

When a person prays, the 'yes' and 'no' must stand equal before him, to avoid despair and to continue to pray for the things he yearns for. He must seek the level of self composure until the 'yes' and 'no' is truly equal before him in all matters. He must contemplate that only Hashem knows what is best for him and therefore subjugate all his desires to Hashem. He should strive to be able to say to himself, "Everything is equal to me, whether I receive that which I ask for - in spiritual as well as material requests - or not.

The essence of proper *hitbodedut* is seeking what Hashem wants from us. Once again, King David asked for this also in his personal prayers, when he said (Psalms 119:35), "Guide me on the path of Your commandments," the commandments being an expression of *Ratzon Elyon* or Divine Will. We too can pray in this manner:

"Master of the Universe, I surely do not know where I stand in spirituality, nor do I know the next step I should make. Show me what my priorities should be, where to put my emphasis, how lengthy my prayers should be for any specific matter, how I should pray on each matter, and how to serve You, especially in light of my intended mission on earth. For You, all things are revealed and known. You know where I stand and what I am supposed to do. Have mercy upon me, give me the words that I need to pray today, enable me to thank you wholeheartedly for all the things that I should thank you for, let me assess myself properly, let me express myself in the prayers that I pray before You today, and please illuminate my heart. Above all, lead me in the path of Your will!"

A person will never walk away from such *hitbodedut* with impatience. All the more so, when he walks this path in pleasantness and patience, Hashem will illuminate his path and he'll be able to properly converse with Hashem.

Improper Hitbodedut

Improper *hitbodedut* results in a weakening of *emuna*. Weakened *emuna* leads to impatience and anger.

If the essence of proper *hitbodedut* is seeking what Hashem wants from us, then improper *hitbodedut* is the opposite, when one fails to seek Hashem's Will during his *hitbodedut*. Rather, he prays to Hashem to fulfill his own physical and spiritual desires, and this is contrary to Hashem's Will. He actually asks Hashem to help him to do what is contrary to Hashem's Will.

Proper *hitbodedut* means that a person seeks to nullify his will to the Will of Hashem. All his *hitbodedut* and his prayer focus on this.

Improper *hitbodedut* means that a person wants Hashem to nullify His Will to his, and all of his *hitbodedut* and prayer focus on his attempts to convince Hashem to do as he wills.

Material requests that have nothing to do with serving Hashem don't invoke Divine compassion at all – this is readily understandable. But in spirituality, one is likely to be fooled into thinking that he is asking for spiritual things yet in truth his requests are not pure in intention and thought. His desire to be a great Torah scholar or tzaddik could be none other than lust for honor, fame, prestige, and even money. He longs for people to kiss his hand and send him *kvittlach* stuffed with hundred-dollar bills. He loves hearing people say, "What a righteous genius! The entire world depends upon him," and so forth. And there too are those who are not interested in any of this - not in honor or fame - yet are motivated by their desire for the rewards in the World to Come, or for their children to benefit from their merits. Although the latter example is much more respectable than the crass desires for personal gain in the former example, Rebbe Nachman still calls this, "filling the belly," in other words, a slightly more refined aspiration for personal gain (see *Likutei Moharan* II:37).

True self composure means searching for and clarifying the truth, asking what Hashem wants, what he himself wants, and differentiating between the two to avoid fooling oneself. Then, one must strive to nullify his will to the Will of Hashem. Hashem surely knows best what's best for each of us.

Self-nullification is just as important in spiritual matters as it is in regard to material requests. We must recognize that in spirituality too we have desires, perhaps more refined desires than our physical ones, but nonetheless personal appetites such as lust for honor, respect, fame, and rewards in the World to Come.

Anger and impatience are signs of improper *hitbodedut*. If a person is asking for his own will to be fulfilled and not the Will of Hashem, then he is impatient to have his requests fulfilled and he falls into anger when they're not. If he truly wants to live according to Hashem's Will, he'll have no sorrow, anger, or impatience if his prayer is not accepted. He accepts this as Hashem's Will and simply continues his prayers and *hitbodedut* with the goal of clarifying truth and getting closer to Hashem. Self-nullification

Proper *hitbodedut* strives to achieve self-nullification, which enables one to be totally encompassed within Hashem. *Hitbodedut* without the aspiration of doing Hashem's will is counter-productive, and will not bring a person closer to Hashem.

Self-serving personal prayer brings about flaws in one's *emuna*. Those flaws invoke stern judgments, leaving the person with feelings anger and discontent.

People suffer from anger and impatience in their *hitbodedut* because they aspire for things that have nothing to do with – or even go against - the will of Hashem. One's own desires are so strong that he becomes impatient and angry. This is heresy and a very serious flaw, for only Hashem decides when, how, and if He'll grant a given request. If the person is obstinate in his repeated request, it's as if the he's arguing against Hashem. Such an attitude certainly doesn't invoke Divine compassion, but the exact opposite, Heaven forbid.

Hitbodedut at every moment

A person should practice *hitbodedut* before anything that he does. Effective *hitbodedut* is a key to success, since it includes self composure, prayer, self-evaluation, and clarification in one's mind of what Hashem truly wants of him at that very moment. A person is much more likely to choose the best course of action when he asks Hashem for guidance and for Divine assistance.

When faced with a test after having clarified his thoughts, firmly establishing in his mind what Hashem's Will is and requesting Hashem's help, a person will not sin. This is so because he has practiced *hitbodedut* properly. On the other hand, if he has not done a proper self-evaluation, if he has not sought out to understand what Hashem's Will is and has not truthfully asked to act accordingly, then he'll likely go against Hashem's Will as a result of his improper *hitbodedut*. This was Eve's mistake at the very beginning of Creation. She was the first person who practiced improper *hitbodedut* and did not truly clarify the truth of the forbidden fruit.

She was therefore easily tempted, resulting in her sin. She lost her *emuna*, and the entire world must labor to find *emuna*.

Chapter Six:

Connecting to the Source

After we have already learned a number of significant foundations to proper *hitbodedut* we must address one of the basic principles, one often neglected even by those who have been practicing *hitbodedut* for many years. And this is the element of concentrated *hitbodedut* which is particularly fruitful.

This then is the rule: For a person to see significant changes in his life, in his *middot* (character traits) and his service to Hashem, to truly merit clinging to Hashem and His Torah, to be continually with joy and vitality and to ascend further and further – one must be thorough in one's efforts. That is to say, to take one issue, such as an unholy desire or negative character trait, and to practice daily lengthy *hitbodedut* on that particular issue until it has been nullified completely, as taught in *Likutei Moharan* I:52.

"For through *hitbodedut* and conversing with one's Maker one nullifies all his earthly desires and bad traits, until he has nullified all of his physicality and is encompassed in his holy source etc. That is to say that he must devote himself a great deal to prayers and *hitbodedut* and conversing with G-d etc. until he nullifies one of his negative traits, and then he must devote himself again to this *hitbodedut* until another one of his desires or bad traits is nullified, and then so forth until all his negative character traits are nullified…"

Not to be "religious"

The rule is that anyone who truly yearns to do *teshuva* must learn how to pray. For *teshuva* requires the "labor of the heart", to deal with the fundamental internal points of Judaism, to correct his middot one by one, and to nullify his earthly desires one by one, until he has nullified them completely – something that can be attained only through prayer. To do so, one must stand in front of G-d for a continual and lengthy period of time each day for several months, and plead for that particular trait to be corrected.

For a person to be called "religious," he doesn't need to learn how to pray. He can suffice in reading from the prayer book along with everyone else, and after one hundred and twenty years can earn the grade "100" in reading skills… Yet if he wants to truly do *teshuva*, he must learn to pray. For a person cannot truly alter anything without continuous daily prayer. A person can be "religious" for a million years, and not merely "religious" but be someone who studies all day long and does mitzvot, yet remain unchanged from within. He may remain with all his negative character traits and physical desires.

Furthermore, even if a person does *hitbodedut* daily - if he does not commit himself to praying on a regular and consistent fashion for a particular matter - he will never realize a true fundamental change in himself. It is true that if he devotes himself to daily "self-examination" he will merit *yirat shamayim* (awe of Hashem) and avoid transgression, and surely his prayers won't go to waste and he will be an upright individual. Ye he will not be able to be cleansed from within of any evil that he possesses, and will spend his life in battle with those evil inclinations.

On the other hand, if one begins to practice daily concentrated prayer, every few months dedicated to another issue, he will begin to see true and significant changes. To discover the validity of this claim one does not have to wait years; even after a week of such concentrated prayer, one will feel significant change taking place. In this way, he will know that he has found the true path to redeem himself of all his earthly desires and bad character traits. He will understand that prayer is redemption!

Give Yourself a Chance

Every person who cares about himself will give this a try: Concentrate for one week on one particular issue, and for a half an hour or one full hour daily do *hitbodedut* on only that sole issue. On your own, you will already understand what we are speaking of here. For one practicing this kind of *hitbodedut* will already see results, and will experience renewed vitality and faith in his prayers; he will not only believe – but see - that through his prayers he can acquire and repair all things.

If a person does not give himself this opportunity, he will bring despair upon himself, when he realizes that another day and yet another passes, another Rosh Hashana and then another, year after year, and still he has not attained any true significant change – so why wouldn't he feel despair? He simply is getting himself accustomed to the notion that he cannot do *teshuva*. And so for him to begin to believe in himself, to believe in the strength of his prayer and believe that he can truly do *teshuva*, he must take this "project" upon himself at least for one week, to pray for a half hour or preferably for one straight hour on a single specific character trait that needs improvement. He will surely see results and receive

great strength to continue and make true repentance.

All of this is relevant to both men and women. Women too must labor to nullify their bad character traits and earthly desires. Every man, woman, boy and girl must do *teshuva*; there are no exceptions. A soul is brought down in order to do *teshuva*. Without anything to correct, a soul has no need to descend to this world at all.

The main element of prayer is to simply request again and again whatever we desire. Even speaking the same words daily over and over, such as "have mercy on me" or "help me to overcome this issue" will already have a dramatic effect with a week or two. With perseverance, we soon see the fruits of our prayers and witness the first ray of light at the end of the tunnel. We begin to understand that the path of personal prayer leads to our entire personal salvation. Even though we must pray for months in order to correct one single trait, we'll already sense a change for the good after one week.

A person owes himself this important favor, to strengthen himself through prayer and to believe in his prayer. If he follows our advice as prescribed here, he will begin to believe in his own prayer, and will recognize that he truly has found the direction to do complete *teshuva*.

Utilizing Your Strength

Deep inside, everyone yearns to return to Hashem, to correct one's negative traits, and to nullify one's bodily lusts. Yet one who does not utilize his power to pray in order to do so resembles someone attempting to dig foundations for a building with his bare hands, without the use of any tools whatsoever. Instead of operating a tractor that can readily and swiftly do the necessary digging, he uses his hands alone and therefore barely scratches the surface.

Prayer is the heavy-duty tool that is always at our disposal. Rebbe Nachman says that prayer is the main weapon a Jew possesses.

A person who receives an answer to his prayer derives enormous encouragement: He might say to himself, "I prayed, and my prayer was accepted! I'll continue to pray for more and more things, and I will attain them all through prayer. And, if I pray only a half an hour or an hour a day for one particular objective - and I see such salvations - who can imagine what I can achieve through praying several hours each day for that one objective?

Rebbe Natan in *Likutei Halachot* writes that the first prayer that a person prays that is answered is similar to a firstborn. In Jewish Law, a firstborn receives a double inheritance.

A woman's faith and prayer pave the way to parenthood: "Master of the Universe, give me the faith to believe that I am capable of bringing children into this world." Yet after she has already given birth and she has already become a vessel for bringing children into the world, then she attains the belief that she is capable of bearing children. Therefore, in effect, all her future children come to this world by virtue of the strength of the firstborn. This is why the firstborn merits receiving a double inheritance, for he has a part in the birth of each and every other child born to his mother. Rebbe Natan explains that the same principle holds true in regard to the first prayer to which a person receives an answer; it is the "firstborn," for through the strength of that first answered, the person is encouraged to continue praying for himself and for others.

Rebbe Natan of Breslev said in a brief conversation, which indeed encompasses this entire world: "Wherever I see deficiency, it was either not prayed for or not prayed for sufficiently." Everything that is lacking in this world is due to a lack of prayer. And the exile too is also due to the lack of prayers, as Rebbe Nachman teaches in Torah 7: "Know, the main reason for the exile is because of a lack of faith." And it is known that in every place where Rebbe Nachman writes the word "*emuna*" (faith) the word signifies prayer. Faith and prayer are one and the same. And the world is so distant from redemption because it is distant from prayer.

Obstinacy and Patience

One of the obstacles to devoting several months of *hitbodedut* to one particular issue is that people tend to expect a renewal each personal prayer session and it doesn't necessarily happen. When the newness subsides they think, "That's it", that they have nothing more to add to their prayer. They have the impression that any further repetition of what has already been said is, G-d forbid, a waste of time.

In reality, no one is capable of always saying new things! One must be simple and steadfast, even if that means repeating the same words the entire hour of *hitbodedut*, and to rehash the same points for months at a time. Rebbe Nachman spoke of this type of prayer with longing, and sighed, "Ay, simplicity". Many great Tzaddikim testified that they attained their high level of holiness through this

labor of simplicity.

When a person recognizes that this is the way of *hitbodedut* and no longer anticipates continual innovation in his conversation, he is awarded the patience that is needed to be consistent in one's prayer. With patience and consistency, he'll discover that he is actually innovating!

One personal-prayer experience during an extended time period enables him to understand new things - this is what gives novelty to his prayers. As one prays for something he learns the issue, which awakens in him originality and new directions to his prayer, as well as altering the emphasis he places on varying themes. He innovates and develops clarity, realizing that perseverance in prayer is truly the way to attain that which he longs for. The main factor is to pray extensively, to beseech and beg Hashem to merit nullifying the particular bad character trait or earthly desire about which he is praying.

The Order of the Prayer

Prayer is essentially self-composure, where we clarify our innermost thoughts. Prayer should answer several significant questions: What is the truth? How are we to behave in each situation? Prayer arouses a person and enables him to internalize knowledge while begging Hashem to have mercy upon him and to grant that which he is praying for.

Personal prayers also encompass one's gratitude for the miracles he has already experienced and for all the help that he has already received in regard to that which he is praying for. They should also include thanks for the privilege of continued praying daily for this specific objective. For if a person is being allowed to continue to pray for something, this is a wonderful sign that Hashem desires to redeem him in this matter, as Rabbi Chanina ben Dosa said: "If I see that the prayer is planted in my mouth then I know it will be accepted. For this, a person must be extremely grateful."

Our prayer must include daily self-evaluation; one must consider where he failed in the matter which he is trying to correct. He must contemplate why he failed. This must be a very careful self-examination since it is connected to the matter upon which he is working to repair. The examination therefore reveals areas of needed improvement that one must pray to rectify. One cannot attain a higher level until he improves himself at his current level. Even if he no longer fails in this matter, he must ask Hashem to help him avoid fooling himself that he's perfect, and to realize that he still has work to do and plenty to pray for with the continued help from Above. Without Hashem's help, we can do nothing.

One must also look ahead to anticipate coming challenges. For example, a man may be making an effort to guard his eyes. He knows that he'll be attending a wedding, a family event, or a business meeting on the following day. He must pray that Hashem will help him precisely at those moments when he'll be exposed to forbidden sights. And as said earlier, the major part of the prayer will be a simple repetition of his request, "Hashem, help me guard my eyes. Help me not to fall into self-deception. Give me the courage and conviction to close my eyes as needed." These prayers invoke Divine assistance and compassion, and merit him a "visa' from Heaven to guard his eyes.

Of course, if a person has yet to achieve a strong and decisive enough conviction to clarify the truth - namely, that guarding one's eyes is only a matter of closing them - then one must develop this conviction through self-composure, as described in the previous chapter. He must clarify his thoughts to the extent that he recognizes the truth and is therefore unwilling to compromise on what's right. When in doubt, he should consult his rabbi and spiritual guide.

The correct order for our prayers is therefore:

* Expressing our gratitude;

* Evaluating ourselves and preparing for upcoming challenges;

* Seeking Hashem's help, with the understanding there can be no success without His help. We therefore must devote much prayer to requesting Hashem's assistance.

* Asking Hashem to help us correct the bad habit or negative character trait that we're attempting to change.

The above is a personal prayer template for all issues. Take for example the characteristic of anger: here too one must develop the self-composure necessary to clarify the truth, until he builds the sound and decisive cognizance that no situation in the world justifies anger or an angry reaction. In truth, anger is a statement that one is actually angry at Hashem. One's personal prayer should also include gratitude to Hashem for the trying circumstances where in fact he did merit to avoid anger or to be less angry then before. Also, he can't be complacent and must pray for success in future challenges. For example if he knows he will be attending a meeting on the morrow which may cause him anger, he should pray, "Hashem, help me to avoid getting angry at all costs." Or "Tomorrow I'll be helping my son with his homework, and I may face a test of anger. Give me patience, Hashem, and help me from getting angry."

Every prayer should include everything that you've learned so far in regard to the issue you're praying for. The chapter "*Emuna* and Emotions" in the book "The Garden of *Emuna*" is a useful aid, for it explains how each trait is founded upon faith. That way, we learn how to pray in attaining a positive trait or in uprooting a negative trait. The main principle is to pray for an extended period of time and with simple words, pleading and begging for mercy; that the Holy One will help us overcome the evil inclination and succeed in correcting a character flaw, ridding ourselves of a bad habit, or nullifying a particular bodily desire.

We must repeatedly emphasize the necessity to dedicate at least one week of concentrated prayer to a particular issue. Once again, if a person does not allow himself the chance to witness the power of prayer and its ability to invoke miracles, he will never attain faith in the power of prayer. This means that he will never attain faith in G-d, for believing in G-d means believing in prayer.

Believing in prayer indicates faith in one's own prayers, a faith that through his own prayer he can bring about salvations and all good. Personal salvation through prayer necessitates lengthy prayers. When one's prayers have not yet been answered it is a sign that one needs more prayers. Rabbi Chanina said: "One who lengthens his prayers, his prayers will not go unanswered".

Pricetag of prayer

When a person yearns to attain something through prayer, he must in effect pay a spiritual price, in other words, a certain number of prayers. Spiritual entities, like material entities, each have a price tag that demands a certain spiritual payment. Once a person completes the payment, he will attain that which he has prayed for. The principle of the prayer quota as a spiritual price tag for both material and spiritual needs is an established spiritual law in Hashem's kingdom.

This principle is learned through the words of our holy sages of blessed memory who expound upon the Moses's prayers to enter the Land of Israel. Moshe prayed 515 prayers and then Hashem asked him not to continue. Why was Moshe asked to stop praying? Why could he not continue praying? Hashem would anyway prevent him from entering the Land of Israel, since that was His express will. We learn from this that if Moshe had added just one more prayer, he would have attained the amount of required prayers to enter The Land of Israel. According to His own laws, Hashem would have had to allow Moshe to enter the Land of Israel.

Rebbe Nachman explains the inner dimension of prayer in *Likutei Moharan* I:2. Prayers build an entire spiritual level, or "storey". Once a person has prayed enough prayers to complete the spiritual construction of the entire storey of that which he has prayed for, he will receive what he prayed for.

Until the price is paid, in other words, before fulfilling the prayer quota for a particular request, a person won't yet attain that which he yearns and prays for. There are those who will witness absolutely no result from their prayers until the last required prayer is prayed. And there are those who will be given glimpses of light so as not to fall into despair and will see that prayers do work. And there are those who see the gradual fulfillment of their wishes. Many variables come into play according to the nature of the request and Heavenly considerations. One thing is surely very clear - that in order to "purchase" one's wish in its entirety, one must complete the full amount of prayers required to attain what he wants.

An empty-handed shopping spree – an allegory about insufficient prayer

Imagine that a person enters a huge department store (*allegorical for the place of prayer*) with sixty dollars in his wallet (*sixty minutes of hitbodedut*). Many items on sale catch his eye (*all the many things one yearns for in material and spiritual goods, all the many blessings one longs to ask Hashem for*). He can't afford them all (*he doesn't have the "prayer time" to obtain what he wants*). Some things cost $100 (*two hours of prayer, for example*) yet in the jewelry department, things cost $1000 and up (*a minimum of twenty hours of prayer*). He only has $60 in his wallet (*only one hour of hitbodedut*). What can he do? He puts a $6 down payment for ten different items (*he prays six minutes for ten requests*). He's spent all his money (*prayer privileges*), yet leaves the store empty-handed. But, if he keeps coming back day after day with his day's earnings of sixty dollars in his wallet (*sixty minutes of hitbodedut*), he'll add an additional sum to the money he has already put down on the items he wants. With perseverance, in a matter of weeks or months – depending on the item – he will attain all his heart's wishes.

Yet, on most days, our allegorical shopper is lazy. He either doesn't go to work, or works less hours and doesn't earn his sixty dollars, so ultimately, he never completes a purchase. In other words he never completes the amount of prayers required to acquire true rectified character traits and spiritual salvations. He continually leaves the "department store" empty-handed. Oftentimes, he puts tiny down payments on new items without having paid for the old ones, spreading his daily wages thinly over many "products".

Our above allegory tells the unfortunate tale of a person that has already accumulated tens of thousands of prayer minutes, which are in effect thousands of spiritual dollars, yet has not "purchased" anything!

One would be much better off by concentrating on one issue and "paying" its price - his hour of *hitbodedut* - or at least thirty of his daily sixty minutes, until he "completes the purchase" and acquires what he has been seeking. Afterward, he can concentrate on another matter, and pay for it with all his thirty or sixty daily personal prayer dollars, until he has made full payment, and so on. In time, such a person will attain a full soul correction.

Our above allegory brings the point home, but in all fairness, it's not completely accurate. Material and spiritual requests have different price tags. Not only that, but in the spiritual realm, when one has acquired a particular good character trait, or nullified a particular physical desire, he can easily conquer his other bad traits and earthly desires. That's like getting a coupon on your previous purchase that's good for your next purchase, for by attaining even one thing through prayers, it's so much easier to acquire more. Also, the improvement of even one small negative trait or bad habit has a profound positive influence on all other aspects of a person's life.

Grasping much is grasping nothing at all

The evil inclination is the culprit that confuses people and prevents them from concentrating on one specific issue in *hitbodedut*. That explains how there are those who have been practicing *hitbodedut* for years already and yet have failed to see the fruits of their labor. They do experience minimal change of course; in comparison to others who have not yet begun to practice *hitbodedut*, their lives are very good, for surely their prayers have an influence. Yet, as we have already mentioned, in order to realize our goals, rectify our negative character traits and truly nullify our material desires, we must focus our prayer power on our current objective for a complete hour each day - or at least a half an hour - over an extended period of time.

Our holy sages of blessed memory teach us that grasping much is like grasping nothing at all. But, when you catch a little, you can indeed taken hold of it. A person who wants to pray for everything, trying to "grasp" a great deal, usually grasps nothing. But, by concentrating on one objective and praying for it over an extended time span, he will grasp it, and systematically in like manner grasp additional objectives. Again, these "little bits" in spirituality are surely not little bits at all, because one by one they influence a person's entire life.

Prayer is redemption and redemption is prayer. For when see how continued daily prayer ultimately redeems us from the prison of a particular material lust, bad habit, or negative character traits, we're not only encouraged but witness our individual redemption with our own eyes.

You too are capable of seeing miracles and your own personal salvation! With focused prayer and perseverance, you can attain virtually all your heart's desires. When Hashem sees your efforts, He will undoubtedly grant you many long years to enable you to pray for everything.

Strengthened by prayer

"Rabbi Chanina says, 'He who prays long prayers, his prayers will not return unanswered' (Talmud, tractate *Berachot* 32)". Moshe Rabbenu (Moses) set this precedent (see Deuteronomy Chapter 9), and said: "And I fell down before the Lord as before, forty days and forty nights." The Torah says directly afterwards, "And the Lord hearkened to me

also at that time". Moshe prayed lengthy prayers, in other words for 24 hours for forty days - nine hundred and sixty hours - and his prayers were answered. Moses shows us that if a person prays long enough, his prayers will be answered.

The Talmud also says (ibid.), "Four things need strengthening: Torah, good deeds, prayer and respectable behavior. In regard to Torah and good deeds, it is said (see Joshua, Chapter One): 'Just be strong and very courageous to observe and do in accordance with all'; be strong – in Torah, courageous – in good deeds. As for prayer, in Psalms we find the passage: 'Hope for the Lord, be strong and He will give your heart courage, and hope for the Lord'

(Psalm 27); and *derech eretz*, respectable behavior – as it says (Samuel II. Chapter ten): 'Be strong, and let us strengthen ourselves on behalf of our people…'"

Our holy Talmud teaches that there are four areas in which a person must fortify himself. We accomplish this by way of self-awakening and reinforcing the heart, by learning relevant books or listening to encouraging words, and by praying for them. Every person must fortify prayer constantly, regardless of his current spiritual level.

The Power to Effect Salvations

Rebbe Nachman of Breslev writes that we must strengthen our belief in ourselves, namely, that we have the power to accomplish everything through our prayers. This is a wonderful incentive for strengthening us in prayer.

A person can't stimulate himself to action if he yet lacks faith in his capacity to achieve. For example, if you would ask a person to go to the moon, and he doesn't believe that he could possibly do such a thing, he would not even begin to contemplate this, much less take an initial step in the direction of the moon. On the other hand, if there is something that he fully believes he can accomplish, he'll make every effort. He rolls up his sleeves and gets to work.

Prayer is no exception. A person who has faith that he can accomplish anything through his prayers never gives up until he reaches his goal, despite the price that he knows he must pay on the way. For example, the pain of strenuous workouts doesn't deter a champion athlete from training for the Olympic finals. All we need to accomplish anything is belief in ourselves and in our prayers. This gives us the power, patience, and perseverance to pray until our prayers are answered and we see our personal salvation with our own two eyes.

The Torah testifies (Deuteronomy 30:12), "It is not far away, it is not in the Heavens." The Torah and mitzvoth are within our reach. Praying is possible! It's not in the Heavens! We pray – and Hashem gives. It's that simple.

Rebbe Nachman's teaching (see *Likutei Moharan* I:52) about character improvement by way of *hitbodedut* at night has been abridged in this chapter. We have slightly modified his words so that everyone

can follow his advice. Few people can practice *hitbodedut* throughout the entire night until they nullify each of their base desires and rectify their negative character traits. We certainly did not want to close the doors of personal prayer to those who are not capable of such *hitbodedut*, for this way of practicing *hitbodedut* is advantageous but not fully required. For those who practice what we have described here, a concentrated *hitbodedut* any time during the day will surely prove effective as time passes.

Overcoming bodily urges

Here's a rule to live by: Speaking to Hashem should be second nature. One should speak to Hashem at every opportunity, at every hour of the day. Most importantly, one should be candid and sincere, speaking from the heart in his own jargon. One should be spiritually sensitive enough to be aware of and ashamed of one's misdeeds, knowing that he has transgressed against a great, loving, and benevolent King. Most importantly, a person should pray extensively, especially asking Hashem to help him overcome his bodily urges.

Bodily urges are certainly no blessing. They are comparable to chocolate-coated poison – they seem sweet, but they're really lethal. Every bodily urge resembles a brick wall that separates between a person and Hashem, blocking out the true sweetness of life which is the illumination of Divine light on that person's soul. The bodily urge fools a person into thinking that he has already achieved his goal of sweetness in life. One must be a valiant spiritual warrior to withstand the strong temptation of bodily urges and their illusion of the sweet life.

How can a human being withstand such strong temptations? The appeal of beauty and pleasure to one's senses virtually captivates a person when faced with a test, and time after time ensnares him. Even when a person discovers the bitter aftertaste of the sugar-coated poison, he'll usually fall into the same trap the very next time he's faced with it. The bodily urge pulls him like a magnetic field against which he can't resist. The more he loses control, the more he loses his powers of reason, until the bodily urge completely subjugates him. How can a person possibly resist and overcome a bodily urge? How can he turn his back on temptation, when every single cell of his body seems to be screaming for him to indulge?

There's only one to rid oneself of a bodily urge, bad habit, or negative character trait: one must turn to Hashem every single day in personal prayer and ask Him for Divine assistance in nullifying and overcoming whatever negative aspect that's sorely impairing one's personal and spiritual development. As with bodily urges, bad habits and negative character traits also impair one's thought process and powers of decision-making especially when subjected to a test of temptation. A person should never give up praying until he has totally overcome his problem.

Words from Heaven

Rebbe Nachman of Breslev writes that Hashem derives immense gratification when a person turns to Him in prayer with an assortment of arguments, trying to persuade Hashem like a son or daughter tries to persuade a loving parent. Not only that, but the *Gemara* (tractate *Bava Metzia* 59b) says that Hashem actually enjoys when a person "out-argues" Him. This sounds strange apparently, for how can a mortal defeat the Omniscient in a debate, so to speak? The answer is both simple and wonderful: Hashem illuminates the person's brain with the right claims and arguments to win his case. In that respect, when Hashem has gratification from a person and from his aspirations, Hashem allows Himself to be convinced, and the person's prayer is answered.

The words that a person speaks to Him are Divinely inspires and tantamount to the holy spirit of prophecy. Just as Hashem sends words to a prophet, He literally puts words in the mouth of those who seek Him. Therefore, a person should speak to Hashem at every opportunity about every subject, always looking for new ways to plead his case before Hashem. Since the words one speaks to Hashem are Divinely inspired, the more a person purifies himself, the more he becomes a worthy receptacle for Divine input. The best way to purify oneself is by guarding the "seven holy candles," a metaphor for the gateways to the brain: two eyes that we must guard from forbidden sights, two ears that we must guard from unwholesome things we shouldn't hear, two nostrils that shouldn't become inflamed with anger, and a mouth that should never lie or slander. The reward for guarding these seven gateways is a pure heart; the reward for a pure heart is more and more Divinely-instilled and inspired thoughts and words with which to speak to Hashem.

Every single request or expression of desire to cling to Hashem helps a person realize his untapped inner potential for greater spiritual and personal achievement. One's yearning for Hashem brings out the best in him. Such appeals as, "Hashem, I want so badly to get close to You," or "please help me guard my eyes," or "help me develop sufficient spiritual awareness to make really beneficial priorities in life." Hashem is more than happy to help us pray with intent or learn Torah with true understanding and proper motives. He'll be glad to help a person to stop smoking or win the battle of overeating, especially when overcoming such bodily urges will be conducive for a person's service of Hashem. All one has to do is ask, persevere and keep asking until he attains his goal.

Speaking to Hashem brings one's aspirations and yearning from the status of inner desires of the heart to the status of tangible self-improvement. Not only that, one's speaking to Hashem is beneficial to the entire world in that it invokes Divine compassion, blessings, and abundance. It's also a wonderful spiritual influence that arouses others as well.

One's *emuna* in the power of personal prayer and his simple and diligent daily practice of it help rectify a person's soul of all blemishes.

The War of Amalek

Be forewarned – there are a number of factors that discourage a person from believing in personal prayer and in its power. These discouraging elements and doubts stem from a source of spiritual impurity known as "the husk of Amalek." As with a fruit, one must cut through the husk (outer shell or peel) in order to partake of and enjoy the fruit. In the case at hand, one must cut through the husk of agnosticism – the doubts in *emuna* and in the effectiveness of prayer, in order to pray to Hashem wholeheartedly. This is the spiritual war of Amalek – fighting against and overcoming doubts in *emuna*.

The Torah tells us about Israel's war with Amalek and that when Moses raised his hands (toward the Heavens, indicative of *emuna*), Israel would prevail. But, whenever Moses lowered his hands, Amalek would prevail.

Our sages say that Moses' upraised hands mean that he prayed, and the Children of Israel followed suit, looking toward the Heavens for salvation. As such, Moses – the tzaddik of the generation – had the power to uplift the Children of Israel to a level of greater *emuna* and prayer, which subsequently led to their victory.

The War of Amalek is still with us today. Every time a terrorist strikes or some calamity befalls the Jewish people, Heaven forbid, Amalek is prevailing. Our only defense is to uplift our eyes and to turn to Hashem in prayer; as such, the tables will turn and Amalek will fall. In any predicament where no solution is in sight, the best and only course of action is prayer.

The prime reinforcement

Rebbe Natan of Breslev writes (*Likutei Halachot, Choshen Mishpat, Nachlot* 4) that people's main obstacle to prayer is their lack of faith in the power of prayer. One cannot expect to have prayers answered immediately. But, with perseverance, one's prayers are eventually answered. Having seen that his prayer really does work, his *emuna* is strengthened. *Emuna* is the spiritual vessel for holding the blessings of abundance, both material and spiritual. Increased *emuna* means increased blessings. As such, perseverance in prayer is the prime reinforcement of *emuna*, for one sees with his own two eyes just how amazingly effective prayer is.

Patience in prayer

Most people doubt the power of prayer and never get off the ground, thinking that personal prayer is a waste of time. Many others begin to pray and quickly become discouraged if and when their wishes aren't fulfilled instantaneously. If they make an effort and pray for fifteen minutes, they feel that they've prayed extensively and are entitled to whatever they asked for. If they pray for something in what they consider a superhuman effort of thirty minutes – and still go unanswered – they lose heart. The evil inclination jumps in the bandwagon of their disappointment to destroy what little *emuna* they have left, telling them that personal prayer is ridiculous, for there's no one on the other end of the line to hear those prayers, G-d forbid.

Patience in prayer means standing before Hashem and praying for as long as necessary. When it seems that prayer is ineffective, it's only because one hasn't prayed sufficiently.

Patience in prayer, when a person prays extensively without looking at his stopwatch, is a clear indication of *emuna* and a statement that he believes in the power of prayer. Patience in prayer and belief in the power of prayer enhance the effectiveness of prayer.

There are two main ploys to increase one's patience in prayer and his ability to pray at length.

First, he should remind himself of the situations when his prayers were answered; this serves as an incentive to pray further. The evil inclination does its best to make a person forget about all the occasions when his prayers were answered, so he'll despair and lose faith in prayer. But, when a person reminds himself of the wonderful times when his prayers worked wonders and he thanks Hashem for those times, he derives renewed strength to pray again at length and with vigor.

Second, he should ask Hashem to help him pray at whatever length is necessary to accomplish his goal. Here's an example of a short prayer that's extremely beneficial as a preface to personal prayer: "Hashem, I don't know how much prayer is necessary to have my request fulfilled. Please, enable me to pray at whatever length is required to attain my needed salvation. Help me persevere with *emuna*, and never to be discouraged until my prayers are answered."

The sixty-minute level

We've previously discussed in this book the importance of several of the most important tasks that we must accomplish during personal prayer. Gratitude to Hashem is the highest priority, followed by daily self-evaluation. These two subjects could easily monopolize an hour's daily *hitbodedut* session. We spoke about the need to pray for character improvement in general and the improvement of a particular negative trait or bad habit until we truly overcome it; this too could require an hour a day. A person must also avoid the pitfalls of ego centeredness and pray for the Jewish people at length. He also needs to pray for his wife and his children, and for his material and spiritual needs. A person that reads this book will certainly desire to implement its contents, but what can a person do? Can he spend entire days in personal prayer?

There are wonderful stories about the tzadikim of previous generations. Rabbi Levi Yitzchak Binder of blessed memory told us about his father in law, Rabbi Aaron Kiblitsher, who would spend twelve hours in the frozen Ukrainian woods in the middle of winter calling out to Hashem. Even today, one can find pious individuals praying to Hashem all night long in the cave of Shimon HaTzaddik or Rebbe Shimon Bar Yochai's gravesite in Meron.

This book, though, is intended to be a practical guide for everyone, even a person taking his first steps in spirituality. Realistically, there are two feasible paths to take:

First, for those who can't devote more than an hour a day to personal prayer, no problem! They should do their very best to set aside 60 minutes a day, and utilize them as follows: spend the first few minutes thanking Hashem and the next few minutes in self evaluation and *teshuva*. To invoke Divine compassion, one should spend a few minutes praying for the Jewish people and for others in need, such as the poor and the sick. The remainder of the hour should be devoted to one's needs, predominantly focused on correcting a negative character trait or habit. This is the path that Rebbe Nachman refers to when he writes (*Likutei Moharan* II:26), "*Hitbodedut* is an attribute that surpasses everything, in other words, to set aside one hour or more for solitary prayer in some room or field, and to converse with Hashem…".

Rebbe Nachman promises that anyone who steadfastly devotes an hour a day to personal prayer will attain a complete soul correction and never see the face of purgatory.

Second, the "lion-hearted" who would love to spend multiple hours in *hitbodedut* but can't, should at any rate devote ninety minutes a day to expressing their gratitude to Hashem, soul-searching and *teshuva*, praying for others, and praying for his own needs in the first half hour. Then, they should devote an entire hour to praying for one thing such as acquiring good character traits or ridding themselves of a bodily urge or bad habit. Such people will certainly become true servants of Hashem.

Who has emuna?

A major misconception people have is that they don't need to pray for *emuna*. In the early days of Breslev, the opponents to Rebbe Nachman's teachings scoffed when his prime disciple Rebbe Natan wrote a book of prayers based on Rebbe Nachman's teachings. Many of Rebbe Natan's prayers are heartfelt requests for *emuna*. The opponents chided, "The Breslever Rebbe lacks *emuna*, because he prays all day long for *emuna*!" They had no idea how far away from *emuna* they were.

Everyone has *emuna* to some extent, but weak *emuna*. Why weak? Stop and think: when someone yells at you, do you believe that Hashem is yelling at you? Do you seek revenge when someone wrongs you? Anytime we attribute anything that happens to us to people rather than to Hashem, we're far away from *emuna*.

The ninety-minute level

The ninety-minute level are for those who seriously desire to make a major character improvement. They devote the first 30 minutes of their personal prayer session to expressions of gratitude and self-evaluation, then devote an entire hour to the particular character trait (or other issue) that they're working on. Even though the 90-minute session is 50% longer than the 60-minute session, the time devoted on the issue at hand in the 90-minute session is double than it is in the 60-minute session, namely, an entire hour instead of a half hour. As such, one can accomplish in 90-days of 90-minute sessions what he would otherwise accomplish in six months of 60-minute sessions. And, if one sees blessings and miracles within 90 days of 60-minute sessions, just imagine the wonderful surprises in store for him after 90 days of 90-minute sessions!

One issue – one hour

Let's discuss the practical side of praying for one issue for one hour, using as an example overeating, something that plagues many people.

First of all, to make our prayers effective, we should learn as much as possible about the subject at hand. In the case of overeating, we should learn how detrimental it is to our physical health, how it presents a barrier in serving Hashem, and the rewards due to the fortunate person who succeeds in overcoming the habit.

One can learn about the root spiritual causes of overeating in *Likutei Moharan* I:47.

Sefer HaMiddot says that overeating is detrimental to *emuna*.

Eating properly is strongly connected to wholesome speech. Therefore, if a person wants to overcome the habit of overeating, he must be especially careful to tell the truth and to avoid angry speech such as yelling or cursing.

Many issues that affect proper eating should be included in the hour's daily prayer. A person should ask Hashem to help him eat slowly and be satiated. He should pray for guidance in eating only what is healthy and what his body needs. He should ask Hashem to help him fulfill all the mitzvas that are associated with mealtime, such as blessings before and after and washing the hands. He should pray that he should never eat anything questionably kosher.

Next, he should evaluate himself and his eating over the past 24 hours. Did he eat in holiness, or as a glutton? Did he eat healthy foods, or did he eat sweets and junk foods? Did he eat between meals? Could he have sufficed with less food?

People have accomplished more in personal prayer than they ever hoped to accomplish by means of any diet or weight-loss program. With Hashem's help, a person can learn to eat properly, lose weight, and serve Hashem with greater agility with no fads, drugs, or artificial means.

By repeating our heart's desires daily and reinforcing our goals with renewed commitment each day, we gradually achieve more than we ever dreamed we could.

The central point

Each bad habit or bodily lust stems from some central point that is the core reason for the bad habit or negative trait. For example, a person might deviate from the truth because of a low self-image; he thinks that people will admire and respect him only if he is greater than what he really is. He therefore fabricates untrue tales about himself.

If such a person would pray for an hour a day asking for help in speaking the truth, his prayers would be lacking in that they wouldn't address the central point or core reason of his problem. He therefore must pray to Hashem to help him identify and appreciate his own very special qualities that Hashem has given him. He should pray for a positive self-image and for emotional independence so that he won't need to depend on others for approval like a spiritual beggar in need of a few "pennies" of constant compliments.

Once a person establishes the central point of his negative characteristic or bad habit, personal prayer becomes so much easier *and* effective. For example, a low-level prayer would be praying for a bottle of aspirin. Better than that would be a prayer to recuperate from the flu. But, the best prayer would be for the central point, asking Hashem to help him realize which misdeed he committed that invoked the harsh judgment of catching a flu virus, and to make *teshuva* for it.

The two-hour level

The disadvantage of the 60 and 90-minute sessions is that one cannot devote an hour a day to self-evaluation and soul-searching, which in essence is the foundation both of *teshuva* and of personal prayer. Two hours a day of personal prayer is for the fortunate few who seek a high level of character perfection, self-awareness, *teshuva*, and clinging to Hashem.

One need not take on the two-hour level as a daily commitment. Yet, two hours of *hitbodedut* is suave for the soul in times of need, such as when a person is faced with a new challenge in life, is sick, or is temporarily unemployed. Such a person has an entire hour for soul-searching and tshuva. A wise person understands that if he suddenly has free time – as when he's hospitalized or unemployed – Hashem is giving him the opportunity to devote more time to personal prayer.

We shall deal with the proper way to judge ourselves in the coming chapter.

Chapter Seven:
The Attainable Good Life

This chapter addresses the main component of *hitbodedut* – self-evaluation and *teshuva*. *Hitbodedut* is the gateway to serving Hashem, for one who performs an hour of *hitbodedut* daily will ascend higher and higher.

Let's examine the best way to approach one's daily hour of self-evaluation, which in effect is personal judgment.

24 Courts

There are 24 heavenly courts, each corresponding to an hour of the day. Each hour, a person is judged according to his deeds; if they are good, he is judged favorably and therefore feels joy and a sense of wellbeing. On the other hand, if his deeds are not good, he is judged harshly and therefore feels sad and tormented, for our sages said (Mishna, tractate *Eduyot* 5:7): "Your deeds will bring you near, your deeds will distance you."

Rosh Hashanah is the main Day of Judgment, determining life and death, livelihood, and other broad issues. Yet, the specifics of each day and each hour - whether good or otherwise - depends on the judgment rendered on a specific day, at that very hour, according to one's deeds.

Here's an example: The Holy Baal Shem Tov met an elderly Jew who made his livelihood as a water-carrier. The Holy Baal Shem Tov asked how he's feeling, to which the water-carrier replied with great joy, "Everything is excellent, I thank Hashem for giving me the strength to earn my living honorably."

A few days later, the Baal Shem Tov saw that the water-carrier looked forlorn. The Baal Shem Tov greeted him, but the latter burst into tears and complained about his bitter fate, that even at his old age he must work so hard to make a living.

The Baal Shem Tov was surprised at the drastic change in attitude. He contemplated this and later remarked: "Finally, an apparent contradiction in the Talmud tractate 'Rosh Hashanah' became resolved in my mind. The Mishna states that a person is judged on Rosh Hashanah, while the Gemara says that a person is judged hourly on each day. A question of course arises – if a person is judged for a whole year on Rosh Hashanah, then why must he be judged once again each and every hour?

The water carrier's drastic mood change is an indication of the answer to the above question. True, on Rosh Hashanah a person is judged for the whole year. Yet, *how* he will receive this judgment, whether it will be in joy or sorrow, is decided upon every single hour, according to his deeds."

On Rosh Hashanah it was determined how the water carrier would continue to earn his living – namely, as a water-carrier. Yet how he'd react to this ruling, whether bitterly or with joy, would be determined daily and hourly during the year. He might be judged favorably by the Heavenly courts during one hour and consequently be happy. Yet during another hour, when the Heavenly courts have ruled adversely against him, he'd experience difficulty and bitterness.

Teshuva, prayer, and charity can change both what has been decreed on Rosh Hashanah and all the daily and hourly rulings of the Heavenly courts.

The above example enables us to understand how and why a person's mood changes from day to day and from hour to hour. During one hour, everything seems to be going his way and he consequently feels good. Later, he suddenly feels unsuccessful and downtrodden. At breakfast, he may have enjoyed harmony with his wife, but at dinner, they began to argue over something petty.

The only reasonable explanation for such dramatic changes is the hourly judgments of the Heavenly courts. They affect one's health, moods, *shalom bayit*, livelihood, and every other aspect of his life.

Divine Providence in all things

We must internalize the knowledge that life's every difficulty - even the simplest of things such as an itch or a mosquito bite - is a tribulation decreed by the Heavenly courts. These tribulations should stimulate *teshuva* rather than be dismissed as a consequence of nature and chance.

The Talmud says (tractate *Chulin* 7): "A person can't lift a finger unless this has been decreed from Above." King David says, "Hashem prepares a man's each step" (Psalm 37:23).

In another instance the Talmud teaches us (tractate *Arachin*, 16): "To what trivial extent should we still consider 'tribulation'?" That is to say, what is the most insignificant thing one can view as tribulation? "Rabbi Eliezer says: A garment that has been sewn that the person finds unbecoming. Rabbi Shmuel bar Nachmani says: no, more than that, even if a person wanted to eat something warm but was served something that has been cooled, or visa versa, that can be considered tribulation. The son of Rabina says: even if his garment is inside-out. And it was added: even if a person puts his hand in his pocket to take out three coins and takes out only two, that too is a tribulation…"

One must internalize the belief that every bit of joy, happiness and pleasure that he enjoys, as well as every hardship that he suffers, is neither by error or happenstance, but a decree from Above by the Heavenly courts according to one's daily deeds.

Hashem is Righteous and Just

One who erroneously imagines that his suffering is a consequence of nature or chance and therefore blames himself and his surroundings for his misfortune will not only become a victim of frustration and resentment, but will invoke severe judgments from Above. This is just like the wayward son who is punished by his father: instead of mending his ways, he blames his brother and picks a fight with his him. Surely the father will be all the more angered by such a son's behavior. "Not only are you not making an effort to correct yourself, you are fighting with your brother!?"

Another frequent misconception is a person's belief that all is a product of Divine Providence, yet simultaneously holds the opinion that Hashem has judged him unfairly.

Rebbe Natan therefore says (*Likutei Halachot, Hilchot Nezikin* 5):

" … and the main cause of assuming misjudgment is the unholy wisdom of the world, of the aspect of flawed judgment, which construes that Hashem is not absolutely fair and just in his judgments. This misconception leads one to believe that we are incapable of standing up to the tests Hashem gives His people. For example, most of the world proclaims it can not worship Hashem properly because of insufficient livelihood. In other words, they claim that Hashem has made warped judgment against them, because they lack the means to fulfill His Will and are unable to spend their time studying Torah because of poor finances. Surely this is not the truth. We must, every one of us, believe that Hashem is just and His judgments are upright and just. Surely Hashem does not expect any one to do what is beyond their means or capabilities; surely He has no grievance against us for what we cannot do. Hashem gives us the test to study the Torah and do the mitzvoth precisely under duress, for as our sages have taught us: 'All who keep the Torah in poverty – will inevitably in the end keep it in wealth'.

"So we must believe that everything that we must endure is given to us by a just G-d, who never tests a person beyond his means\ capabilities. Even if one's mind tells him that what he is suffering is beyond his capacity to suffer, he must still believe that Hashem's ways are just and fair, and so all the things that a person must endure and suffer in his lifetime are given to him justly and for his own good."

Frequently people fail to believe that Hashem is just and that all His judgments are just and merciful. As such, they are far away from *emuna*. By way of tribulations and suffering, Hashem calls them in order to bring them closer to Him, for King Solomon says

(Proverbs 3:12), "Hashem chastens the one He loves". Those who fail to understand this principle impair their faith. Rather than their suffering leading to them to a spiritual awakening, they descend to heresy, believing that Hashem has ruled against them unjustly. They are erroneously concluding that Hashem has no desire for them or for their efforts to grow close to Him. They even become angry at Divine Providence, as we often see when people who have suffered claim that Hashem has acted cruelly and unfairly against them, G-d forbid.

Just as we must believe that everything that happens to us is from Above, so too we must have complete faith that Hashem is righteous and upright and no injustice whatsoever comes from him, Heaven forbid. We must have faith that all our trials and tribulations are actually products of Hashem's great mercy, their sole purpose being to enable us to come closer to Him.

Hashem's Great Mercy

The path to becoming a tzaddik is not easy, nor does one become a righteous person overnight. What, then, should a person do until he has attained complete *teshuva*, for he still fails and continues to sin? How can he be saved from daily judgment, from the self-induced suffering invoked by his sins? After all, everyone wants to do *teshuva* and return to Hashem and act according to His Will. Yet if the path is such a long one, then what should a person do in the meanwhile? How should he act? Is he doomed to live his life in torment?

Hashem in His infinite mercy has given us an amazing solution, called "Judging oneself." There is no double jeopardy in the Heavenly Courts, for if a person judges himself daily then he is exempt from being judged by the Heavenly Courts. The Midrash states explicitely, (*Midrash Rabba, Mishpatim* 5): "When there is judgment below, then there is no judgment held Above."

The Zohar reveals that when a man judges himself, while conducting a daily self-evaluation of his deeds, confessing his wrongdoings, asking Hashem's forgiveness, and resolving to do his best not to repeat those transgressions, then the Heavenly Courts cannot and do not judge him. Only Hashem judges him.

Here's the good news: Hashem judges a person with such unfathomable mercy that the latter always is found innocent. On the other hand, the Heavenly Courts are exacting in every letter of the law to the extent that one is almost always found guilty there. Hashem both judges people favorably and rewards them for their *teshuva*!

Therefore, if a person longs for relief from tribulations and suffering, he must learn to judge himself. This means to devote one hour of each day to self-evaluation of all his thoughts, words and deeds – if he is conducting himself properly. He must do *teshuva* for those things which fall outside the limits of propriety. By judging himself, he won't be grilled in the meticulous stern judgment of the Heavenly Courts.

Going Through Life with a Smile

One who practices daily *hitbodedut* will be pronounced innocent even on Rosh Hashanah, for he has done *teshuva* on every day of the year. The Midrash elaborates on a passage in Ecclesiastes 9:8, "Your clothes shall be pure [white] at all times," and quotes Rabbi Eliezer who says: "A person who does *teshuva* the day before he dies." His pupils asked him how one can know the day he is going to die. Rabbi Eliezer replied, "Precisely, one must do *teshuva* today, for he may die tomorrow. In this way he will be doing *teshuva* all the days of his life."

Imagine that in this physical world the court system in your area offered every person the chance to admit to his crimes; by means of this confession, he would not only be pardoned but would even be rewarded. Who wouldn't take advantage of such an opportunity?

Think of this hypothetical example: A person is driving a car. He drives straight through a red light and is stopped by a policeman. The driver steps out of the car, confesses and does *teshuva*. He says: "Master of the Universe, I confess that I ran through a red light; I totally regret this act and ask You to forgive me for this serious transgression. I solemnly resolve to forever heed the traffic lights and laws to the best of my ability..."

Upon hearing this confession, the anger of the policeman subsides. He smiles at the driver and says, "At first I planned to give you a stiff fine, as well as to revoke your driver's license and subpoena you. Since you've expressed such sincere remorse in driving through that red light, I forgive you. Not only that. I would like to reward your act of repentance." And with this the policeman takes out his checkbook and writes out a check for one hundred thousand dollars, blesses him and sends him on his way!

Mind boggling? A fantasy tale? That's just how judging yourself works from a spiritual standpoint! As with our hypothetical example of the red light violation, is there a driver in this world who would not prefer on-the-spot penitence to a stiff fine, losing his driver's license and facing a court-case, as well as missing out on a one hundred thousand dollar reward for doing *teshuva*?

This is exactly how Hashem governs the world! If a person believed in the power of *teshuva* - that Hashem gives every person the chance to rectify any sin in the world - then he would surely do *teshuva*. He would not forfeit such a golden opportunity! He'd daily examine his own actions, rectify his deeds, and spare himself the headache and heartache of severe judgment. He definitely wouldn't make the excuse that he doesn't have the time for self-evaluation, especially when his alternative would be wasting tons of time and money running after doctors and lawyers, seeking their help in coping with all the severe judgments he has to deal with.

With the above in mind, are we now ready to believe what's written in the Zohar and many other holy books about the lofty merits of daily *hitbodedut*? Would we prefer tribulations and untold suffering in this world and the next because of our uncorrected transgressions? Are we so inane to forfeit boundless rewards for *teshuva*?

Hashem in His mercy gives each person the opportunity to examine and judge himself, and thereby avoid the danger of standing before the Heavenly Courts. He offers such a person reward for this as well! Who is the fool who would be too lazy to save himself from all the grievances against him and from all the torment of this world, leaving himself exposed to what may be waiting for him in severe judgment in this world and in the next? Advice

Everyone must practice 60 minutes of *teshuva* daily. This can be any hour that is convenient, during the day or at night; it can be conducted any place where one can be alone – in a garden, a forest, a room, or a porch. Total privacy is essential, with no interferences or distractions. One can stand or sit, or walk. The most recommended manner is to walk, for walking prompts a person to talk.

Ther hour of personal prayer should begin with speaking words of gratitude. Then, one can speak of everything that has transpired since the previous day's *hitbodedut* session. One should speak of all the good things that he would like to thank Hashem for, as well as judge himself for everything he did. He must confess the current day's misdeeds and repent for them, and request that Hashem fulfill all his needs, both material and spiritual.

How Does One Do Teshuva?

The "SCAR" treatment is easiest way to do *teshuva*:

Hashem is a loving and forgiving Father who's always waiting to hear our voice. By talking to Him for an hour a day, we can painlessly do *teshuva* for all our wrongdoings. Transgressions scar and blemish the soul, but here's more good news: the *teshuva* process is a simple 4-step spiritual treatment that cleans **all** the scars off one's soul. That's why we call it the "SCAR" treatment.

Here are the 4 steps:

Stop what you're doing wrong – the first thing we have to do is to put an immediate stop to whatever we're doing wrong.

Confess to Hashem every misdeed – once we confess, the *Yetzer Hara* (Evil Inclination) has no right to say anything bad or accusatory about us, nor can the Heavenly Court judge us.

Apologize to Hashem for our misdeeds – we certainly have remorse about hurting someone we love, and our transgressions cause extreme anguish to our loving Father in Heaven.

Resolve to do better in the future – here, we ask Hashem to strengthen us in *emuna*, *yir'a* (fear of Hashem) and *ahava* (love of Hashem) so in the future we can enhance our good deeds and diminish our bad ones. Self-Judgment

People do judge themselves, but according to distorted concepts. They consequently arrive at twisted conclusions. For example, they assume that they're faulty or unsuccessful, a "loser" with no chance of ever being rectified. They conclude that they deserve to be depressed and more often than not persecute themselves. This is a serious misconception that causes a person to despair and feel alienated from G-d. It may even lead him to heresy, Heaven forbid. The evil inclination is not so much interested in a person committing a sin as he is in that person's subsequent depression and sense of hopelessness that follows a misdeed.

Sin itself is not what creates a barrier between a person and Hashem, but rather the despair and sadness that he feels after a failure. If a person were to judge himself correctly, his sinning would in effect bring him even closer to G-d, for he would be awakened by his transgression to make an even greater effort to rectify himself.

Judgment Together with Emuna

Remember that Hashem is not filled with grievances against us! Hashem knows that we're not angels. Hashem's only complaint when a person has sinned is why that individual did not turn to Him and seek His help. People erroneously think that they can overcome their evil inclination without Hashem's assistance. That's wrong!

Hashem knows that He created man out of physical matter and that man has a tendency to fail. He expects a person to do *teshuva* after transgressing. Hashem surely doesn't expect a person to be perfect and never transgress. But, in virtue of a person's *teshuva*, he can surely free himself of sin.

Even if one has transgressed a great deal, he must remember that *teshuva* doesn't mean descent into an abyss of depression. Indeed, one should rejoice that Hashem has given us the opportunity to rectify at any given moment. The gift of *teshuva* is enough to make a spiritually-cognizant person sing and dance until his 120th birthday. Therefore before anything else the person must say to himself: "There is no one other than Him! Hashem wants to show me that I cannot manage without Him, because He loves me and wants me to be close to Him. The proof of this love is that I tried to "do it alone" and look how I failed... Yet, now that I have failed and sinned, what does Hashem want from me? Does he want me to be depressed? To persecute myself? No! He has given me the gift of *teshuva*! Hashem wants me to be happy and believe, *Ain Od Milvado* - there is no one other than Him! This *emuna* will lead me to prayer and to *teshuva*."

Thanks are now in order. After a setback, a person should say, "Thank you Hashem, for showing me that I cannot succeed without You. From now on, I'll depend on Your loving assistance in everything I do..."

Forfeiting the Crown

Rebbe Nachman of Breslev tells a story that helps us internalize what we've just learned:

"I will tell you how to be happy. Once there was a king who had an only son. The king desired to give his crown to his son while he was still living. He made a great banquet. Surely when the king makes a banquet he is filled with joy, and now he was especially joyous because the banquet was to celebrate transferring the rule of the kingdom to his only son. All the king's men, ministers, and dukes were certainly joyous because of this banquet.

The people of the kingdom too were joyous that the king was handing the rule of their kingdom over to his son in his lifetime. This was a great honor for the king, and therefore brought them tremendous joy. The banquet was the most joyous of occasions, with orchestra, magicians and entertainers taking part as well.

The king stood up and turned to his son: Because I have the gift of prophesy, I see that in the future you will forfeit the crown. I ask of you that even when this happens, you should not lose your happiness. And if you will continue to be joyous, I too will be happy. Even if you become sad, I will continue to be happy. For if you cannot continue to be in a state of joy when you lose the crown, that will mean that you are not worthy of kingship. But when you are happy, then I will be happy… I will be exceedingly happy…"

Let's examine this story:

"This is the tale of a king who had an only son" – The first message of this story is that every single person is an only child of Hashem. Every person has a unique mission in the world and is special in the eyes of G-d.

"and the king wanted to hand the crown to his only son during his lifetime…" – this means that Hashem wants His son to pray, for through his prayers he will rule heaven and earth, in other words, merit kingship. Prayer is an aspect of kingship, for it reveals Hashem's monarchy more than anything else in the world. When a person prays and his prayers are accepted, then we all witness that Hashem is King and rules the entire world. Hashem wants everyone to be a "master of prayer," and for this purpose, He created this world. A master of prayer can rule by way of his prayer.

Rebbe Nachman teaches (*Likutei Moharan* I:102) that Hashem created the world for the purpose of revealing His sovereignty. Prayer reveals His sovereignty and thereby vanquishes the evil inclination. As such, everyone must aspire to pray and to subsequently reveal Hashem's monarchy. Rebbe Nachman also writes (ibid., 107) that the Hashem created the world for those righteous ones who will rule through their prayer. Consequently, the more a person immerses himself in prayer, the greater he is fulfilling Hashem's Will. Through his prayer, he is revealing Hashem's glorious rule over the entire world.

One reveals Hashem's kingship only through prayer. Even if he proclaims that Hashem is the ruler of the universe - as long he is not praying for Hashem's assistance in every endeavor and as long as he is not invoking Divine abundance through his prayers - he is not living with the *emuna* that Hashem is the One and Only King who did, does, and will do all things. So as long as he is not asking Hashem for help in every endeavor, he is not acting according to his proclamation that Hashem is King. Only when he prays for everything and sees the effectiveness of his prayers does he reveal that Hashem is the One and Only King.

"… and he made a great banquet" –Hashem delights when a Jew has earned kinship through prayer.

"This was a great honor for the king" – This truly is Hashem's

honor, when we pray and act through our prayers.

Here is the crucial point that is essential for true *teshuva*:

"Because I have the gift of prophesy, I see that in the future you will fall from the crown. I ask of you that even when this happens,

224 | In Forest Fields

you should not lose your happiness." - The king's message is for all: "I know you will have times of setbacks and failure, but I warn you – Be happy! Don't despair!

Pay attention! This is a message from the King Himself! The very same King who commands us to rule over our urges, not to sin, and to be careful about fulfilling every commandment of the Torah is telling us that He knows that we'll not be able to be absolutely perfect always. There will be times that we will fall and not live exactly as commanded in the Torah. He nevertheless tells us to be happy always!

Hashem knows that becoming a tzaddik requires years of hard work. Our path is laden with times of setback and failure. Hashem knows this, but we don't! We tend to think that we can instantly become angels and be totally free of any evil inclination while never failing.

As long as a person is distressed and persecutes himself for being less than an angel, and as long as he cannot forgive himself, he'll be depressed. He is dejected because he fears that he's not capable of *teshuva*. Herein lays a serious contradiction: on the one hand, he demands perfection of himself, so that he'll never sin. On the other hand, the minute he fails, he goes to the opposite extreme, becoming depressed while regarding himself as an absolute failure incapable of anything.

By falling into sadness as a result of his failures, his self-judgment is totally warped and nears madness. Therefore the King comes to warn him very explicitly – do not be sad! Be happy and do *teshuva*. By this a person saves himself both from illusions of grandeur and a sense of inferiority.

…**and if you will continue to be joyous I too will be happy** – Here Hashem tells us, "Maybe you think that I am sad because of your failings? That's not true! If you remain in a state of happiness then I will not be saddened by your failings, because I knew that you would fail. Only one thing does bother me —your sadness! Once you have sinned, move forward! You still possess your freedom of choice. You can choose whether to continue to be happy or to fall into despair. When you choose not to be sad – then I will be happy.

We're bound to ask, "But what about my transgressions? Don't they impair The King's happiness?" The answer is an emphatic "No!" If we don't fall into sadness, then our sin will not sadden The King. An intrinsic part of life's journey is to fail, fall, and face difficulty.

Rebbe Nachman said that even if he would commit a great sin, he wouldn't fall into despair; he'd be happy because he'd do *teshuva*.

A person who maintains happiness will ascend and ascend more and more, for he'll continue to serve Hashem and do *teshuva*. For this reason, a daily hour of *teshuva* is so vital. It keeps a person is at peace. He knows that he doesn't have to walk around with a blemished soul or far away from Hashem. He can repent for every sin and setback that he suffered during the last 24 hours. In this hour, he deals with his shortcomings and therefore can be happy for the rest of the day.

"And even when you become sad I will continue to be happy. For if you cannot continue to be in a state of joy when you lose the crown that will mean that you are not worthy of kingship." Here the king relays a very clears message: only a person who remains happy when his crown is removed is worthy of kingship! The world thinks that if a ruler is removed from the throne, it's proof that he was unworthy. They also think that the tzaddikim, the righteous ones, never fail and are therefore deserving of kingship. This is not true. The true test of royalty is precisely when a person is removed from the throne and yet does not fall into sadness and despair. All the righteous ones, contrary to what people assume, also suffer tremendous setbacks. Yet, they maintain their joy and thereby continue to ascend.

Rebbe Natan said that every tzaddik earned his elevated spiritual status precisely because of the manner in which he strengthened himself when he was down. He revealed that he too merited whatever he attained through strengthening himself by faith reinforcement during difficult times.

Why is this strengthening of one's happiness despite one's failings the key to being worthy of kingship? One who strengthens himself in *emuna* can maintain happiness, and therby demonstrates to the world that he believes that everything is from Hashem, both his successes and his failures. If he loses his happiness and falls into despair, he is saying that he lives according to his flawed imagination that he himself and not Hashem is responsible for his successes and failures.

"... but when you are happy, then I will be happy... I will be exceedingly happy..." There is a significant difference between Hashem's happiness when a depressed sinner has been removed from the throne and His joy when one holds onto his happiness despite a setback and is consequently worthy of kingship. Hashem is therefore "exceedingly happy", a complete joy in that His beloved son is indeed worthy of ruling (through his prayer). This is surely the pleasure of The King and His motivation in creating the world.

Serve Hashem in Joy

Few people serve Hashem in joy. Those who do are always happy, no matter what. They know that there is no place for sadness in the service of Hashem.

We should maintain our inner joy even on the 9th of Av. Although lamentations and mourning the destruction of the Temples are the order of the day, we are expressing our yearning for Hashem, but not depression or despair. We are broken-hearted that our sins caused the destruction of the Temples, but we desire to rectify. We long for the rebuilding of the Holy Temple and are therefore not sad. Sadness and broken-heartedness are quite the opposite, for only a person who had previously been joyous can then become broken-hearted.

In that respect, even our prayers on the 9th of Av should be prayed in joy. Even then, we sing our halleluiahs in joy, as we do every day. On Tisha b'Av, we recite Psalm 100, the Psalm of thanksgiving, which says, **Serve Hashem with joy**. So even on Tisha b'Av we first pray in joy, and only afterwards sit on the floor in mourning. One who worships Hashem must be joyous when it is time for joy, and weep when it is time to be broken-hearted. Our service to Hashem should not reflect our own personal emotions but rather the Will of G-d. When He commands us to be happy – we should be joyous; and when He commands us to weep – we weep. The essence of our service is, of course, our prayers; we should pray them in joy.

Joy and not Illusion

Without joy, a person cannot do proper *teshuva*. Once someone said to me, "Rabbi, I found that every time I examined my deeds, I fell into despair and sadness, so I just stopped looking at my shortcomings altogether and look now only at the good in me."

So I replied, "That's great! But please tell me, now that you no longer look at your misdeeds, does that mean that you no longer have flaws to rectify? Since you no longer look at yourself truthfully, does that mean you are perfect, with no shortcomings? You should learn how to evaluate yourself in the correct manner, for that will protect you from becoming sad. That way, you won't have to fight against yourself all the time. You will no longer have to struggle to ignore your shortcomings, for you will have learned how to face them without falling on your face."

What is the correct way of looking at oneself? One must assume in advance that he surely has shortcomings, and will have inadequacies in the future as well. One must recognize that Hashem knows that we have faults, and still expects us to be happy while gradually correcting those faults.

The way to rectify these shortcomings is to practice an hour of daily *hitbodedut*. During this hour, one should examine what it is that he needs to correct in himself. He must be truthful with himself. He must open his eyes and see his shortcomings. Yet on the other hand he must not persecute himself because of these faults. He must keep in mind constantly that he is in fact a human being and not an angel. Hashem doesn't expect him to act like an angel. Consequently, there is no reason to despair because of one's shortcomings. A person cannot be perfect, and if he is unwilling to look objectively at his faults, then he surely has a problem with arrogance and self- delusion. After all, we are brought down to this material world to correct our souls. This is the purpose of our lives – to *rectify* rather than to ignore our shortcomings. By doing so without falling into despair, we accomplish our life's mission.

If a person really does not know how to practice *hitbodedut* correctly, then it is preferable that he only look at his good points and be happy. Ignoring one's shortcomings is preferable to sadness and depression. Yet a person should be honest with himself and admit that certain character flaws need correction. Self-evaluation does not necessitate sadness. Hashem is not only patient and tolerant with all of us, but is happy to help us become better people. What more could one ask for?

Most people think that they're OK, but when they discover that they do suffer shortcomings, they become sad. Some will subsequently persecute themselves for their shortcomings and others less so. Yet, Hashem tells us that despite our shortcomings, we must continue to be joyful. Sadness reflects pride, while joy reflects humility. The humble accept that they have shortcomings and are indeed happy that they have the opportunity to rectify those faults.

One who practices *hitbodedut*, who looks at himself honestly and admits to his failings without becoming sad, will actually take pleasure in striving for character improvement.. **Humility**

Rebbe Nachman's story of the king and the royal banquet reveals the depths of wisdom encompassed within the king's commandment to continue happily even after the greatest failure or during the most difficult of tribulations; this is the true expression of humility. The King – the Holy One, blessed be He - knows that a person will undergo times of highs and lows. Yet He commands us to be unconditionally joyful, even during those times of difficulty. Just as the king presented his son with success, so too he desires that his son will be happy even at times of failure. In like manner, Hashem commands us not to sin and he also commands us not to fall into despair once we've transgressed.

Hashem loves us and rejoices in us! He is happy when one is "king", that is to say when one succeeds, and He is happy when one is removed from the throne, i.e. when one has failed, so long that he remains joyful at those times too. Hashem loves the person who remains happy despite a setback because it shows that he doesn't fool himself that he's perfect, but rather accepts the fact that he is only human with things to improve. Rather than being surprised and upset when he fails, he is overflowing with gratitude at times of success. He understands that triumph over sin is achieved through Hashem's abundant kindliness that allows him to overcome his evil nature.

Hashem wants us to "rule", so to speak, but He wants us to be worthy of kingship. The true sign that one is worthy is when he can forfeit that reign without becoming sad. The greatest proof that a person has in fact attained this level of humility and truth is when he remains joyous even when kingship and his successes have been taken away from him. True happiness is not something which should be dependent upon anything, but independent and unconditional.

One must recognize that he is the son of the King, and that he rules only through the grace of his Father. He knows that he is only flesh and blood with an evil inclination that waits in ambush at all times to ensnare him in its traps. He must understand that without the King, he cannot overcome his evil inclination. Therefore, at times when he does succeed to triumph over evil – the times when he is called "king" - he must realize that his success is a gift from Hashem and His kindliness. He should consequently be very grateful to Hashem for those times when - through Hashem's mercy - he does succeed in defeating his evil inclination. When he does "fall from the throne," in other words, when he fails, then he should not see it so much as a fall but rather as a reflection of his true spiritual level. This time, Hashem decided not help him overcome his nature. Consequently, one must beware of arrogance following successes and despair and guilt feelings following a failure.

Why are there times when Hashem does in fact not help a person overcome his evil inclination? Why does He allow His son to fall from the throne? This happens when a person fails to bear in mind that he needs Hashem's assistance, and forgets that his power to rule comes from Hashem. He erroneously imagines that he is succeeding on his own. This happens when he thinks: "I am good, I am a righteous one, through my own strength I overcome all that is evil, I am king …" For when a person in inflated with ego and attributes his successes to himself, he forfeits Divine assistance and will soon be rudely awakened from his delusions of grandeur and returned to his actial spiritual proportions.

We all must realize that we're nothing without Hashem's help; Hashem gives us our monarchy, otherwise there's no reign at all.

By remaining firm in one's happiness despite failing, one in fact rectifies the very cause of his failure. How can that be? He surely failed because he forgot that his power and strength are gifts from Hashem. When he falls from his spiritual standing and remains happy despite that fall, Hashem sees that he knows that his abilities are Divine gifts. This spiritual awareness enables him to return to his former pre-transgression spiritual level and even ascend further.

In our prayers we say, "He humbles the haughty to the ground, and raises the lowly to supreme heights." In other words, the purpose of humbling the arrogant is to enable them to make spiritual growth and to allow them to be raised in a manner that's beneficial to their soul. This of course is on the condition that the humbled person accepts his setback joyfully. Yet if, on the other hand, he complains and rebels against the circumstance of his fall, then Hashem sees that he has neither relinquished his haughtiness nor accepted his lowered station. As such, crying and complaining prevent him from being elevated once again.

King David sinned once – and he remembered that sin for the remainder of his lifetime, as he testifies, "My sin is ever before me" (Psalms, Chapter 51). He indeed recognized the reality that he could sin again and never forgot this possibility. For the rest of his life, he wasn't complacent for even a moment. Always on guard, he constantly prayed that Hashem save him from his evil inclination so it wouldn't overcome him. He was therefore always happy, never ceasing to sing and praise and thank Hashem even during the most devastating times of tribulation, even when his own son Absalom rebelled against him and plotted to kill him!

Superficially, King David had every reason to blame himself harshly for his predicament with Absalom: he could have blamed himself for not having educated his son properly, he could have concluded that Hashem despises him if he had fallen to such a lowly state, or he could have succumbed to dozens of more negative thoughts and emotions. Yet, in this very circumstance, King David proved just how worthy of rule he was. Hashem indeed vowed promised him the throne of Israel for posterity and that the King Messiah would also be of his descendents.

King David proved how worthy he was of the throne when he maintained his happiness despite being removed from the throne. This was the clearest of testimony that King David recognized that his rule was a gift from Hashem and not of his own merit. For he acknowledged: "Hashem gave and Hashem took; may the name of the L-rd be blessed" (Job, Chapter 1).

King David didn't care whether he'd be a shepherd or King of Israel. In his eyes, they were both the same. His sole desire was to serve Hashem. He saw himself as "David", not as King of Israel, and understood that the monarchy would be his only as long as Hashem so desired.

Anyone who truly wants to serve Hashem should think and act in the same manner. He should ignore self-intersest and concern himself with serving Hashem. When he succeeds, he should be grateful to Hashem and continue on without any hesitation. When he doesn't succeed, he should pray to Hashem that he'll merit living with humility and be happy with his current lot in life no matter what.

The following prayer is conducive to *teshuva*, humility and *emuna*: "Master of the Universe, forgive me that I imagined that there can be anything outside of Your reign or any power other than You. Pardon me for having imagined that I can succeed, much less exist, without You. Forgive me for my thoughts of grandeur, for my arrogance, and for my complaining, sadness and anger. Forgive me for persecuting myself as if success or failure were in my hands;

forgive me for letting my earthly desires dictate my life rather than seeking my true pleasure and source of vitality. Forgive me for trusting other people; from now on, help me put my trust in You alone."

When a person does *teshuva* in this way, recognizing his faults and shortcomings while turning to Hashem and asking his forgiveness, he is doing true *teshuva*. Without this, even if he confesses and regrets his wrongdoings, his "*teshuva*" will be dictated by his conceit. He'll be crying that he's not a perfect angel; he'll be persecuting himself for having an evil inclination, and sorrow that he's not superhuman. He'll gripe that he's not Moshe Rabbenu, or the Moshiach, or even Hashem…why isn't *he* King … why isn't *he* the sole reality!?

The Eight Parameters of Judgment

Generally speaking, there are eight basic parameters that affect Heavenly judgments of a person:

Joy: Hashem wants us to do *teshuva*, but not in sadness. We must always ask ourselves, "What does Hashem want from me? Despair?" Of course not! Hashem wants us to maintain our joyous mindset and to do *teshuva*! Joy mitigates severe judgments.

Confession: According to the principles set forth by Rebbenu Yona in "The Gates of Repentance," the first stage of *teshuva* is a verbal confession to Hashem, followed by regretting the misdeed, asking forgiveness, and resolving to do one's utmost to avoid repeating that transgression. One who readily confesses defuses the prosecution's accusations.

Hashem's Fairness: Hashem is absolute justice and fairness, never demanding more than a person is capable of doing. In other words, He never tests a person with a situation that he cannot bear.

So, if we're tested with any type of test situation in the future, by recognizing Hashem's fairness, we do have the power to prevail.

Learning: One must set aside a specific time each day to learn what he can about the issue in which he has failed. He must study the pertinent laws that govern behavior in that given situation, such as the laws of Shabbat if he violated the Sabbath or the laws of *Lashon Hara* if he slandered someone or listened to gossip and slander, for example. He must also take advantage of other resources on the subject such as CDs and video lessons wherever available. He must review what he has learned again and again, until he is proficient in all the relevant advice and statutes. One should preferably take notes on all that he studies as well. By learning, a person knows what to do, sins less, and avoids stern judgments.

Self-Composure: If a person's self-composure is strong and decisive, then the truth will be clear to him at all times. The more he is able to internalize this clarified truth, the less he sins, thereby circumventing harsh judgments.

Prayer: Through prayer all is possible! A person should devote daily time to praying for one specific thing, believing that his many prayers will enable him to rectify all matters and overcome all faults. He should not erroneously expect immediate results, while avoiding the feeling that he "deserves" what he is praying for. With prayer, harsh judgments can be mitigated, or even rescinded altogether.

Humility: Hashem owes us nothing. With that in mind, one should pray with humility, merely asking for Hashem's mercy and unmerited gifts. As such, he'll be patient until his prayers are answered, not worrying that because time has elapsed, his prayers won't be heard. On the contrary, when a person acts and prays with humility and recognizes that he does not deserve anything, he will be capable to pray in a steadfast manner even over a very lengthy period of time, sustaining his belief that no matter how long it takes, he will be able to attain anything through his prayers.

Gratitude: A person should seek out, recognize and express gratitude for every tiny blessing every single day. This enhances one's awareness, reinforces faith, and prevents taking things for granted. Gratitude mitigates harsh judgments and is a true manifestation of one's belief in Divine Providence, for gratitude reflects a person's belief that everything is an unmerited gift. If a person does not thank Hashem, it is a sign that he does not understand or feel this way. One who aspires to connect with G-d must begin by expressing gratitude before anything else.

We Want Teshuva!

Those who seek spiritual gain should strive for *teshuva* and proficiency in the above-mentioned eight parameters. Sometimes, when a person begins to learn what ideal character traits really are, he may well become discouraged by his present faults and shortcomings. Intellectually, he understands "*teshuva*" to mean that he must blame himself for his wrongdoings and shortcomings. He confuses *teshuva* with self-persecution, despairing that he'll never attain complete rectification.

These thoughts of despair and hopelessness all stem from one's evil inclination. By learning the aforementioned eight parameters, one realizes that every character flaw is the result of precise Divine Providence. One understands that his task in this material is to rectify those particular flaws and that the varying obstacles in the way of his spiritual advancement are for his own good, enabling him through prayer to build himself spiritually and ultimately merit complete rectification.

Suppose a person suffers from a bad temper and aspires to overcome his tendency to anger. Here's how he should apply the eight parameters:

Joy: Every time he judges his own actions, every time he gets angry, he must ask himself: what does Hashem want from me now? That I despair? That I persecute myself because of this? That I should despair so that I will never be able to correct my bad traits? Or maybe Hashem wants me to maintain my happiness, my faith, my hope! If I remain happy, I'll be able to find the strength to both do good deeds and to continue to work at improving myself. Surely Hashem wants me to remain happy and continue making spiritual. With such self-encouragement, one can continue to the next stage…

Confession: One must make a verbal and detailed confession every time he fails to overcome his anger. He should sincerely regret his setbacks and ask to be forgiven. Following this request for pardon, he should move on to the next step and resolve to avoid future transgressions to the best of his ability. Despite his best efforts, he can't expect to be perfect in the future, so he can be consoled by the next parameter…

Hashem's Fairness: Remembering that Hashem is fair and will not test a person with a challenge that he cannot withstand will give him the encouragement that he **can** succeed, despite the peripheral pressure and stress. One also has the capacity to overcome his anger through learning and through prayer.

Learning: This person should learn all about the bad trait of anger on a regular basis, not only learning in detail about the damages of anger but about the benefits of overcoming anger as well.

Self-composure: Now that he has learned about anger he must compose his thoughts, evaluating himself as to whether certain stress situations really warranted his anger. For example, he must ask himself if anger is justified for the sake of educating his children. With honest introspection, he'll come to the conclusion that it's not.

Prayer: He must devote time daily praying to rid himself of his anger, clinging to the full belief that through prayer, he can fix anything! By praying for something repeatedly, one achieves true wisdom. Soon he'll see that he is no longer incensed by the same type of situations that previously ignited his anger. Since anger is mainly the result of a deficiency in *emuna*, he must pray to Hashem and seek true faith.

Gratitude: This person must thank Hashem daily for the privilege of praying to rid himself of his anger. He should thank Hashem for every situation that arose in which he succeeded in overcoming or at least in curbing his tendency to get angry. By thanking Hashem for every bit of progress, he'll be encouraged to make further gain in ridding himself of his anger. Hashem will certainly help him in virtue of his sincerely expressed gratitude.

An Escape Route

As taught in the Zohar and other holy sources, one who practices daily personal prayer will not only circumvent judgment by the Heavenly Courts but will be rewarded for his *teshuva* as well. Since Hashem forbids double jeopardy, by one's scrutinizing and judging himself, he won't have to face additional judgment. On the other hand, the person who fails to judge himself should not be surprised to find that his life is heavy with tribulation and hardship, having incurred the severe judgments of the Heavenly Court.

Why people fail to take advantage of the wondrous and merciful opportunity Hashem offers us to do *teshuva* and to be exonerated of judgment is the result of gross spiritual unawareness. Why go through life with the burden of judgment weighing heavily upon us, in this world and the next? Let's see what it means to circumvent Heavenly judgment:

The True Courthouse

Imagine that one day, all of the prisoners in the state penitentiary – from the pettiest criminals to the worst felons - receive the following letter.

With G-d's Help

To all Prisoners!

Subject: The New Law Offering Every Prisoner to Judge Himself

Dear Prisoners!

According to the new law passed in the State Legislature, I am happy to inform you that from this day forward you will have the option to choose from two alternatives of how you will be judged for the crimes you have committed against the laws of the State:

The first alternative is to stand before the Supreme Judge. The prisoner must confess all of his wrongdoings before Him; he must express remorse and ask for forgiveness, as well as resolve to do his utmost not to repeat such a crime in the future. The new law establishes that any criminal who indeed chooses this option will be found not-guilty and will be immediately released from prison. All charges against him will be dropped and forgotten forever. In addition to being exonerated and released from prison, the criminal choosing this option will also receive a package of benefits upon his release. He will receive help in his livelihood and assistance in any and all aspects of his life. As well, he will be awarded with free entrance to all government agencies for any assistance he might require, as well as special pension benefits and a substantial retirement monthly income.

The second alternative is the regular court process and trial for each wrongdoing. The prisoner choosing this alternative will suffer the severity of the law and subject to the most severe penalties, including monetary fines and incarceration, as set forth by State Law.

The choice is in yours, Minister of Justice

Who in the world who would choose the second over the first option? Who would prefer to be judged and punished by a typical court of law to the leniency of judging himself? Who would want to be exonerated of all punishment and receive a treasure of benefits, in this world and in the next?

The analogy here is obvious. In this world we are all prisoners, waiting at each moment to be judged. We have the option to judge ourselves and be exonerated, for every person is being judged by the minute in 24 Heavenly Courts. What's more, when he dies, he must face the Supreme Court Above. The Holy One Blessed be He is all-merciful to those who do *teshuva*. But to those who do not, He judges without leniency. He tries them for every crime and wrongdoing they committed during their time on this earth.

Every trial and tribulation a person suffers in this world is a consequence of the judgments handed down every minute of the day and night. Yet, all of these judgments can be avoided if one judges himself!

Let's ask ourselves: are we not acting as prisoners who receive such a letter, being told that we can judge ourselves and therefore be exonerated of all our crimes and the ensuing punishments? Are we so inane as to go through the regular Heavenly court system and suffer endless trials and tribulations?

Teshuva always

Teshuva is always effective, no matter how serious the transgression.

With daily *hitbodedut* and concerted effort to judge oneself, a person will be cleansed of all sin and freed from all the suffering and tribulations that have tormented him until now.

With daily *teshuva* and self-evaluation, a person will stand in front of Hashem on Rosh Hashanah clean of all sin. He'll pass his Day of Judgment with a smile on his face, for he hasn't waited for the last minute to do *teshuva*. Otherwise, he would have to recollect and confess each and every flawed thought, word and deed of the last 365 days! How can he possibly remember what every tiny misdeed from three, six, or nine months ago? Impossible!

By consistently practicing daily *hitbodedut*, a person can rectify everything in this lifetime. He'll leave this world as sinless as a newborn infant. He won't have to be judged nor will he have to be reincarnated. He'll receive magnificent rewards for his daily hour of *hitbodedut*.

There was a Breslever *chassid* who was dying. The *chevra kadisha* (burial society representatives) came to him as they customarily do during one's final moments on earth, to assist him to make a final confession of his sins before he dies. The dying chassid opened his eyes and asked, "Tell me, how is it possible for me to confess all the sins of my days in my last weak moments? Every day I did an hour of *hitbodedut*. Today too I did *hitbodedut*; I did *teshuva* for the wrongdoings of my last day on this earthly world... I have confessed all that I need to confess..." He then said "Shema Yisrael", closed his eyes and died.

How can a person achieve such amazing self-composure on his death bed? There's one way only - by practicing *hitbodedut* every day of his life. If we contemplate this matter, we'll see that one can't possibly recollect, confess and repent for all of the thoughts, words and deeds of a lifetime.

Hashem's Mercy

Don't confuse self-judgment with self-punishment! The essence of one's self-evaluation is simply to ask himself if he has acted correctly; if not, he merely needs to acknowledge his misdeeds and confess them. He must then ask Hashem to forgive him as well as to help him rectify his flaws. That's all! He is then cleansed of his sin and rewarded for having done *teshuva*.

The Gemara teaches that in merit of one person's *teshuva*, the entire world is pardoned! We can't fathom the magnitude of Hashem's mercy. We can now appreciate the Zohar's saying, namely, that just as Hashem's magnitude is beyond our grasp, so too is Hashem's mercy!

Our Weaponry

Life is overflowing with trials and tribulations, especially during the adolescent years when physical desires are overpowering. Adolescents don't yet know how to cope with these physical desires, nor do they possess the tools needed to overcome their mighty evil inclination. If they would "meet" with Hashem on a regular daily basis, opening their hearts out to Him and telling Him everything that's happening in their lives, they'd outsmart their growing evil inclination. Without *hitbodedut*, the tests they face are virtually insurmountable.

Adolescents who were raised in a Torah environment are especially embarrassed seek advice from people they know, fearing that their mounting evil inclination attests to the fact that are bad, unwholesome, and beyond rectification. They've been conditioned to believe that a person with shortcomings is terrible. Yet, no one gave them the tools to strengthen themselves. They try to conceal what they feel and do. In attempting to deal with their problems on their own - without talking to Hashem and without asking for His help, they fall even lower, lacking the spiritual stamina to fight against their evil inclination.

Without *hitbodedut*, we have trouble enduring the trials and tribulations of this world! This world is a difficult battleground for anyone who does not practice an hour of *hitbodedut* each day. Rebbe Nachman of Breslev teaches that the most powerful weapon a person has is prayer. How can a person fight a battle without a dependable and powerful weapon?

The Gemara teaches that we daily face the challenge of our powerful evil inclination; without Hashem's help, we can't overcome it. Hashem helps those who turn to Him and ask for His help. He has given us the freedom of choice to try to manage on our own or to ask for His help; Hashem never turns away those who seek Him.

A Good Friend

When we look at the world through spiritual eyes, the material world has nothing to offer us. Once I had a pupil who had begun to stray from Torah. I phoned him and said, "Starting from today, I want you to be my friend. Okay?"

He replied sheepishly, "Of course Rabbi."

I continued, "Listen, I want you to promise me something. If you find something better than my yeshiva, then take me there with you. If we're going to be truly good friends, then let's be so all the way. You won't leave me here in our Yeshiva if you find something better, so if you do, please tell me. In fact, I'll take all the students of the yeshiva along with us to that better place."

A person must yearn for the truth to the extent that he'll be willing to do absolutely everything for it. If he thinks that climbing walls is the true thing to do, then he should do his utmost to climb walls. We all say we want the truth, but are we must be willing to live according to the truth!

With Hashem's help, I'll prove to you that a daily hour of *hitbodedut* is the truth!

Find the Differences

Let's compare the following two images:

In the first image, we see a child who is extremely troublesome. He plays in the mud and gets into trouble all year long, but he approaches his father once a year and cries, "Dear Father, I am sorry I upset you all year long; I gave you a lot of trouble. I'm so sorry."

In the second image, we also see a troublesome child. However, this child comes to his father every single day and says, "Father, I want to please you and behave according to your will, but the evil inclination keeps overcoming me. I am sorry Father, I am so very sorry." He speaks to his father in this manner every single day, even telling his father every unacceptable deed that he has done.

Are the above two images identical? Is the child who approaches his father each single day identical to the child who comes once a year? Of course not! They are as different as day and night! One apologizes daily for every small misdeed while the other can't possibly recall what he has done a whole year long. His apology is therefore not much more than lip service, since he barely remembers what he's apologizing for.

As such, the circumstance of a person who practices daily *hitbodedut* is completely different than that of a person who only asks forgiveness once a year on Rosh Hashana or Yom Kippur. The latter, after all, cannot truly remember even what he did wrong!

Think back to our allegory of the prisoners who received a letter from the Department of Justice. In that letter, the prisoner was given the option to do *teshuva* and subsequently not only be released from prison but to be rewarded for his *teshuva*. We are all prisoners! Family strife is a prison. So are difficult children, financial stress, and bad character traits. All the trials and tribulations of this world are in actuality a prison that incarcerates us. Let's get out of prison! Now! And at the very same time, we'll be rewarded for doing *teshuva*!

People tend to imagine that doing *teshuva* is very difficult; that's not so. One does not have to be an astronaut on the moon to find truth or to do *teshuva*. "It is in your mouth and in your heart, so that you can fulfill it" (Deuteronomy 30:14). All a person has to do is to speak to Hashem; Hashem is waiting to hear your voice! Just call His name…

A Beautiful World

A fundamental principle of this world is there is no tribulation without prior transgression (Gemara, tractate Shabbat 55:2). There is no such thing as a person suffering for no reason. If a person has nothing to rectify, he won't suffer. He should therefore correct what needs to be corrected and smile, in this world and the next.

Without the above underlying principle, the world surely seems a very cruel place, with no justification for its brutality. It gives the impression of a very ugly place indeed. But, if we keep in mind the principle that there is no suffering without sin, we understand that everything in this world is justice from Above. From a spiritual standpoint, there's really nothing but good.

One tends to perceive suffering as bad. Suffering stimulates *teshuva*; *teshuva* mitigates harsh judgments and exonerates from sin. Until one does do *teshuva*, the suffering he encounters serves as penance for his transgressions. This is also good. So, we see that there really is no bad in the world, only justice. A person must believe that Hashem is "my rock in Whom there is no injustice" (Psalm 92); that He is righteous, honest, and rules this world with true justice. So if a person suffers, he must know that he has to do *teshuva*. And as we have said, *teshuva* is not a difficult task; it simply entails speaking to Hashem.

Belief in the Truth

People often ask me, "How do I know what I have to do *teshuva* for?" My answer is that initially a person must believe with a full heart that his suffering is a consequence of his transgressions. He must fully acknowledge that any tribulation and suffering he faces is a result of his sins. The very first step of his *teshuva* must be to recognize with no hesitations that if he suffers, this is a sign that he has to rectify a flaw or misdeed. His suffering reflects Hashem's Will that he act somewhat differently.

With the awareness that tribulations are the outcome of transgressions, one will be motivated to stand for hours on end, begging Hashem to reveal to him the misdeed that is the root of his suffering. He will be able to stand endlessly before Hashem and plead, "Master of the Universe! Have pity upon me! Please let me know and understand what it is that I must rectify. Please have mercy upon me! I beg of You to show me what it is that I need to correct; what I must do to please You and live according to Your Will. Why have You inflicted me with these tribulations? Please show me the right way; I want to do *teshuva*." Such an individual will surely merit recognizing his flaw and learning what Hashem wants of him. He will enjoy salvation!

Shabbat: The root treatment

The following is my personal story: It was Shabbat. One of my teeth caused a horrible swelling. The pain was horrific. I obviously needed a "root canal" treatment. Yet, I didn't ask myself where I could find an emergency dentist on Shabbat. I asked myself why the painful swelling appeared in the first place. I must have sinned. I knew in my heart that if I did *teshuva*, the swelling would disappear.

So I spoke to Hashem for nearly two hours. "Master of the Universe! Please show me what sin I have committed to bring about such pain, such inflammation. Perhaps I spoke slanderously? Perhaps I spoke undesirable words? I want to do *teshuva*! Please remind me what it is that I did to bring about such pain. Perhaps I ate something that was forbidden?" And I searched harder and harder in order to reveal my sin. When I did discover the transgression that I sinned I repented, and the swelling went down almost immediately. Within minutes, the pain was gone! I have seen such miracles frequently, in all realms of life. I did *teshuva*, and immediately saw miracles!

The only reason we receive tribulations is that Hashem wants us to do *teshuva*. Once we do, Hashem releases us from the imprisonment of our suffering and rewards us as well with *emuna* and joy. We receive true faith in the Holy One Blessed be He, that Hashem is above the laws of nature. We enjoy belief in the power of *teshuva*, in the power of our own prayers. We are awarded great joy and a reason for living that enhances our spirituality. Financial worries dissipate and our home becomes a place of harmony. Who could want more?

Why would a person choose to remain in prison, because it's hard for him to speak to Hashem? It's not difficult! We can ask Hashem to help us find the right words. We can ask Hashem for everything, even the words to phrase our requests. Everything is easy when we cling to Hashem and understand that everything comes from Him.

Unfathomable mercy

Teshuva is the vessel that makes our lives beautiful. We really cannot fathom the infinite magnitude of the Holy One's mercy. Hashem is not at all like human judges. When a person confesses to his sins and expresses remorse, Hashem's pardon is complete. In merit of our *teshuva*, Hashem even forgives the entire world!

As we said earlier, Rebbe Nachman of Breslev asked his disciples: "Why do you let Hashem make judgments against you?" The disciples looked at one another in total bewilderment. Can one individual prevent the rendering of Divine judgments? Rebbe Nachman says an emphatic yes; even the most insignificant person has the ability to prevent the rendering of stern judgments during the time that he speaks to Hashem. The Zohar teaches that when a person turns to Hashem, He tells all the celestial beings not to disturb Him during His conversation with His cherished son or daughter. We cannot begin to grasp the infinity of Hashem's mercy!

Unmerited Gifts

One who opts against daily self-evaluation is not only willingly forfeiting exoneration from judgment, he is actually bringing upon himself suffering that exceeds the tribulation he deserves! How so? When a person fails to judge himself on a daily basis, he in effect declares unaccountability for his actions. If he is unaccountable, then the Heavenly courts judge him with no leniency, ignoring what might be mitigating circumstances. The result is a severe verdict that leads to painful afflictions. Yet if a person does make a daily account of his deeds and proves his accountability for his behavior, then the Heavenly courts act in moderation and in mercy, giving him the necessary minimal tribulations to stimulate his *teshuva* process. And, if he confesses to Hashem before his misdeed comes to the attention of the Heavenly courts, he won't be tried by the Heavenly courts at all!

Rabbi Yoseph Chaim of Baghdad the "Ben Ish Chai" tells a wonderful parable: There were two men, Reuven and Shimon. Reuven slapped Shimon once on his cheek. Then Shimon hit Reuven back – three times.

Reuven asked, "Why three slaps? After all, I only hit you once."

Shimon answered, "I have made no error. I gave you one slap for the slap you gave me. The second slap was a fine for as it says in the Torah a thief must pay double retribution. And the third one came as an unmerited gift from me to you."

Reuven complimented Shimon and said, "You judged well; you spoke well." And then approached Shimon and slapped him thirty times on his cheek!

Shimon accepted the blows silently, thinking to himself that once Reuven finished, he would give him back twice over! He would slap Reuven thirty times in return for the thirty blows he slapped him, and another thirty as a fine, and then he would even slap him one more time – as a "gift". But when Reuven finished and Shimon wanted to strike him back, Reuven turned and walked away. Shimon shouted out to him, "Hey! Where are you going? Stand still and let us make an account of what I now owe you."

Reuven replied that there was no account to settle, because the thirty blows he just dealt Shimon were given as "unmerited gifts", as Shimon himself had given him. It was Shimon who had declared that one could deliver a slap as an 'unmerited gift' that was beyond the account that could be done.

Shimon continued his argument, "But I gave you only one slap as an 'unmerited gift'. How can you give me thirty?"

Reuven responded that since they were delivered as unmerited gifts and not through a precise account then it did not matter if it was one blow or a hundred; they were after all unmerited gifts...

The parable is obvious: when a man keeps an exact account of his misdeeds, then the tribulations sent to him are indeed limited and a precise reckoning according to the account that has been made. The 'blows' are measured, and are limited only to what is absolutely necessary to awaken him to *teshuva*. Yet if a person does not make an account of his actions and ignores his shortcomings and sins, it appears that he shirks responsibility for his actions and does not differentiate between sinning a single time or committing hundreds of transgressions. The suffering he is then administered is also without account, as a turn for a turn.

Making the Time

A person must therefore make the time for daily self-evaluation and personal prayer. Without an hour of hitbodedut a day, we lack the necessary self-composure to make adequate reckoning of our deeds.

One shouldn't postpone *teshuva* and soul-searching until the month of Elul. There's no way a person can remember what he did for a whole year. Worse still, how can he live with an average person's tremendous burden of sins until Elul? How can he bear the suffering he will suffer as a result of his sins? Is it not sweeter to be exonerated from judgment by making a self-accounting of one's deeds and doing daily *teshuva*? If a person does this daily self-reckoning, he will arrive at those holy days of Elul without the weighty burden of all his previous sins. He will therefore be able to use those special days for a deeper level of *teshuva*, and to merit a true spiritual ascent.

The Good Life

For the health of our souls, *teshuva* must be an integral and inseparable part of our daily existence. *Teshuva* in fact guarantees a beautiful life, a good life, in this world and in the next.

Hashem created a beautiful world over which He governs with absolute fairness. Nothing a person experiences is the result of a mistake or random chance. No one suffers tribulations and agony for no reason or purpose. It is anathema to think that Hashem created humans just so they'd suffer haphazard pain and injury.

Since we are humans with a tendency to err, Hashem offers us the option to do *teshuva*. Anyone that speaks to Hashem on a daily basis, confessing his transgressions and asking for forgiveness, will definitely not suffer; indeed, he'll live a good life.

One who believes that his suffering is not a consequence of his sins is denying the concept of Divine providence. He is no different than the heretics who claim that Hashem left the sovereignty over this world to nature and fate.

This world is overflowing with pain and suffering. There seems to be no end to hardships – financial problems, marital strife, difficulties in raising our children – the list is long. This suffering would not exist if we would all practice an hour of daily *hitbodedut*.

As mentioned previously, the Gemara teaches that an underlying principle in creation is that there is no suffering without sin. All tribulations are for a reason, as the spiritually-aware realize. Such people know that it is possible to attain a good life by walking innocently in the path of Hashem's will. He therefore will not suffer anguish.

Daily self-evaluation provides the basis for a good life. Despite our best efforts, we all transgress from time to time. These transgressions are liable to invoke stern judgments and consequent suffering if gone unchecked. By daily self-reckoning - our hour of daily *hitbodedut* – we can identify our wrongdoings, confess and judge ourselves, resolve to do better, and all-in-all stimulate character improvement. As such, we are constantly maintaining blemish-free souls, tribulation-free lives, and making phenomenal personal and spiritual growth as well. We not only attain the real *dolce vita* – the sweet life – we perfect ourselves and make the most out of our personal potential. Who could wish for more?

Don't be fooled into thinking that Hashem requires perfection. A person should do *teshuva* the best he can; Hashem will forgive him even though he may still be far from true and complete *teshuva*.

One who knows that nothing in this world is left to chance or nature enjoys a great measure of inner calm and composure. Knowing that Divine Providence governs the universe, a person can live a secure and joyous life, without worry or bitterness. He knows that so long as he endeavors to follow a righteous path, there is no reason for him to encounter suffering. Even if he errs or fails, Hashem will hint to him through some tribulation what to correct and how to correct it. Such a person lives without fear or worry, without sadness or despair. His life is a reality that excludes all bad.

Knowing that all is good and just, a product of truth, fairness and morality, one lives a pleasurable existence, enjoying clarity of thought and self-composure. This level of existence also produces a heightened clarity of consciousness, which resembles a spirit of prophecy.

Most of the tribulation we suffer is because we do not understand Hashem's rule of this world. Subsequently we question His ways so often, feeling we are being punished unfairly. We tend to place our belief in the laws of nature. Full of worry and fear, we unceasingly both blame ourselves and harbor endless complaints against others. We readily conclude that we are being unjustly persecuted and thereby sink into an abyss of depression and despair.

With no conception about how Hashem runs this world, a person fails to search for the Divine wisdom that underlies every occurrence. Such a person is hopelessly distant from the knowledge that all is good. He is prone to fear and worry, full of bitterness and harboring endless complaints. He suffers, believing that he is being unfairly persecuted.

On the other hand, one who trusts in Divine Providence is confidant, calm, and composed. He understands that life's difficulties are for his own good and designed to help him rectify in his life and thereby get closer to Hashem.

Knowing that Hashem rules this world justly and honestly gives us peace of mind. Such awareness in itself brings us closer to Hashem and affords us limitless spiritual gratification.

Accepting Responsibility

Knowing that there are no tribulations without prior transgression is both comforting and encouraging. But, it requires intellectual maturity and the acceptance of full responsibility for our lives, knowing that we ourselves are to blame for our troubles. We can no longer blame our spouses, our children, our inlaws, or our business competitors for our troubles, nor can we point a finger at fate or at nature.

Grievances, anger, sadness, bitterness and despair all become non-sequiturs once a person recognizes the Divine Providence in his or her life. There is no reason to think we are suffering unfairly. And even though our suffering is a consequence of our sins we need not even blame ourselves, but rather realize that Hashem is helping us make spiritual and personal growth. As such, we constantly feel G-d's loving intervention in our lives and enjoy a sense of happiness. This is a level that even the simplest person can attain by way of a daily hour of personal prayer and talking to Hashem.

Anyone who chooses to accept full responsibility for his actions will certainly mitigate all stern judgments against him. The greater and clearer one's trust is that there is no suffering in this world without sin, the more motivated he'll be in asking Hashem to reveal the core misdeed or shortcoming that is the cause of his current suffering. Hashem will undoubtedly take pity upon such a person and show him what he must rectify, sending him endless hints and thoughts from Above that will help him on his way. One who accepts responsibility will therefore pay close attention and contemplate everything that happens to him and subsequently understand the way Hashem is communicating with him. Once again, such a level of spiritual awareness is tantamount to a spirit of prophecy. What more could a person hope to attain in this world?

Seeing our flaws

Despite the realization that our suffering is designed to stimulate *teshuva*, we might still doubt that we are capable of true *teshuva*. After all, who knows how many sins we carry from previous incarnations? And even without taking all those sins into account, how many sins have we already transgressed in this lifetime? And even without taking all our past sins into account, how often do we unwittingly sin in the present? Every day we add more sins! So how can we do *teshuva*? Are we doomed to suffer?

Such a mindset makes the knowledge that there are no tribulations without prior transgression a source of despair rather than encouragement...

Let's put things in proper perspective: Hashem knows that a person cannot know what sins he transgressed in previous incarnations; He therefore does not make a person suffer in order to awaken him to do *teshuva* for them. Furthermore, Hashem does not make us suffer to stimulate *teshuva* for sins of this lifetime that are so long in the past we do not recall them. What remains are the sins of the present. Even in the regard to present sins, Hashem knows what we are capable of doing, each person on his current respective spiritual level. As such, Hashem only hints to us to do *teshuva* for those flaws that we are capable of rectifying at present.

We are only expected to rectify the present. Hashem allows us to make a new beginning and wipe the past's slate clean, as long as we do *teshuva* for the day that has just transpired. This surely is not so difficult. Such a process enables us to see our flaws without being overwhelmed with mountains of past debts. Once Hashem sees that we are doing what we can to improve, He will no longer make us suffer. Living with the principle that "there is no suffering without sin" ultimately leads us to live a good life!

According to the Zohar (see *Parshat Balak*), one who labors to do *teshuva* for all those sins he is conscious of will merit correcting the misdeeds that he wasn't aware of as well.

Regarding the laws of checking for *chametz*, unleavened bread derivatives that are forbidden on Passover, one need not search for crumbs in crevices of the home that are above the rafters or beneath the floorboards. A thorough cleaning and examination of all those places in his home that are in eye-view and arm's reach are all that religious law requires.

Religious law regards *teshuva* in the same way. One need not confess each and every wrongdoing he has done since the day of his birth, including all his misdemeanors as a small child. He is also not expected to confess to sins he was not aware of transgressing, nor the sins he has forgotten; the former are likened to the crevices in a person's home that are above the rafters or beneath the floorboards. We need only confess to those sins that are apparent to us. When we confess to the transgressions we are aware of having committed, the remainder of our sins will be forgiven as well.

We can now conclude that the doctrine of no tribulations without prior transgression is taught for the sole purpose of bringing us peace of mind and spirit; happiness, security and tranquility.

Incomparable Mercy

The hints Hashem gives us so that we can identify what we must rectify reflect His incomparable mercy. Would a person prefer to fool himself his entire life? On the contrary, one should take the greatest pleasure in identifying his flaws, enabling him to strive for perfection and ascend in spirituality. During daily self-evaluation, one should not be preoccupied with thoughts of suffering. He should bear in mind one thing: where is the truth? Where am I mistaken? He who desires to rectify will ultimately succeed, for the Gemara testifies that, "a man is taken on the path he desires" (tractate Makot, 10b).

On the other hand, a person who examines his actions only for the purpose of freeing himself from current tribulations will have difficulty in finding where he must correct himself. Such a person is not truly interested in finding the truth, and he does not care if he continues to live a lie just so long as he is rid of his suffering.

For this, he is willing to do "*teshuva*". But, since he's not sincerely seeking the truth, he'll have difficulty uprooting the root of his misdeeds and is likely to continue sinning in the future. This explains why there are those who practice daily *hitbodedut* and yet continue to suffer, while the harsh judgments against them seem only to increase, G-d forbid.

One who asks Hashem to cease the torment without his making true *teshuva* is in essence asking Hashem to capitulate - this is a great flaw. For example, would a father who lets his son eat chocolate all day long be categorized as merciful? Not at all! He'd be cruel for allowing his son to harm himself. In like manner, one who wants Hashem to be lenient and allow him to live his life in falsehood is asking Hashem to freely enable him to blemish his soul. Such leniency would be the epitome of cruelty when a person discovers the excruciating soul corrections he'll have to undergo in the next world. Even in this world, discovering at age eighty that one lived a lie for all his life is purgatory in itself.

Any intelligent being will surely not wait complacently for suffering to torment him, but rather will precede its undesirable arrival with daily self-examination and *teshuva*. Otherwise he will be contradicting himself. On the one hand, he seeks the truth and yearns to rectify himself in this lifetime. He does not want to arrive at the world-to-come and discover he lived his life in falsehood. Also, he knows there is no suffering in this world without prior sin and believes as well that Hashem does not concede to sin and transgression. Yet on the other hand, he is waiting for tribulation to awaken him to do *teshuva* … why?

Why do people wait to suffer trials and tribulations in order to be awakened to *teshuva*? With our parable of the prisoner and the Justice Department's offer of self-judgment, we have illustrated this principle at length. Hashem gives us the key to live a good life through our own sincere daily self-evaluation.

A person must be truthful with himself. Can he live an entire lifetime free of sin and spiritual setbacks? Of course not! So long as a person has not attained the true humility of Moses and cling to Hashem with every single breath, there will be times that he falls. Pride, in fact, is the root and essence of our evil inclination. As long as a person possesses even one iota of arrogance, he will inevitably sin. Hashem knows this. He knows the spiritual standing of every person, and therefore does not expect any of us never to sin. He does, however, expect us to do *teshuva*.

When a person judges himself each day - even if he doesn't evaluate every single act and thought - all judgment against him will be mitigated. Again, we may conclude that there is truly a path by which a person can live a good and beautiful life according to the principle "there is no suffering without prior sin". When a person does *teshuva* everyday he won't have to suffer at all.

Proper Judgment

Let's take a closer look at how one should properly judge himself. Many erroneously conclude that self-judgment means self-punishment. In a regular court of law, a person is punished when found guilty. This is not the intention of self-judgment, for the essence of self-judgment is to attain a clarification of the truth. Without such self-evaluation and truth-seeking, a person will continue to err, unable to recognize the truth. How? One must seek the truth of the Torah's commandments and then act accordingly, otherwise he'll remain a slave to the evil inclination and its accompanying bodily appetites and drives. For example, if one thinks that anger is acceptable behavior according to Torah, he'll continue to yell at his children when in truth he is violating the Torah commandment that prohibits causing grief or insult to another human being, including one's spouse and children (see Leviticus 25:17 and relevant commentaries). He'll probably convince himself that he is acting properly when in fact he is sinning. If he does not seek out to clarify where the truth lies, he will be misled to accept all kinds of falsehoods. For this reason, judgment is called the "attribute of truth".

Hashem wants us to seek truth, acknowledge the truth, and recognize where we have erred. This is best accomplished by personal prayer and self-evaluation, together with extensive Torah learning in order to familiarize ourselves with what the Torah cites as proper conduct in all phases of life. Willful ignorance of Torah is no excuse for the transgression of Torah.

Rebbe Nachman teaches (*Likutei Moharan*, I:169) that one's judgment of oneself mitigates judgments. Hashem gives us the wonderful opportunity of evaluating ourselves as to whether our deeds have been worthy and correct.

Once a person has acknowledges, comprehends and truly feels that he has made a mistake, he'll be sincerely remorseful. He'll reach the understanding that no matter what trial he was facing, his deed was not the proper thing to do according to the truth of Torah, and so he must confess and ask forgiveness for acting against the Will of G-d. The main issue is to understand that his behavior was wrong, so that he will take it upon himself to rectify his ways. The deeper his recognition of his error, the greater his repentance will be, and too, the stronger his determination to avoid making similar mistakes in the future.

A person's greatest strength is in his intellect. Once he clarifies truth in his mind beyond a shadow of doubt, he'll have the strength of firm conviction to act accordingly and overcome his evil inclination.

The true purpose

The true purpose of our lives is to know Hashem. Without clarifying the truth, this is impossible. If a person lives a lie, he is distanced from Hashem. We therefore don't want to live a lie. One who denies the truth is only cheating himself.

The aspiration to admit and return to the truth is the core of self-evaluation. Hashem doesn't want us to lead lives of lies and delusions. Punishment and tribulations aren't the main issue. The question that every person must ask in the mirror is, "Do I want to live a lie?" Hashem - Who is Truth - will not accept our living a lie. Our beloved Father in Heaven is not a parent with misguided pity who refrains from disciplining a misbehaving child by withholding tribulations. Despite His infinite love and mercy for us, Hashem won't yield the truth despite the consequent tribulations we must suffer. Hashem grieves when His children suffer, but He's willing to do so in order that we learn the truth. This is true mercy.

People today are burdened from head to toe with tribulations – debts, family strife, difficulties with children, emotional anguish, and overall insecurity. Why? Hashem tells us, "First of all, breathe deep. Calm down. Take time out to have a good look at yourself and your life. Seek understanding of who you are, where you are, and what you're doing on this earth. Don't look for quick answers and instant solutions. Don't expect overnight rectification of all your shortcomings. Put aside your tribulations and torment for an hour; just forget about them and designate a 60-minute time slot to clarify truth. In this manner, one should begin to practice daily *hitbodedut*. Remember:

Forget your tribulations for this one hour;

Don't expect to correct everything in one day;

Seek the truth with all your heart;

Yearn to grow closer to Hashem with all your strength;

Talk to G-d an hour a day.

If you practice the above, you will witness Hashem's mercy and enjoy daily salvations!

Rational expectations

There are those who feel that Hashem expects too much of them. Yet, an intrinsic aspect of free choice is that Hashem never demands more than one is capable of doing, otherwise that person would be doomed to failure. Hashem knows better than anyone that a person cannot attain his best potential in one day.

Then, what does Hashem want from us?

Hashem only wants us to acknowledge the truth. King Solomon teaches, "He who acknowledges [a misdeed] and abandons [the wrongdoing] will enjoy mercy" (Proverbs 28:13). In other words, one who confesses and subsequently avoids sinful behavior invokes Hashem's mercy. Even if a person does not abandon all of his wrongdoings immediately, but merely *begins* to recognize the truth while trying his best to avoid sin, he too will enjoy Hashem's mercy. Hashem knows that such *teshuva* takes time.

We therefore have no need to be compulsive or hasty in our soul-searching. We needn't beat our chests, roll on the ground in tears, or shout our remorse without giving serious thought and sincere deliberation to our words. As we showed earlier, remorse that is motivated exclusively by hopes of being freed of tribulation merely awakens more severe judgment. Insincere self-evaluation won't have the capability of mitigating stern judgments.

Our search for truth should be calm, conscious, and with self-composure. The tranquility and self-composure that we benefit from secluded personal prayer enable us to ponder what exactly Hashem wants of us. Seeking truth is so spiritually significant that even if it takes weeks and months to determine the truth, the search itself will allow us to sweeten all of the judgments in the meanwhile.

By aspiring for truth, one connects with truth. On the other hand, if one's *hitbodedut* lacks this yearning truth, then there won't be real communication between this person and G-d. Hashem might hint to the person that he must correct himself in a certain manner, yet the person in turn will not pay attention to Hashem's messages, especially when those messages negate that person's preconceived desires. Rather than doing what Hashem is constantly hinting him to do by heeding Hashem's subtle messages, that person will deliver lengthy orations, apparently outpouring his aching soul. Hashem won't be listening as long as that person is seeking only personal relief that's devoid of *teshuva* and truth-seeking.

Hashem wants us identify and improve our weak areas. We must recognize the truth that we need to improve. Yet, Hashem doesn't demand full instantaneous *teshuva*; all He wants is that we work on ourselves, seek His help, and improve a tiny bit every single day. 365 tiny bits of improvement add up to wonderful *teshuva* and phenomenal character improvement at the end of the year, that is, if one has been perseverant in devoting at least an hour a day to *hitbodedut* all year long.

Lies and Truth

Be careful of haste in *teshuva* and in prayer; the desire to correct something completely and immediately sometimes reflects a desire to be rid of tribulation and not a sincere commitment to correct one's fault. It may reflect the impatience to persevere in *teshuva* in an orderly and gradual manner. This is not the way things should be done. A person must make spiritual growth step by step, but with tenacity and perseverance, investing daily effort in achieving the desired goal. In this way, the yearned-for rectification will be attained – slowly, gradually, and truthfully.

Approach your daily self-evaluation session with calm and self-composure. Don't be tense – your hour together with Hashem is the hour of delight and relaxation for your soul. Calm down – outside pressures and anxiety melt away and mean nothing when you're spending time with Hashem. Ask yourself and ask Hashem, "Where is my flaw? What do You, my beloved Father in Heaven, desire from me? What direction should my *teshuva* take?" Leave the rat race back in the office. Don't hurry and don't look for immediate solutions just to be rid of the tribulations. Take it easy; some matters indeed demand years of work. When Hashem sees that you understand that character improvement and *teshuva* aren't instant coffee or instant chicken soup, then all the judgments against you will be mitigated. Hashem's purpose in the first place when He sent you the tribulations was to help you open your eyes to the truth.

Practicing such self-judgment is the sweetest hour of the day! Hashem wants our submissiveness, our surrender to the truth. We must therefore calmly and truthfully identify our faults and weak areas and do our best to rectify them. Hashem facilitates our *teshuva* and does not have impossible expectations of those who sincerely yearn to get close to Him.

Opposing Forces

The Torah in Parshat Korach relates a shocking episode. Korach, one of the most prominent Jews, along with a following of another two hundred and fifty community leaders, rose up in opposition to Moses and were consequently punished in a most severe manner.

Korach was a great scholar, blessed with the spirit of prophecy and considered to be of high moral standard. How on earth did he walk a crooked path despite all the Torah he learned? How is it possible for a person who is so learned in Torah to make such a tragic error?

If the Torah itself does not guard a person from such mistakes, what does?

Our answer lies in the following Torah portion, Parshat Chukat. Here too we find a bewildering narrative. We learn of the red heifer, whose ashes are used to purify one who has become ritually unclean by touching a dead person. This commandment is one of the most baffling statutes in the Torah: the person preparing the ashes is made unclean by the ashes of the heifer, yet those who are unclean become purified when the ashes are sprinkled on them. Apparently, the ashes of the red heifer possess two opposing powers: they can purify the unclean or contaminate the clean.

How is it possible for one element to attain both opposing results? Since we know we cannot understand Hashem's ways, we could accept this as a law of G-d that is simply beyond our grasp. But another significant question remains. For the Torah reading begins with the words, "This is the statute of the Torah," and then continues with a detailed description of the red heifer commandment. Why does this Torah portion begins with the generic phrase, "This is the statute of the Torah," and not with a seemingly more relevant opening as, "This is the statute of the Red Heifer"? After all, the chapter deals with the mitzvah of the red heifer.

The principle of one element attaining two opposite results is an intrinsic principle in all of Torah and in all of creation. It's easy to understand that with nuclear power, one can illuminate the world or destroy the world. Likewise, the ashes of the red heifer in some circumstances purify the unclean but in other circumstances contaminate the pure. As such, the Torah can be a life-giving remedy to those who so merit, but it can also be a drug of death for those who do not. Since Korach used the Torah for personal interest and gain, it became a deadly poison for him.

We still ponder two profound questions in regard to our Holy Torah: first, why didn't the light of Torah protect Korach and lead him to *teshuva*? And second, how can the Torah encompass such opposing forces, life and death?

Better or not?

We find our answer to these dilemmas in the Talmud (tractate *Eruvin*, 13b). Here we learn about a disagreement between the School of Shamai and the School of Hillel on a certain issue, a disagreement that lasted two and a half years until it was resolved and a decision was reached.

Let's pause for a moment and contemplate who headed this dispute. These were not simple people by any means, nor were they the scholarly of contemporary times. Rather, they were *Tannaim*, Mishnaic scholars who had the power to revive the dead, comprehend the languages of animals, decipher Heavenly messages and much more. Yet for two and a half years, they debated the issue in question, each taking diametrically opposed stances in a question of religious law. For two and a half years they dwelled on this subject, with deep discussion, hard proof, spiritual logic, and profound arguments supporting each opposite opinion!

What was the debate about? One school said that it would have been better for man not to have been created. The other school said that it's better that man has been created than not. They concluded that it's better that man has been created, now that he has the ability to evaluate himself.

The School of Shamai and the School of Hillel argued this truly existential question. Is man's existence in the world for the good? They ultimately concluded unanimously that in the end it would have been better if man had not been created at all! In other words, it was not worthwhile for man to have been created, but…and yes, there is a "but"…

But, now that man has been created, there is hope to transform his existence into something worthwhile, and this hope rests in his self-evaluation, examining his deeds on a regular basis. These holy Tannaim ruled that man's existence is not worthwhile without *teshuva*, without evaluating himself and correcting what needs to be corrected.

We can now understand why this discussion lasted for such a long time before a ruling was reached. For these scholars knew that their decision would establish the underlying meaning of man's existence! Man's role, his very purpose in this world, would be defined by this ruling. In other words, this ruling would reveal what Hashem wants us to accomplish in this world. Practically speaking, the only meaningful reason for our existence is daily self-examination during *hitbodedut*!

The Talmud here establishes that without daily *hitbodedut*, it would have been better that man not have been created at all. Rabbi Moshe Chaim Luzzatto writes in his classic book "The Path of the Righteous" that self-evaluation, literally translated as "accounting of the soul," means that a person will examine his thoughts, words and deeds daily; if he discovers that he has sinned, faltered, or exhibited less than upright character traits, then he must do his best to rectify.

Just as a textile merchant feels a fine cloth to determine its quality, so too we must feel our deeds, the mitzvahs that we perform, in order to determine their quality. Have we performed the commandments with real enthusiasm, with joy and sincerity, or have we done them perfunctorily merely to fulfill our obligation? We must examine each one of our deeds in this manner, examining them for flaws and/or for areas that need improvement. We must do this self-examination daily, and if not – according to the Mishnaic sages, it would have been better if we had not been created in the first place.

Rabbi Yechezkel Levinstein of saintly and blessed memory, one of the prominent rabbis of the famous Ponivitz Yeshiva, wrote in the introduction to his famous book *Or Yechezkel*: "If a person does not do daily soul-searching, it is not worthwhile for him to exist at all!"

Let's stop and think: these Torah and Talmudic giants, the holy *Tannaim*, who knew all the secrets of the Torah, following years of deliberation and discussion, reached the conclusion that man would have been better off if he had not been created in the first place, but now that man's existence is a given fact, the sole justification of his being is on earth is to practice daily self-assessment and do *teshuva* by way of daily personal prayer. This is man's purpose and the sole justification of his existence. Without daily self-assessment and *teshuva* – even if a person learns Torah - it would have been better if he did not come into existence at all.

Even the Most Righteous

Let's go back to the question of Korach, namely, why the Torah he learned did not protect him from such a transgression; also, let's now see how the ashes of the red heifer can be both a means to purify the unclean and to contaminate the pure.

The book *Lekach Tov* explains the profound difference between Aaron and Korach. Aaron performed daily self-assessment to the extent that he "felt" his deeds. Every person, even the most righteous, must "feel" his deeds and judge their quality according to his present spiritual level. The most righteous will, when "feeling" their deeds, sense how distant from perfection they still are. Indeed, in their humility, they will feel that they are on the lowest spiritual level. Breslever tradition tells of one of Rebbe Nachman's disciples who heard the Rebbe during *hitbodedut* cry to Hashem with a broken heart: "Master of the Universe! How long will I continue my life in such uselessness?"

Imagine the exalted Rebbe Nachman of Breslev, who at every moment attained phenomenal revelations and Torah nuances, felt that he was living his life in uselessness! This is because he "felt" his deeds, felt so distant from the absolute holiness of Divine Light. Since The Almighty is infinite, one's capacity for spiritual gain is also endless. When the righteous tzaddik feels the quality of his deeds, he can see that he is still far from absolute perfection; he therefore feels that he is still lowly.

The tzaddik's feeling of imperfection is also manifest in the letters Rebbe Natan of Breslev wrote to his son Rebbe Yitzchak. Rebbe Yitzchak was filled with a bitterness of the spirit, as if he saw himself as groping in the darkness of his sins. His father, Rebbe Natan, had to encourage him to look for his good points. One can reach the conclusion from this correspondence that Rebbe Yitzchak, G-d forbid, had fallen into a cesspool of countless sins and transgressions, while in truth he was a righteous tzaddik. Yet he saw in himself someone horribly distanced from Hashem.

Every human being, each according to his respective level, must examine his deeds; Aaron the High Priest was no exception. Aaron too, at his lofty spiritual level, knew he had acted in a way that was far from perfect. As such, Aaron the High Priest felt distant from Hashem. Despite his righteousness, he was humbled by what he realized during the self-assessment of his deeds. He too asked how and when he'll be able to do true *teshuva* and rectify himself. When Moses came to anoint him, Aaron was appalled. He called out to Moses: "Moses! What are you doing? You want to anoint me with the anointing oil! It is forbidden! It is strictly forbidden to anoint someone who is unworthy of the high priesthood with this oil, and I am not worthy!" Moses in turn replied that he was fulfilling Hashem's commandment to anoint Aaron, and thus reassured him.

Korach, on the other hand, lacked self-assessment and consequently thought that there was no one more righteous than he. He felt that he alone was worthy of all the positions of authority, including president and high priest. He reached that mistaken conclusion because he did not evaluate himself and his deeds on a daily basis.

Purifying the impure

Here's how the Torah can contaminate the pure: If one considers himself pure and exempt from the need to practice a daily self-evaluation, then the Torah that he learns contaminates him in that it feeds his arrogance and makes him swell from self-pride. The Torah inasmuch contaminates the pure, namely, those that perceive themselves as pure, inflating their egos even more than its current oversized proportions.

On the other hand, if a person does perform a daily self-evaluation and feels the shortcomings of his deeds, he will inevitably realize he is still impure. He develops a true sense of humility. The Torah purifies such a person, giving him more and more humility. And so we can see that the Torah truly purifies the unclean, or rather, purifies those who perceive themselves as impure.

One who fails to practice a daily hour of *hitbodedut* devoted to self-evaluation must surely feel that he is above such self-reckoning, that he is perfect and therefore worthy of the highest posts, as Korach believed he was. Such a person can learn Torah but his learning contaminates him. He accumulates more knowledge but his ego swells simultaneously. He thinks, "I was already perfect, and now that I have studied more Torah I am even more perfect." He fulfils another commandment and says to himself: "What a great tzaddik I am! Even before this mitzvah I was so righteous, and now even more so! Who can compare with me?" For him, the Torah becomes a deadly poison instead of a life-giving potion.

Our two questions are now answered: the Torah couldn't protect Korach from sin becaise Korach failed to practice daily *hitbodedut*; he did not devote an hour to self-evaluation and soul-searching, examining the quality of his deeds. His Torah learning contaminated him because it fed his arrogance and inflated his ego. Really, he had nothing to be proud of, because he didn't learn the Torah the way it should be learned. One who learns but is filled with arrogance is in fact more impure than one of a much inferior spiritual level.

The Light Within

We can now understand why people study Torah and the Talmud and yet do not do *teshuva*. Rebbe Nachman reveals (*Likutei Moharan* I:15) that one can merit seeing the concealed light of the Torah through practicing *hitbodedut* that includes self-judgment. As such, one obtains the fear of G-d, or *yirah*. Rebbe Nachman stresses that this fear must be accompanied with wisdom, for without it, one's fear is intelligence will be foolishness (see Job 4:6). Foolish fear is the notion Hashem is a like policeman, waiting to catch us making a mistake and eager for the opportunity to punish us, G-d forbid.

Hashem Himself instructs us to be joyous even after transgression. So why should we fear Him? Is it not sufficient that the King Himself is telling us to remain happy despite our misdeed? What more do we need? The King is smiling, so what are we afraid of?

Our fear of G-d must be coupled with wisdom so that we can understand that Hashem Himself is asking us to do His Will; when we fail to do so. He requests that we repent and ask for forgiveness. Hashem doesn't want us to persecute ourselves and despair – that's foolishness. He only wants us to repent – to confess to Him where we've failed and ask His help in bettering our ways.

Hashem's not a policeman but an all-merciful father. For sure, he doesn't let us get away with our sins. Yet if a person daily does *teshuva* for his sins, Hashem will forgive him. If he learns to assess himself and his deeds every day, the King promises not to judge him. What can be more merciful?

Through daily self-judgment, a person acquires the lofty fear of Hashem that's accompanied with wisdom. When a person attains this level, he will merit understanding the revealed Torah as well. Subsequently, teaches Rebbe Nachman, with added prayer and deep devotion, one can merit learning the concealed dimension of the Torah.

Without daily *teshuva*, a person cannot even comprehend the simplest and most literal meaning of the Talmud. He does not see the Torah at all; he is not seeing Hashem's message within the words but rather merely his self-pride and his own cleverness.

How is it possible to learn about the dispute between the School of Shamai and the School of Hillel without beginning to practice a daily hour of *hitbodedut*? This is only possible if the person studying the tractate does not truly understand even the literal meaning of the section. The Divine illumination of the words remains concealed from him because of his lack of daily self-judgment.

Our sages of blessed memory have taught that if a person witnesses a Torah scholar transgressing during the day, he should not think badly about him, for surely he will do *teshuva* for this sin at night.

How can our sages be certain that the Torah scholar will do same-day *teshuva* for a sin? The answer is amazingly simple: one is not a Torah scholar – by the Talmud's definition (see tractate Berachot 19a) – if he doesn't practice a daily hour of *hitbodedut* that includes self-judgment and *teshuva*. We can therefore be certain that the Torah scholar did *teshuva* at night for the sin we witnessed him transgress during that day. Many people have studied this famous teaching of our sages every single day but haven't yet taken upon themselves the practice of daily self-evaluation. Why? They apparently don't understand what they are studying.

If one fails to grasp the intrinsic wisdom and practical advice of the Talmud, then he can revert to Rebbe Nachman's explicit teaching: only a person who practices daily *hitbodedut* and therefore does daily *teshuva* merits understanding the revealed dimension of the Holy Torah.

Self-assessment is therefore the key that unlocks Torah. Daily self-judgment and *teshuva* lead to an understanding of the revealed dimension of the Torah and to the literal plane of the Talmudic wisdom. Only afterward, through extensive devoted prayer, one can also merit an understanding of the hidden dimension and lofty secrets of the Holy Torah.

Learning for the Sake of Prayer

Let's address another apparent contradiction: we learned that by learning Torah, we achieve the level of praying with true devotion. Yet in reality, when a person learns Torah, he is drawn to continuing his learning and not to prayer. He prays more out of a sense of obligation, like a burden that he'd rather free himself of. How can this be? Simple - since he hasn't yet grasped even the revealed dimension of the Torah, he is not yet motivated by the Torah to pray with devotion. This process doesn't yet start without self-judgment on a daily basis.

How can people who study the Talmud lack motivation for *teshuva* and returning to Hashem? They lack daily soul-searching and evaluation of their deeds. After all, both the School of Shamai and the School of Hillel did not say that since man has been created they should study Torah; rather, they concluded unanimously that since man has been created, he should engage in self-assessment. What could be clearer? King David writes (Psalm 50:16): "But to the wicked man, Hashem said, "For what reason do you recount My statutes, and bring up My covenant on your mouth?" Hashem asks, "Why do you learn Torah, if you do not do *teshuva* each and every day? If so, I will not give you My Torah. What do you need My book of statues for if you do not do *teshuva*?"

The Torah is not, G-d forbid, a mere book of folklore. The Zohar in the name of Rabbi Elazar the son of Rabbi Shimon bar Yochai curses one who thinks that the Torah is merely a book of tales. The stories of the Torah are told for the sake of teaching us how to live upright and productive lives.

We all talk about daily *teshuva*, but this is something most often said without true conviction. Let's realize that only a person who practices at least one hour of daily *hitbodedut* can claim that he does *teshuva* every day. Otherwise, he might speak of *teshuva*; he might even give lectures and deliver sermons on the topic of *teshuva*, but in actuality, for one to really live a life of *teshuva*, he must do at least one hour of *hitbodedut* each and every day.

Baal teshuva, Baal Emuna

Through the issue of *emuna*, we can understand just deep we are in exile. Today, we witness a most astonishing phenomenon: it's easier to teach the advice of daily *hitbodedut* to those who are far from Torah and mitzvot than to already practicing Jews. Someone who until now was distant from the Torah and now yearns to get close to Hashem easily grasps that *hitbodedut* is the best means to attaining this closeness. He understands that *hitbodedut* is the main form of prayer according to the Torah, as elucidated by Maimonides. Unfortunately, many practicing Jews erroneously conceive of *hitbodedut* as *bitul Torah,* a waste of time that should be spent learning Torah, or as strange practice of eccentrics. Such a view reflects the depths of the horrific exile to which we've descended.

All of the Jewish people prior to the codification of today's liturgy by the *Anshe Knesset HeGedolah* (the Men of the Great Assembly, some 2000 years ago) would practice *hitbodedut*. They did not have prayer-books; each person, according to his own capability and his own spiritual level, would speak to Hashem. This is a practice they inherited from our holy patriarchs.

A "practicing Jew" is not enough; one must also be a "*baal teshuva*". He must do *teshuva* each and every day. He must spend an hour each day in self-evaluation. This is like an hour of "Shabbat" during his weekdays. With Shabbat comes rest, a rest from the constraints of this earthly world and a break from life's mad race. One must daily search his soul and assess the quality of his actions; this is Talmudic advice and not Chassidism. As we've seen, the Talmud states unambiguously that if a person does not search his deeds then his existence is not worthwhile.

Torah and Teshuva

The claim that the study of Torah is a means to search one's deeds and sense the quality of one's actions is not true. This is not what the greatest personages of Torah have said. All of them, from all the varying factions of the Jewish world, instruct that every person delegate time devoted to self-reckoning. They do not teach that Torah learning comes in the place of such self-searching. On the contrary, if a person that studies Torah without daily *teshuva* is surely not studying Torah for the sake of the Torah. Nachmanides wrote his son: "And when you finish studying the book, seek out whether you have learned something from your studies that can be fulfilled; evaluate your deeds morning and night, and in such you will be doing *teshuva* all the days of your life…"

The discussion that was conducted between the School of Shamai and the School of Hillel did not differentiate between those who do and those who do not study the Torah. In fact, they did not judge whether a person's existence is or is not worthwhile by his Torah learning. Their stipulation was whether a person evaluates his own deeds. Therefore, even if a person studies Torah from morning till night, if he doesn't assess himself, his existence is not worthwhile! Better that he not have been created; his Torah study contaminates him.

We definitely must learn Torah, the more the better. Without Torah learning, we lack the tools to evaluate our deeds. If we don't learn what is permissible and what is forbidden, what is pure and what is impure, how can we judge our deeds? How will we know how to distinguish proper behavior? How will we know how to define good character traits? The Torah reveals to us the Will of G-d; through practicing *hitbodedut*, we can fulfill G-d's Will.

A Torah scholar with simple faith who talks to Hashem and engages in daily self-assessment will inevitably attain a very lofty spiritual level. His endeavors in Torah will be fruitful and his existence in this world will be truly worthwhile.

Daily *hitbodedut* is a necessity for both men and women.

Some may argue with what we said here, claiming that the Schools of Shamai and Hillel did not use the term "*hitbodedut*;" they therefore question the necessity to do such self-evaluation for one hour each day. Anyone who harbors such doubts should ask himself truthfully if he in fact fulfills the advice – as the Gemara says literally - to "rummage through and feel the quality" of his deeds without daily *hitbodedut*. One who does not practice an hour of daily *hitbodedut* yet claims that he in fact assesses his deeds is fooling himself. He will have a rude awakening at some point during his lifetime, but perhaps only when it is too late, like when his children have already strayed away from Torah, for example. Such a person is delaying the coming of Moshiach. If he's persuading other people not to practice *hitbodedut*, he is perpetuating a grave sin.

The Debate

Why are people against the practice of *hitbodedut*? Rebbe Nachman has already explained: "Why do people oppose me? Because I'm all about prayer!" The Talmud itself mentions (tractate *Berachot* 6b) the elevated and lofty attribute that people regard with contempt - prayer. Since people resist and show contempt for prayer, they will inevitably have contempt for and resistance to he whose foremost issue is prayer.

Let's think about what would bring people to oppose Breslev: does Breslev encourage or allow even the slightest deviation from one small letter of Jewish Law as brought forth in the *Shulchan Aruch* (Code of Jewish Law)? Of course not! Indeed, Rebbe Nachman is adamant that not even one day should pass without us learning from the *Shulchan Aruch*. In fact, the Chofetz Chaim of saintly and blessed memory once instructed his student who thirsted for Chassidic thought to associate with Breslever Chassidim, because "they surely abide by the *Shulchan Aruch*!"

Do Breslevers study a "different" Torah? Of course not! We study the same Torah, the same Talmud, and the same *Shulchan Aruch* as every other Jew, allowing for no deviation whatsoever. So what are the grounds for this opposition to Breslev? Simple - Breslev's foremost issue is prayer. Any person who becomes attached to Rebbe Nachman draws closer to prayer. This is surely not something the evil inclination wants to happen! Therefore, the evil inclinationt arouses controversy and opposition against Breslev, to distance people from the significance of prayer.

To the Point

We are left with the very direct and simple question: How can a person possibly live without practicing an hour of daily *hitbodedut*? This world is drowning in anguish and suffering. How can one survive without an hour of *hitbodedut* each day? How can he live without an hour that sweetens harsh judgments; an hour that allows a person to receive counsel and strength, resources and wisdom? What does he do without the hour that offers him salvation and joy, the opportunity to be forgiven his sins? Daily *hitbodedut* fortifies a person with at least 365 prayers a year, and these prayers are rewarded with endless assistance from Above, the creation of angels that accompany him and give him heavenly support. How can a person possibly relinquish such a blessing, preferring to live a life burdened with strict judgments?

Can anyone attain true rectification without endless prayer? A person who does not practice daily *hitbodedut* is treading upon millions of uncorrected sins and evil thoughts, G-d forbid. No wonder he feels a heaviness of the soul…

Imagine you are hammering a nail into a wall and the hammer hits your finger instead. Has this happened for no reason? Has the Heavenly Court made your house tremble so that the hammer would miss the nail and hurt you instead all for the pleasure of causing you pain for absolutely no reason? Of course not! Rather, you did something wrong and invoked a stern judgment from Above. If you had practiced an hour of *hitbodedut* each day, you would have already done *teshuva* for whatever you did that was wrong and you would have probably been spared the pain of a bashed finger.

If someone denies the veracity of the above example – based on the Talmudic concept already discussed at length earlier in this chapter that there are no tribulations without prior transgression – he is a heretic, denying the entire Torah. How can most of the world therefore doubt the veracity of daily *hitbodedut*? This is the sour fruit of the evil inclination's labors, to conceal the light of *teshuva* and prevent a person from getting close to Hashem. Only through an hour of daily *hitbodedut* can a person overcome this concealment; only through *hitbodedut* can attain a life of *emuna* and true tranquility of the soul.

No Shortcuts

There are no shortcuts to *teshuva*. Without devoting a daily hour to self-reckoning and *teshuva*, one will remain – unwittingly or not – stuck in his approach that whatever happens in the world is the consequence of nature and chance. His refrain from spending one hour a day in striving for *teshuva* mitigation of the stern judgments that could be pending against him reflects his lack of belief in the concept of ongoing Heavenly judgment. It shows a lack of awe of the Divine and the nonchalant attitude that one need not make a reckoning of his deeds before Hashem.

We mentioned previously that Rebbe Nachman remarked that when the Moshiach comes, every person will have to do an hour of *hitbodedut* just like they all put on tefillin for the morning prayers. *Teshuva* and this hour of self-evaluation are the core of a person's *tikkun,* of his soul correction.

Rebbe Natan has said that just as Moshe Rabbenu has given us the Torah, so Rebbe Nachman has given us the key to keeping the Torah. In particular, his instruction of daily *hitbodedut* gives us the means to true observance of the Torah. We thereby understand why *teshuva* is the foremost element of *hitbodedut*, and why *hitbodedut* is not just about us asking things from Hashem. Certainly, we must all ask Hashem for our many needs, both in the spiritual and the material realms. Yet the main part of daily *hitbodedut* must be directed to self-examination of our deeds and deportment, and *teshuva* for what the shortcomings we discover by way of that self-reckoning.

Suppose a person asks a rabbi for his blessing. That's fine, but the blessing won't rectify that person. Many people have lived in proximity to great rabbis and righteous people and have even served them. Yet, they stayed essentially the same. One must make his own personal efforts at spiritual gain.

A person once asked for my blessing in guarding his eyes. I told him, "I will bless you that you beseech Hashem with all your heart and praying many many prayers devoted to guarding your eyes." A blessing is surely wonderful but the main issue is a person's individual efforts, his own lengthy and frequent prayers.

Suppose that a person wants to succeed in guarding his eyes. He must devote at least one half an hour of prayer to this endeavor every day. If he does so, he will surely succeed in guarding his eyes. After all, he is praying to fulfill Hashem's Will, and Hashem will therefore help him. Yet, without a half an hour of daily *hitbodedut* devoted to this matter, he can't hope to succeed. He will not find the strength to stand the repeated tests; for only with Hashem's help, can he manage to truly guard his eyes. No one can do true *teshuva* without the help of Hashem.

To be without prayer means to be without G-d. If a person tries to do *teshuva* without prayer, he is in essence attempting to do *teshuva* without G-d. Hashem is prayer; prayer is Hashem. If a person tries to do something without prayer, he is in actuality doing it without G-d. This then is the essence of repentance: to pray to Hashem to help him do *teshuva*.

Chapter Eight:
Hope for Hashem!

Be prepared – a person who wants to pray will inevitably face endless obstacles. Most of these obstacles are figments of the mind. When people begin to pray yet their prayers remain unanswered, they frequently lose heart. If so, how can a person be encouraged to continue praying, despite the fact that he hasn't yet seen results?

In this chapter, we'll look for encouragement even during the times when we don't feel that our prayers are effective. Remember these two facts:

No prayer is prayed in vain.

Hashem hears all prayers.

The Midrash says (*Midrash Raba, Va'etchanan*), "The gates of prayers are never locked!" A number of reasons explain why our prayers sometimes go unanswered. This chapter addresses them and examines several concealed aspects of prayer.

The Time will Come

Each prayer is answered in its own respective time. Moshe prayed for forty days, Daniel's prayer was answered after twenty days, but Jonah's prayer was answered after three days. Some prayers – like those of Elijah the Prophet – received same-day answers. King David's prayer was answered within a matter of hours.

Hashem answers some prayers before they're even uttered: "And

it shall come to pass that, before they call, I will answer" (Isaiah, 65:24). This verse exalts Hashem and His closeness to those who cry out to Him. That notwithstanding, it's not always for the best for a prayer to be answered immediately. The Gemara (tractate *Taanit* 25) tells about a community that set a fast day in order to pray for the termination of a severe drought. Suddenly, it began to rain even before daybreak, when the community would begin the fast and their prayers. Everyone saw the rain as a marvelous sign from Heaven. Yet, the Talmudic sage Shmuel HaKatan explained that this was not praiseworthy but rather a dishonor; it resembled a slave who comes before his master to ask for a reward, but before he opens his mouth, his master says to the servants, "Give him what he wants quickly, so I won't have to hear his voice…"

We can learn this principle from the curse set upon the snake: "Dust shall be the serpent's food" (Isaiah 65:25). After all, dust is found everywhere. What curse is there in his food being so readily available and abundant? Wouldn't we all be content if our income was always available to us, without any required effort or labor? The curse in fact lies in the fact that the Hashem was so disgusted with the snake that He no longer wanted to hear its voice again. He therefore made his food so available so that the snake would never again need to pray. All other beings lift their eyes to the Heavens and ask Hashem for their sustenance: "All of them wait for You, that You may give them their food in due season" (Psalm 104: 27). The snake is the only living thing that does not need to ask for food from his Maker; this is truly a bitter curse.

Receiving something without having prayed for it is not necessarily advantageous. If one receives abundance without having prayed for it, he should indeed be concerned that perhaps Hashem is angry with him and therefore doesn't want to hear his voice. Despite the fact that a person has what he needs without prior prayer, he should immediately thank Hashem for the abundance he has received and ask for future needs as well, thus acknowledging that his abundance is Heaven-sent.

Our patriarchs, matriarchs, and the greatest tzadikim had to pray a great deal until their prayers were answered. We cannot really know when a prayer is answered quickly whether it is truly a blessing or not. We have no concept of the Heavenly calculations and considerations that determine when and how prayers are answered. King David simply tells us to, "Hope for Hashem, be strong and He will give your heart courage, and hope for Hashem" (Psalms 27:14). Never give up! Hope, pray, and don't be discouraged –at the right time, our prayers will surely be answered!

One can't know in advance how much prayer he must offer until his request is fulfilled. Just as a material object has a price tag, so does everything we pray for. Whatever we desire requires so many hours and/or words; just as one can't expect to buy a new car for the price of a bag of popcorn, one can't expect to attain the biggest blessings in life with a few perfunctory prayers.

As King David teaches, one should pray and continue to pray, always with the hope that in due time he will receive that which he is praying for. Hashem does everything for the best, including not answering one's prayers immediately. Only Hashem knows the best time for a request to be fulfilled. One must strengthen his *emuna* that Hashem loves him and is dealing with him in the very best way, while waiting patiently and continuing to pray for salvation. There's no room for despair!

The erroneous assumption that effective prayers are answered swiftly discourages many a person. If we'd realize that each prayer has its respective time to be fulfilled, we'd never despair.

Moses's prayers were not immediately answered; neither were our forefathers' prayers. Why then should we expect immediate salvation?

Our descendants reap the fruit

Our sages teach that a person's prayers are never in vain. If one's prayers remain unfulfilled in his lifetime, then his descendants will enjoy their fulfillment. There are times when a person prays a great deal yet sees no response from Above. He's liable to assume that his prayers were in vain. This is not the case at all, for his prayers will be answered at a later time, to the benefit of his descendants.

We too enjoy many blessings that we have not really prayed or toiled for. These blessings may be material in nature – such as excellent livelihood and good health, or spiritual – such as *teshuva* or success in Torah. These blessings that come without effort or endeavor on our part may well be the products of our ancestors' prayers.

Exact Calculations

Rabbi Ephraim of Sidelkov in his book *Degel Machane Ephraim* says in the name of his grandfather the Holy Baal Shem Tov that there are times when a person prays for something and yet he receives something else. And there are other times when a person prays and the prayers are only manifested in the higher worlds. My esteemed teacher Rabbi Levi-Yitzchak Bender of saintly and blessed memory explained that there are times when a person prays for a particular thing that he feels he needs desperately; Hashem, on the other hand, knows that while he can survive quite well without that particular thing, there is something else that he needs much more. Maybe there's a pending harsh judgment against that person of which he is unaware, and salvation from that judgment is surely more important than the object of his prayer.

In such circumstances, one's prayers devoted to a particular matter accumulate and are applied toward the more important or urgent salvation, such as the mitigation of a severe judgment. In that regard, one's prayers are rewarded with the most important of salvations, though he has no knowledge of this. We must consequently cling to prayer always, whether or not our requests at hand are fulfilled. No prayer is lost or wasted!

Imagine that a small child asks his father for a candy or chocolate, a request that in his childish mind is most appropriate. The child of course imagines that this candy is the most important thing in the world! His father knows full that there are countless things more important than that candy. He decides that his child can live without the candy. So, every time the child asks for a candy or chocolate, his father - instead of buying him the sweets - puts aside its monetary equivalent until he has accumulated a significant sum. Suddenly one day, the father reveals to his son, "You must wonder why I didn't buy you all the candies you wanted. In its place, I saved the money and have purchased a new penthouse for you." In like manner, our "nickel and dime" prayers accumulate magnificent credit especially when we devote daily effort to prayer.

The Holy Baal Shem Tov taught that there are times when our prayers only manifest themselves in the upper worlds. This refers to times when it is urgently necessary to draw down Heavenly abundance upon the world-at-large. Without this abundance, something harmful may happen to the world. The sincere prayers of an earnest individual can literally save the world.

All delays are for the best

Any delay in a response to one's prayers is for the best. We have seen countless examples of this in conjunction with our students who prayed for certain things such as a place to live, a marital partner, children, and a livelihood. When they prayed for an extended period of time without receiving the longed-for answer from Above, they came to me seeking encouragement. I would tell them not to lose hope, only to continue praying, for in the end they will surely be blessed!

Numerous couples marry quickly, without obstacles or delay, rather than after lengthy prayers. Shortly after the wedding, they begin to suffer marital problems, divorcing as quickly as they married. Maybe they stay together but suffer because of a lack of domestic harmony. Contrastingly, we see individuals who waited a very long time for their match, praying for years until they found the right partner, who ultimately live with their spouses in true harmony and endless blessings.

Easy come, easy go

This principle is applicable to our learning as well. For some, learning comes easily, yet in the long run they either lose the desire to learn or suffer from a complacence that leads them to arrogance or loss of interest. On the other hand, we witness those who have to pray long and hard for the privilege of learning Torah, but ultimately, the gates of comprehension open. Those with desire and perseverance usually outdistance the naturally sharp minds that are prone to arrogance. The time and effort they invest in prayer to attain their learning skills make the Torah all the more cherished in their hearts. What's more, they are forever grateful that Hashem opened the gates of learning for them. In contrast, the "shpitz" with the naturally sharp mind often attributes his success to himself.

This is true in every realm. We must trust with perfect faith that every word we utter in prayer is significant, heard, and - as the Holy Baal Shem Tov teaches - accepted. If the prayed-for deliverance tarries, we must have absolute faith that this delay is for our best, most likely to entitle us to something exceeding our anticipation and limited comprehension. Maybe our prayers are accumulating to be used for something that we will need much more than that which we are presently praying for. It could well be that our prayers are contributing to the salvation of the entire world!

When our matriarch Sarah finally conceived, all the barren women of her generation also became fertile, since her prayers brought salvation to all the childless women of her time. The Midrash reveals to us that when Sarah would pray to receive a child, she prayed for all the women of her generation. She even proclaimed that if the other barren women could not conceive, then she asked to also remain barren. This Midrash thus teaches us the lofty level of our matriarch who put the good of the entire world before her own personal happiness. Our prayers too might contribute to the salvation for the entire world.

Humility is prayer

One must cast aside any doubt in the power of prayer, even the seemingly humble thought of, "Who am I to pray before the King of kings?"

Rebbe Yaacov Yosef of Polnoi in his book *Toldot Yaacov Yosef* writes in the name of his holy teacher the Baal Shem Tov that there are times when a person's meekness distances him from Hashem. This results when he asks "Who am I and what is my life worth that my prayers should be listened to, much less answered?" He doubts that the prayers of a simple person can have any affect; that it can create and sustain angels, bringing blessings upon the entire world. If he believed in the power of prayer, he'd speak every word of prayer with care and worship Hashem in great joy and awe.

The evil inclination's main aspiration is to prevent a person from praying - this is its most powerful battle against us. He therefore disguises himself in humility, weakening a person's belief in the power of his own prayers. Yet, true humility has no connection to despair and sadness. On the contrary - true humility brings a person closer to joy and faith. A truly humble person says to himself, "Sure, I am nothing and I deserve nothing. I therefore put all my hopes and trust in Hashem. If He provides for the birds and the insects, He'll certainly provide for me too, especially when He gives me the privilege of talking to Him whenever I want."

The Torah tells us, "Moses was exceedingly humble, more so than any person on the face of the earth" (Numbers, 12:3). Moses prayed tirelessly until his prayers were finally answered, praying for unmerited gifts as if he deserved nothing.

Pride in the guise of humility

In truth, the "humility" weakening a person's efforts to pray is arrogance. Why should a person be discouraged to pray because of his low worth? Why should he feel that it's not appropriate for him to turn to Hashem? If he really believes that he is nothing, what would be preventing him from asking Hashem for a free gift? In actuality, he doesn't turn to Hashem because he doesn't want to lower his pride; he's only willing to ask for that which he thinks he deserves.

If this person had true humility he would realize that no one is ever deserving of any of the gifts that Hashem gives us. Everything we receive from Hashem is a free unearned gift, regardless of our respective spiritual standing or social station.

Know the enemy! The question, "Who am I and what is my life worth?" is none other than the ploy of the evil inclination attempting to weaken our prayers, arrogance disguised as humility. True humility is turning to Hashem and requesting an undeserved gift, praying for all that we need.

There was a Chassid who saw his own lowliness, physical desires and vices every time he prayed. At first, he thought that this was a positive phenomenon, leading him to a heightened sense of humility. Yet in truth, it weakened his power to pray. One day he thought, "Why do these thoughts of 'humility' came to mind only when I begin to pray? Why do they not come at other times, like when I eat or drink?" Once he realized that this was in fact the ruse of the evil inclination in an effort to weaken his prayers, he returned again to the enthusiasm and joy that previously accompanied his prayers (*Shivchei HaBaal Shem Tov*).

You are children of Hashem, your G-d

Even a wicked person's prayers are heard. There are times when a person's faith in his prayers is weakened upon realizing that he's far from upright. He begins to doubt that his prayers will be heard. He should drop such a thought immediately! One must turn to Hashem as a child turns to his father, as the Torah says: "You are children of the L-rd, your G-d" (Deuteronomy, 14:1).

Even a most evil person who has not even yet begun to do *teshuva* must pray. By turning to Hashem in prayer for what he needs, he will merit the light of *teshuva*. The worst criminal can cry out to Hashem, "Master of the Universe! Help me! Have pity on me, save me and strengthen my faith. When I see how You are listening to my prayer and helping me, my *emuna* will also be strengthened. Help me walk the right path…"

If a convicted criminal will pray in this manner, with sincerity, then Hashem will certainly help him. The Almighty is all-merciful. He does not desire the death of the wicked but rather their repentance. When such a person sees that his prayers are answered, that the help he needs comes in response to his prayers to Hashem, his *emuna* strengthens. He'll soon conclude that he should be praying for repentance too. He will realize that he can ask Hashem to help him leave his old ways and cleanse him of years of wrongdoing.

Preparing for challenges

Precisely at times of difficulty, we desperately need to pray for deliverance from our tribulations. For then, the evil inclination fills us with despair in an attempt to steer us away from prayer. Therefore, we must reinforce our faith in prayer **before** challenging times arrive. We must strengthen our understanding that all prayers are important, heeded, and effective.

We must always keep in mind that our first prayers are like "firstborns". A firstborn gives his mother the confidence that if she mothered him, then she is capable of bearing more children as well. And just as the firstborn grants his mother the faith that she can bear children, so our first answered prayers give us the faith that our additional prayers will be answered too, even if not immediately. Thus, a person won't lose heart during tough times. He will remember how his other prayers had been answered and will remain confident that Hashem will answer his current plea as well.

The simplest advice

Prayer is the best and simplest advice of all. We can all open our mouths and speak to G-d! Turning to Hashem in prayer has no preconditions. We don't need money or inside influence in arranging an appointment. We must simply open our mouths and speak to Hashem! Here we see that since prayer is such a great thing, it is accompanied with a multitude of obstacles. Many people who have practiced *hitbodedut* for years are still faced with frequent obstacles in this regard. Some get drowsy during *hitbodedut* while others become inexplicably lazy every time their hour of personal prayer rolls around. In that respect, we must pray daily for the privilege of being able to do our *hitbodedut* with a freshness of renewed enthusiasm, speaking to Hashem from the depths of our hearts.

Once more, "Hope for Hashem, be strong and He will give your

heart courage, and hope for Hashem" (Psalms 27). Rashi explains, **"Hope for Hashem:** and if your prayer is not accepted, reinforce your hope." We must review these concepts daily, consistently reinforcing our faith in the power of prayer. Anything so vital to our overall welfare as prayer – especially personal prayer - requires constant reinforcement and encouragement.

It's so important to seek the great tzaddikim who inspire us to do *hitbodedut*. Their teachings, so profuse with *emuna*, reveal the value of our prayers and guide us on a path leading to Hashem and true *teshuva*. One must therefore review this book at regular intervals to derive constant reinforcement and encouragement in the practice of proper *hitbodedut*.

When Moshiach comes

Let's examine the status of prayer throughout the history of the Jewish people. The first redeemer of the Jewish people was Moses. The Zohar reveals to us that his soul is indeed the soul of the Messiah. Moses was occupied predominantly with prayer. The Midrash teaches that for most of his sixty years between the ages of 20, when he escaped from Egypt, until the age of 80, when Hashem revealed Himself to him in the Burning Bush, Moses was busy in prayer, beseeching Hashem in behalf of His people and with *hitbodedut*. He spent most of this time praying for the salvation of the Jews who were enslaved in Egypt, entreating Hashem to redeem His people.

Moses prayed that Hashem awaken the hearts of the Jewish people to cry out for themselves and beg for their redemption from slavery! The Jews suffered such horrific suffering and still remained in slavery, yet as soon as "…they cried out, and their cry ascended to G-d from the toil," Hashem heard them and immediately began the process of their salvation (Exodus 2:23). Hashem then says to Moses: "And now, behold, the cry of the children of Israel has come to Me, and I have also seen the oppression that the Egyptians are oppressing them. So now come, and I will send you to Pharaoh, and take My people, the children of Israel, out of Egypt" (Exodus 3:9-10). When the Jewish people finally cried out for salvation, Hashem immediately revealed Himself to Moses in the Burning Bush and sent him to redeem them from slavery.

Although Moshe prayed so much on behalf of the Jewish people, salvation came only when *they* cried out to Hashem. Here we learn an invaluable principle: even if a person goes to the Tzaddikim and asks them to pray on his behalf, which in itself is a very good and important thing to do, Hashem wants that he will also pray on his own. The power of the Tzaddik's prayer on his behalf is that it sweetens the judgments against him so that the individual can begin to pray for himself. Stern judgments impair one's ability to pray on his own behalf. Once a person opens his mouth in prayer, salvation is on the way.

When the time comes for Hashem to redeem a person, He gives that person the words of prayer that will unlock the gates of salvation. When a person cannot open his mouth properly in prayer, he should recognize that this is from Heaven. He must therefore beg with all his might for a mitigation of the judgments set against him. He must then ask the Tzaddik to pray on his behalf, so that he be given the opportunity to pray for his own salvation. Once he can pray properly again, he should know that the power of prayer is a gift from Hashem; he must make good use of this opportunity to pray until he is blessed with his personal redemption.

King David too is an aspect of Moshiach. His main preoccupation was prayer. The Book of Psalms, history's all-time greatest bestseller, is a record of King David's personal prayer sessions, his cries to Hashem for salvation, and his thanks to and praise of Hashem. The Book of Psalms is the book believers turn to when they need help. The Psalms comprise a major portion of our liturgy today.

Moshiach, our final redeemer will make personal prayer an integral part of our lives and our daily service to G-d.

The War

Redemption is prayer. We must ask ourselves: Why am I the way that I am? Why can't I control my bad character traits and bodily appetites? Why can't I seem to achieve any significant goal? Why? Simple - I lack the essential ingredient of salvation – prayer.

How can a person hope to change without the help of G-d and without prayer? Our holy sages of blessed memory teach that one cannot overcome his evil inclination without Divine assistance. The evil inclination makes daily efforts to conquer us; only through Hashem's loving grace, it doesn't succeed. We must therefore beseech G-d's help on a daily basis if we want to prevail.

The evil inclination recognizes that personal prayer leads to redemption and consequently concentrates its efforts to creating doubt and controversy in this regard. We've all experienced heavy opposition, both from other people and from within ourselves, to personal prayer. When we finally succeed in setting aside our hour and finding a quiet secluded place, suddenly our heads fill with distracting thoughts; uncertainty and a feeling of "what am I doing here" gnaws at our hearts until it seems we cannot utter a single word with true conviction. Know the enemy – we've now caught the evil inclination red-handed; that's who's infiltrating our hearts and brains and trying to stop us from speaking to Hashem.

Look at the evil inclination's cunning strategy: as soon as we want to speak to Hashem, this nagging little voice in our heads tells us there's no time. Suddenly, we're presented with a long list of other urgent things to take care of and one hundred different preoccupations that are vying for our immediate attention. When that doesn't work, the evil inclination puts on its Torah-scholar disguise and is willing to give us nuances in our Torah learning; it's willing for us to open up a Gemara and review the Tosefot commentary that we had difficulty in understanding just so long as we don't go to the field or the park and spend an hour talking to Hashem. When that doesn't work, the evil inclination finds someone – even a rabbi - to ridicule us and discourage us from speaking to Hashem. What a battle...

Why the war? Why does an attempt to pray arouse such opposition and ridicule, even among those who have a genuine awe of Hashem?

Why don't we face similar challenges in fulfilling other mitzvas? We see how Jews rush to welcome the Sabbath with greatest desire or how they hurry to build their Succah after having fasted for 26 hours. They'll stand for hours to choose the most perfect etrog and approach other commandments with awe and yearning, willing to devote all their energies and resources in fulfilling each commandment to the letter of the law.

Yet, when it comes to prayer, suddenly there's no time. People organize special quorums that enable them to pray in haste; they'll complain if the prayer lingers on even a bit longer than usual.

Notice how a thousand distracting thoughts fill our minds as soon as we pray the "Eighteen Benedictions." As soon as the prayer is over, we can't even remember what we said. At best, we will remember that we were in the synagogue, but other than that – our minds sailed far away...

What's happening here? The evil inclination's first priority is to impair our concentration on our prayers. If we are truthful with ourselves, most of us will admit that we say our prayers in order to be done with them. Most people consider reciting Psalms as a waste of time. And *hitbodedut*? Again, the nasty little voice appears and says, "That's idiotic, true madness! Secluded prayer? Talking to the trees? What, do you think I'm nuts?" The evil inclination's insistent opposition only shows us how lofty personal prayer really is.

Remember that redemption is prayer! Once we are brave enough to overcome the opposition and spend our daily hour in speaking to Hashem, then we begin to see and feel the light of Moshiach.

The robber

Since our lives depend upon prayer, the "dark side" tries to disturb and distract us whenever we pray. That's why unpleasant and embarrassing memories, thoughts and worries bombard our brains as soon as we start to pray. Often a person finishes his prayer session and only then realizes that the evil inclination has robbed him of his prayer.

This phenomenon is unique to prayer. On the whole, we successfully concentrate when performing other mitzvas. The difference is that prayer is the master key that opens the doors to the Heavenly throne. If a person would succeed in praying each word with concentration and sincerity, he would receive all the longed-for salvations he seeks, whether it be a suitable marriage partner, domestic harmony, a good livelihood, the blessing of children, or understanding and wisdom. All the gates of abundance and salvation open wide with prayer. Remember though: wherever there are riches and abundance, there are also robbers lurking in the dark. The evil inclination doesn't want us to be happy; if he robs our prayers, he robs our abundant blessings. That's how he tries to rob us of our happiness.

Just as we don't let robbers enter our private domain, we don't have to allow the evil inclination to rob us of our prayer. As soon as we feel the extraneous thoughts attacking our concentration, all we have to do is stop for a moment, refocus, and start praying again. Rebbe Natan says that thoughts are like a unruly horse – it's up to the rider to grab the reigns and lead the horse in the right direction, rather than letting the horse run off the path into the woods. **Truth**

Rebbe Natan also teaches that one of the greatest obstacles to prayer is a weak commitment to truth. If a person attempted to pray truthfully, he would undoubtedly succeed in praying with genuine intent. For example, one begs for the ingathering of the exiles and for the rebuilding of Jerusalem during the eighteen benedictions we say three times a day. Over half of the eighteen are supplications that deal with the full redemption of our people. Yet, do we really want to see Hashem's Presence return to Jerusalem? If Moshiach appeared right now and gave us a ticket for Israel as part of the ingathering, would we get on the plane? The further away our heart is from our tongue, the weaker our prayers.

Rebbe Nachman reveals (see *Likutei Moharan* I:9) that the darkness that envelops a person during his time of prayer consists of a multitude of extraneous thoughts and unholy layers of the evil inclination, the *kelipot* that block Divine light. But, there are many openings in this darkness; truth illuminates them, for truth is the Light of G-d.

During prayer, one must therefore do his utmost to speak each word with truth. For example, when one says the words, "Grant us, Hashem, wisdom, understanding and knowledge," he should yearn at that very moment to be blessed with these attributes. He should pray one word at a time, concentrating separately on each one, deliberating on each individual word as if it were a one-hundred dollar bill.

When a person prays the *Amida* - the Prayer of the Eighteen Benedictions - with conviction while contemplating, deliberating, and concentrating on each individual word with all his heart, he sees Hashem's Light and invokes the Divine Countenance for the entire world. Such prayer is capable of igniting the souls of other people.

This physical earth is a world of darkness. The Almighty seeks points of truth that are the worthy vessels for His Divine Presence. The Amida, therefore, when prayed with sincerity and truthful intent, enables Hashem's Countenance to illuminate in this corporeal world.

Universal redemption – more about the "Amida"

Both our own personal and national exiles are a consequence of our lack of conviction and deliberation during our prayers. If we were to say the words "And Jerusalem shall be rebuilt" or "Speedily cause the offspring of David, Your servant, to flourish" with true conviction, three times a day and with all our heart, **Jerusalem would be rebuilt!**

The same holds for personal issues. If we'd say, "Grant us, Hashem, wisdom, understanding and knowledge," begging with genuine longing to receive from Hashem's wisdom, then surely the Holy One Blessed be He would illuminate our brains. Since foolishness and a lack of knowledge and wisdom are the source of our misdeeds, and our misdeeds lead to our tribulations in this world, then once we attain wisdom, understanding and knowledge, our lives become so much more gratifying and pleasant.

It's so vital to pray the Amida's words, "Speedily cause the offspring of David, Your servant, to flourish" with sincerity, for the full redemption of our people surely depends on that blessing. King David's prowess is prayer, and so when we pray for the flourishing of his offspring – the Messiah, may he come soon - we are in fact praying that the light of prayer will illuminate the entire physical world. This becomes clear through the continuation of that benediction, "for we hope for Your salvation all day long". With those words, we ask for the revelation of Hashem's sovereignty which of course will be revealed through prayer.

Hashem rules the world. Just as He established the laws of nature, he also established that the redemption will be brought about through prayer. Rebbe Nachman says emphatically (*Likutei Moharan* I:7): "The principle reason of exile is a lack of *emuna*". Since we know that *emuna* – the full and complete faith in Hashem - is synonymous to prayer, we may conclude that a lack of *emuna* signifies a lack of prayer. In Exodus 17:12, we find the expression, "Hands in faith," which Oncolos translates, "hands extended in prayer". So, as we pray the words "for we hope for Your salvation," we are praying for the illumination of prayer and for the entire world to finally awaken to the supreme value of prayer.

The holy Arizal revealed that the final redemption would not come about through Hashem's loving kindness but rather through a vast multitude of prayer devoted to ending our exile.

King David wrote, "I am prayer" (Psalm 109:4); he therefore became Hashem's anointed, "Moshiach". Rebbe Nachman teaches us in the name of the Holy Baal Shem Tov that Moshiach – the Messiah and a direct descendant of King David, may he come soon - will teach us how to pray the Amida, the Eighteen Benedictions, with a pure heart; that's what the world truly lacks.

Torah learning in contemporary times is more profuse than ever. New books are being published all the time, new yeshivas are being established and a marvelous selection of audio and video source material is readily available. Everyone is studying – men, women, young people, retired people, even soldiers in combat zones. With Hashem's mercy, this phenomenon is increasing daily.

Yet, Torah learning is designed to stimulate a thirst for prayer and emuna, as well as the need to express our gratitude to Hashem for each and every blessing in life. The inner light of the Torah arouses our hearts to yearn for Hashem.

The best blessings

Sincere and wholehearted prayer unlocks the safe of life's best blessings - the wellsprings of wisdom, a sound memory, salvations and an ample livelihood. Hashem is glad to enable a person that yearns for more prayer time to spend less hours working overtime in making a living.

Practically speaking, in order to pray the Amida prayer as he should, one needs a good half an hour. He could then say each word with intent and conviction, and walk away from the prayer with a pure heart, happy and content. He would feel reinforced faith and clarity of mind. He'd no longer have to waste time and energy worrying about his livelihood or working insanely long hours. By redirecting worry time into prayer time, a person is rewarded with ample livelihood, a good soul-mate, enhanced Torah comprehension, or whatever else he needs.

Hashem gave us the wonderful gift and privilege of standing before him in prayer three times a day. We should surely take advantage of this gift at least once a day, praying at least one of the three Amida prayers slowly and deliberately, with sincerity and devoted concentration. Why are we in such a rush? The angels laugh at us, for the things which we rush through the prayer for are precisely the things that we should be praying for. The joke's on us – we rush through our prayers because we're rushing to work, only to be caught up in rush-hour traffic. Prayer is a fantastic investment; an extra hour of prayer saves untold hours of wasted effort in trying to seal deals and make the extra dollar. Try it! See how an extra fifteen minutes of prayer saves you several hours in performing whatever tasks you need to at work, at home, or at school.

The King's Treasury

The fantasized reasons that lead us to rush through our prayers are of course ploys of the evil inclination. We frequently rush through our prayers, but as soon as we finish praying, we seem to have all the time in the world, lingering then to talk with friends or sitting to enjoy a leisurely meal. A naive person spends his days with the evil inclination stealing all his prayers...

The heart of the prescribed prayers is of course the Amida – Hebrew for "standing", since we stand to say the silent prayer of the Eighteen Benedictions. The songs and psalms we pray before the Amida are very important, but they're mostly a preparation for the Amida itself. Many take painstaking effort to all the necessary preparations – immersing in the mikva, reciting the preliminary passages of the ritual sacrifices and the psalms of praise – yet, when they reach the heart of the prayers, the Amida, they rush right through it.

Imagine that you're taken inside the royal treasury. The king tells you that you can take as much as he can. Yet, you grab a gem or two and run away...

Hashem wants to give us everything, yet we mumble your prayers in a rush as if they're a burden that we're happy to be rid of. Little do we know that we can enter the King's treasury with our Amida prayers, so where are we rushing off to?

In all fairness, many rush through morning prayers because they have to catch the train, bus, or ride to work. But what about the afternoon and evening prayers? More excuses? We're cheating ourselves! How different our lives would be if at least once a day we'd pray the Amida prayer as it should be prayed. Life can be so much brighter, so much more beautiful....

One should commit himself to reciting at least one lengthy Amida prayer a day. This will surely affect his other prayers as well. In time, he will realize how much he is missing by rushing through his other prayers. By saying at least one Amida prayer this way, he will surely be rewarded with Divine Abundance, both material and spiritual. He'll develop the will and ability to pray with enhanced devotion and concentration, just like the great tzaddikim do.

Our sages of blessed memory teach that a person who prays long prayers will similarly enjoy long life.

List of Priorities

In a congregation that prays fast, one should not concern himself with speeding through the prayer so that he may respond to the Kiddusha or Kaddish. Praying with intent and deliberation is highest priority. Ideally, the entire congregation should be praying with unhurried concentration, enabling everyone to respond to the Kiddusha and Kaddish. But, if a person finds himself in a congregation that rushes through the Amida, he should not feel that he must do so on the grounds that he has to finish together with the other congregants in order to reply to the Kiddusha.

One should ask oneself what's more gratifying to Hashem: should I rush through my prayers and take part in the Kiddusha, or should I pray with solemn intent and deliberation, concentrating on every word?

Funny, but those people who do pray word by word are those who are elevating skyward the prayers of the entire congregation. Without those individuals who pray at length as they should, the service may well be called "A Congregation's Reading" rather than "A Congregation's Prayer". Who would want to finish his 120 years on earth only to discover that in the eyes of the Heavenly Court, he never prayed a single truly earnest prayer. Shocked, such a person replies, "What are you talking about? I prayed every day… and not on my own but with the congregation!"

The Heavenly Court responds, "Your prayers never reached us…"

A prayer devoid of devotion cannot ascend; it's like a body without a soul. Can a body devoid of a soul move? Can it ascend?

Once the Holy Baal Shem Tov passed by a synagogue. He commented, "This synagogue is jammed pack with prayers!" His pupils understood their rebbe's comment to be a compliment, but the Holy Baal Shem Tov quickly corrected them: "My intent is that this synagogue is full with years of prayers that have never ascended… these prayers said without devotion and deliberation cannot ascend."

One tzaddik always insisted on praying alone instead of with a congregation. When the townspeople asked him to explain this custom, the tzaddik replied, "What congregation? There is no congregation!"

"What do you mean?" they asked bewildered, "A large congregation gathers in the synagogue each day for prayers."

"I do not see any living soul there," replied the tzaddik, "only benches and bookstands. Every congregant is in an entirely different place, for one is where his thoughts are, and here, everyone's thoughts are in other places but not in the synagogue. One is milking the cows, another is feeding the chickens, and a third is selling fresh herring in the market… the synagogue itself is actually empty of congregants!"

Prayer is our true service of Hashem. Prayer is *emuna*, and since the purpose of Torah learning and the observance of the mitzvas is to bring a person to the level of *emuna* where he'll desire to pray each and every word with deep sincerity, concentration, understanding and contemplation.

Praying with a whole heart

According to Halacha, the first three and last three benedictions of the *Amida* may not be altered or repeated. On the other hand, there is no prohibition to adding one's own personal words to the twelve middle *Amida* benedictions, although this is not customary. Since the prayer was established by the Great Assembly, the benedictions as they appear are indeed profound and encompass all that a person can possibly need both in the physical and spiritual realms. One may repeat the words of the prayer as long as he doesn't repeat the benediction and G-d's name itself.

While praying each benediction, we should repeat the contents of the section again and again. For example, when one is praying for Hashem to grant us wisdom, understanding and knowledge, he should repeat these words again and again, concentrating on each word its meaning. One who prays this benediction in such a manner, with true concentration and conviction, will surely discover that his mind is opening to knowledge, that he better absorbs and retains his Torah learning.

Why are we in such a hurry? Where are we rushing to - our problems, our tribulations, our persecutors? If only we would stop and pray more slowly and with more thought, we would ascend higher and higher in every way. Who is foolish enough to rush through the King's treasury without filling his pockets with the world's most valuable gems? Like rare jewels, all the best blessings can be ours – we simply have to ask for them in devoted prayer.

The Grab Battle

How it is possible to concentrate on one's prayers when our thoughts seem to wander off the minute we begin to pray?

Rebbe Nachman answers (see *Likutei Moharan* I:76), "There are those whose minds are pure and unblemished, who can learn without prior deliberation. There are others who need to elevate their thoughts before they speak because otherwise their speech will be void of thought." Most of us must consequently contemplate each word of the Amida before we speak it for it to have true devotion and intent.

The evil inclination will still fight to garble our thoughts, but if we contemplate each word before we say it, surely we will manage to say at least some of the benedictions with true intent. Without this advice, most of our prayer will lack deliberation and conviction. Anyone who considers himself to be of such pure mind that he need not adopt this advice should read carefully the continuation of Rebbe Nachman's abovementioned lesson. He subsequently explains that only a person who has done complete *teshuva* to the point where not even the slightest trace of sin lingers within him is of a truly pure and unblemished mind. Anyone who has not yet reached such a lofty level must indeed follow this advice and reflect upon each and every word of his prayer before he utters it.

Unfortunately, many people feel incapable of concentrating on the words of the Amida, so they don't even try. Instead, they simply mumble the words to fulfill their obligation, without even attempting to say them with thought. If they'd only slow down, thinking about each word before speaking it, they'd discover that they are in fact capable of praying with concentration. The evil inclination will indeed fight this capability; don't be discouraged - with courage and perseverance, we all can overcome the evil inclination's obstacles.

How do we obtain the ability of praying with true concentration and deliberation? First, we should devote many *hitbodedut* hours to asking Hashem for the ability to pray word-for-word with intent and devotion. Second, we must never give up. Many times, a person tries to concentrate on the words of his prayers and succeeds for a while to pray properly, only to lose his concentration shortly thereafter. Yet, every little gain is encouraging – don't give up! In time, more and more of our prayers will be heartfelt and sincere as long as we invest continued effort.

A person should pray word-for-word. Even if he is distracted at some point by foreign thoughts, he will succeed in concentrating on at least part of the prayer. On the other hand, one who rushes through his prayers will have prayed with no genuine contemplation at all.

Some claim that it is better to pray as swiftly as possible, in order to get through the prayer before the evil inclination has a chance to introduce foreign and unworthy thoughts into our minds. Rebbe Nachman teaches that hasty and thoughtless prayers belong to the *sitra achra* (the "other side", the side of the unholy). Yet, praying word-for-word it is similar to a "snatching battle" – the evil inclination grabs several words, and then the person praying overcomes this inclination and snatches some words; the stronger a person becomes in praying, the more he'll grab from the evil inclination.

The Chofetz Chaim tells the following parable, so appropriate to the issue of prayer: A widow sells apples. She places all the apples in a basket. A group of hoodlums pass her by and upset the basket, and all the apples fall down and roll into various directions. The hoodlums start snatching up the apples and putting them into their pockets. The widow stands there shouting bitterly, "These hoodlums are snatching up my apples. Without my apples, how will I make a livelihood?!?" A passerby turns to her and says, "Instead of standing in one place and shouting while the hoodlums are snatching all your apples, why don't you rush and grab some of them yourself? Even if you recover only one, it's better than nothing."

Our prayers are much the same. We despair as the evil inclination distracts us, so we rush through the Amida perfunctorily to fulfill our obligations. We'd be smarter to "grab" at least some of his words and deliberate on them, for every sincere utterance of prayer is worth a great deal and are surely preferable to nothing at all.

Even if a person "wakes up" when he reaches the final benediction, he should not say to himself, "What's the point, I've already lost my prayer." Instead, he should concentrate on these last words. These few final words, when spoken with true sincerity and reflection, are priceless.

What did you get from the Rebbe?

I traveled to Uman to be at the gravesite of Rebbe Nachman of Breslev on Shavuot. There I met many Jews from very different walks of life. I met Jews who were visiting the gravesite for the first time, and I met Breslever Chassidim who had been many times to Uman. Among the latter were those who travel to Uman several times a year to be by the gravesite of Rebbe Nachman. Many of them approached me with similar anguish, feeling weak and disoriented. They turned to me and asked, "What will be with me? Won't I ever merit my true soul correction?"

I tried to understand this perplexing phenomenon. How was it possible that Jews who traveled several times a year to be by Rebbe Nachman were still so broken? How was it possible that those who were connected to Rebbe Nachman were still denied salvation, strength and spiritual ascent? Finally, I realized that the problem lay in the fact that they were not connected to prayer! They failed to become the Rebbe's true pupils – those who pray in earnest!

Later, I delivered a lesson about *hitbodedut*. These very Chassidim asked questions about prayer that were similar to the questions of those who were new to Breslev! I then understood just how far they were from prayer and the proper practice of *hitbodedut*.

Rebbe Nachman declared that his main issue was prayer. If a person does not learn about prayer from Rebbe Nachman, then his bond to the Rebbe can't be any more than marginal. True, Rebbe Nachman promised to rescue from purgatory anyone who came to his gravesite, gave a coin to charity, and recited the *Tikkun Klali*. But, he also said that anyone who practiced an hour of *hitbodedut* each day would never see purgatory in the first place! Why depend upon the promise of rescue from purgatory, if you can follow Rebbe Nachman's advice about *hitbodedut* and avoid purgatory altogether? **Promises**

Whenever I encounter a Breslever *Chassid* who doesn't devote an hour daily to *hitbodedut*, I ask him: "Do you really love Rebbe Nachman? Then why do you force the Rebbe to enter purgatory to pull you out?"

The Chassid stares at me in total bewilderment and asks, "Who, me? I put the Rebbe in purgatory?!"

I reply, "Yes! After all, you went to Uman, you gave charity and said the Tikkun Klali. The Rebbe promised that he'd pull anyone out of purgatory who'd come to his gravesite, give charity and say the Tikkun Klali. The Rebbe will certainly fulfill his promise. But why must you make him enter purgatory in order to pull you out from there? Why don't you do an hour of *hitbodedut* daily? In that way, Rebbe Nachman won't have to enter purgatory to rescue you!

We see this concept in the Psalms: "You will not abandon my soul

to the depths [of purgatory]; **You shall not allow Your pious** one to see the pit" (Psalm 16:10). This verse means, "Hashem, don't let me fall into purgatory so that Your righteous one, Rebbe Nachman, will not have to come after me and "see the pit" because of me.

My forte – prayer!

Prayer is Rebbe Nachman's most fundamental teaching. He explained that his emphasis on prayer was what triggered such controversy and opposition against him.

Why does the issue of prayer result in such severe resistance to Rebbe Nachman? Rebbe Nachman answered this question by way of a passage from the Talmud: "What thing is exalted and yet regarded in contempt? – it is prayer!" Since Rebbe Nachman's foremost issue was his emphasis on prayer and prayer is the exalted subject that suffers people's contempt, surely it is that issue which generates such contempt and opposition.

The evil inclination surely knows that the redemption is prayer. Therefore the main weight of his efforts is placed against our prayers. This explains why prayer suffers so from controversy; why though the Talmud states that prayer is a most exalted thing it becomes the subject of man's contempt and antagonism.

The evil inclination strives to arouse controversy against prayer both on a personal and on a broader level. It attempts to introduce doubt into our hearts, to weaken us in this issue, to destroy our patience to pray as we should, to impart the feeling that we don't have the time to pray properly and so forth. In a more general way, the evil inclination endeavors to cause opposition and division against those who teach prayer, especially against the great Tzaddik who came down to this world in order to instruct us how to pray and how to do *hitbodedut*.

Maybe you're thinking that all the Tzaddikim spoke about prayer. That's true. But, it is Rebbe Nachman who emphasizes the solemn obligation to practice a daily hour of personal prayer, *hitbodedut*.

Prayer and love

Seeing the fruition of our prayers gives us remarkable encouragement. Even before witnessing personal salvation brought about through prayer, we gain joy and self-confidence as an immediate dividend of praying. We should simply ponder the wonder that we're actually standing before the King of kings in prayer. Hashem is personally opening our hearts and giving us the privilege of speaking to Him for as long as we like! Such reflection implants in our hearts the awareness that Hashem loves us.

Imagine how we would feel if a mortal king would say to us: "You may have an audience with me any time, day or night. You need not receive permission from any of my guards or ministers. You may enter my inner chambers without advance notice; simply step inside, stand before my throne and speak to your heart's content. Tell me anything that you want, ask me anything that may be on your mind, or pour your heart out before me. Stay as long as you want. I will listen to you - to every word you speak – and I will give you my full attention because I love you and want the best for you…"

Does this not reflect the king's supreme love for us? If someone we don't care for comes knocking at our door, we won't open it? We all have "Caller ID" on our cellular phones and on most modern home phones so we won't have to answer certain calls and callers. Yet if you truly love someone, you'll take his call at any hour, greet him with boundless joy.

That's just how Hashem welcomes us. What could be greater testimony of His love for us than the way He listens to our prayers?

A person who contemplates and comprehends this will turn to Hashem in prayer at every opportunity, whether or not his prayers are answered as he hopes. Conscious of Hashem's love for him, such a person willfully prays, trusting that Hashem will only do the very best for him.

There are those who complain bitterly and declare, "I have prayed so much! Why aren't my prayers being answered?! This means that Hashem does not love me." Such a claim is nonsense. For the fact that the King grants us unconditional free entrance to His chambers is in itself proof of His great love for us. A person who grasps this appreciates the incredible opportunity that Hashem is offering us. It's encouraging enough to know that Hashem listens to us. We therefore need not concern ourselves as to how He will answer our prayers, because we realize something so much more basic, important and magnificent – namely, that Hashem loves us and listens to us. Since He loves us, He will surely do the best for us.

Let's now give prayer a new additional definition: **Prayer is Hashem's love for us!** Come before Him whenever you want; tell Him anything you want, ask for His advice, share your sorrow with Him. The Divine "listening ear" is the hallmark of Hashem's love for us! What have we done to deserve such unconditional love?

Calculations in prayer

From now on, let's stop making calculations in regard to our prayers - which have been answered and which have not. Our sages teach that a person who makes such calculations will inevitably suffer and that all his sins will be recalled. One who questions why his prayers have not been answered is making a statement that he deserves what he has asked for. In Heaven the response is, "He thinks he's deserving? Let us examine all his deeds and all his sins and see precisely what he deserves." Then comes the rude awakening that all his blessings in life have been free gifts that he hasn't deserved at all...

A person who is absolutely certain that he "deserves" what he has asked for has obviously missed the true purpose of prayer. He doesn't realize the great love Hashem has for him. He is obviously not grateful for the magnificent gift Hashem grants us when He welcomes us to stand before Him in prayer.

Contrary to popular misconception, prayer is not a tool devised to acquire one's desires. Prayer helps us attain the ultimate goal - to get to know Hashem and to cling to Him.

Rebbe Nachman teaches that prayer is the main source of our vitality. Food, drink and sleep give us vitality, but only prayer satisfies the soul. Even a physically healthy individual can't get out of bed in the morning unless his soul feels the hope, joy, and strength that true prayer gives.

After all, what we are always praying for? Attaining the sweet and beautiful life of *emuna* and prayer is not that difficult. The Torah promises (Deuteronomy 30:14), "It is not far away... Rather [this] thing is very close to you; it is in your mouth and in your heart, so that you can fulfill it". A person who practices daily *hitbodedut* will enjoy a good life. If a person thinks he knows better than Rebbe Nachman and decides not to practice *hitbodedut*, he has no right afterwards to complain that his life is bitter and difficult. On the other hand a person who strives for prayer and *hitbodedut* will be truly happy. His face will shine and he'll bring gratification to Hashem, bringing the final redemption closer.

In conclusion, life without prayer is the same as life without G-d. The opposite is also true - life with prayer is a sweet and beautiful life with G-d.

Chapter Nine:
The Foundation of Prayer

Prayer is built on one central foundation - guarding one's personal holiness (*shmirat habrit*). Rebbe Nachman teaches (*Likutei Moharan* I:2) that prayer is a person's main weapon. Those who guard personal holiness succeed in prayer, but those who blemish personal holiness don't.

Rebbe Natan of Breslev writes (*Kitzur Likutey Moharan*), "All the battles that one must win - whether conflicts with the *Yetzer Hara*, or conflicts with all adversaries - are fought by way of prayer, the source of one's vitality. So, whoever seeks Jewish holiness must strengthen his prayers and discourse between himself and his Maker because this is the main weapon to win the war."

The service of prayer is a wonderful gift that a person receives from Hashem. Prayer, like everything else, comes from Hashem. One receives this wonderful gift through self-discipline in personal holiness. With the power of prayer, he can go through this world securely and prevail over all opposition. But Heaven forbid, if one does not guard himself in personal holiness, then he loses the power of prayer.

When a person incurs even the slightest blemish in personal holiness, he loses the motivation to pray and prayer becomes burdensome to him. The Torah says emphatically, "Holy shall you be for I Hashem am Holy." In other words, a breach in personal holiness prevents a person from connecting to Hashem. Also, we recite in the *Shemonei Esrei*, "You are holy, Your Name is holy, and the holy shall praise You each day." Someone who is holy in personal holiness has the power and desire to praise Hashem constantly.

Rebbe Nachman adds that charity before prayer is conducive to fluency in prayer. Charity saves a person from extraneous thoughts while praying. He'll be able to focus on his prayers without his mind deviating in any direction. Charity is also conducive in correcting personal holiness. The notion of giving charity before our prayers is codified in Jewish law (see *Shulchan Aruch, Yura Dea* 249:17).

Personal holiness as defined by Jewish law includes guarding one's eyes and modesty in dress. A single person must refrain from touching a person of the opposite sex other than a parent. Married people must also refrain from touching a person of the opposite sex outside of their spouse, parents, or children, as well as observe the laws of family purity and mikva.

A person who has not yet achieved the level of personal holiness that is required for effective prayer need not despair. In the meanwhile, he can bind his prayers to the true Tzadikim of the generation. When one has a spiritual connection with a true tzaddik, his prayers ascend together with the prayers of the tzaddik, for the tzaddik has the capability of elevating the payers of those who are connected to him. He can do this by saying the *hitkashrut* (connection) prayer before each of the prayers that he says: "I hereby connect myself through this (*shacharit, mincha, maariv, hitbodedut, or any other*) prayer to all the true Tzaddikim in this generation and all the true Tzaddikim who have departed, 'the holy ones interred in the earth', and especially to our holy Rebbe, Rabbi Nachman the son of Feiga, may his merit protect us."

Reinforcing personal holiness

There are many levels of personal holiness; the holier a person is, the more he is able to pray. A simple understanding of Rebbe Nachman teachings indicate that any person who makes an effort to maintain personal holiness in any aspect can merit the power of prayer, as we'll soon see. Only someone who has no intention of correcting his ways has no connection to prayer. None of the lectures that he'll hear on the subject will help him and he won't be able to pray. As mentioned earlier, prayer is the connection to Hashem. Holiness is the prerequisite to prayer. So, without personal holiness, there can't be a connection with Hashem.

On the other hand, one who develops the slightest desire to attain holiness will undoubtedly yearn to pray, especially if he listens to lectures on prayer and reads this book. His prayers will be steppingstones to personal holiness. As such, prayer and *hitbodedut* are cogent remedies in correcting personal holiness. Although a person who has continuously breached personal holiness may experience great difficulty and bitterness in his initial efforts to pray, if he nonetheless perseveres, his prayers will become a magnificent personal atonement and correction of the soul that ultimately sweeten his entire life (see *Likutei Moharan* I:50).

Enormously powerful

In further elaborating on the wonderful advantages of personal holiness in regards to prayer efficiency, Rebbe Nachman writes (ibid, II:83) that by correcting personal holiness, prayers become as pointed and as powerful as arrows from a bow.

The more a person succeeds in guarding personal holiness, the more he prays. The more he guards his eyes, the more he is capable of praying at length. The difference is vast between the prayers of one who guards his eyes and those of one who doesn't. Blemished eyes mean blemished and weakened prayers. But, the prayers of one who makes every effort to guard his eyes become enormously powerful.

The boundaries of Halacha

The Torah relates the episode of Er, one of the grandsons of our forefather Jacob (Genesis 38:7): "Er, Judah's firstborn, was evil in the eyes of Hashem, and Hashem caused him to die". What sin did Er commit to be called "evil in the eyes of Hashem"? Rashi explains that that Er would spill his seed so that his wife would not become pregnant and her beauty would not diminish. From here, we learn that a person who spills his seed is called evil in the eyes of Hashem. One who is evil in the eyes of Hashem cannot possibly cling to Hashem.

The transgression of spilling one's seed is codified in Jewish law (see *Shulchan Aruch, Even HaEzer* 23:1), which refers to it as "the worst sin in the Torah." One is not allowed to waste seed, especially manually, as the prophet admonishes (Isaiah 1:15), "Your hands are filled with blood", comparing masturbation to bloodshed, as if spilling the seed is tantamount to killing a soul.

The Torah commands (Numbers 15:39), "And you shall not stray after your hearts and after your eyes." The Midrash explains that "after your eyes" is sexual immorality. Halacha thereby forbids gazing at women whether they are married or not. Our sages teach that immorality and lust begin with the eyes, for one craves what one sees. Jewish law explicitly prohibits looking at the pinkie finger of a women with the intention of deriving pleasure.

Holiness applies to women as well. If a woman's appearance causes a man to look at her and covet her beauty, have lewd thoughts about her and spill his seed, her punishment is very grave and she'll be denied any connection to Hashem.

The Spirit of Holiness

One who harbors vulgar images in his mind's eye virtually creates an iron curtain that blocks out holiness. Unwholesome speech is also devastating to prayer and spirituality. Just as one would refuse to eat from a garbage pail, prayers can't be acceptable if they're emitted from a mouth that utters vulgar speech.

Today's media, especially the internet and cellphones, enables thousands of forbidden images to enter a person's heart and brain every single day, Heaven forbid. These images create a spirit of impurity that is mutually exclusive with both holiness and *emuna*.

The spirit of Godliness cannot dwell in a heart that's contaminated with the spirit of debauchery, impurity, and immorality, thereby closing the door to holiness, *emuna* and prayer. The barrier of personal holiness is therefore called "foreskin", indicating a coarse concealment which seals the heart from any input of holiness. One can't pray with a hermetically-sealed heart.

Rebbe Nachman explains that spilling one's seed dulls the intellect. Since the seed originates in the brain, one who wastes his seed virtually loses a piece of his mind, and his intellectual prowess is consequently diminished. What's more, explains Rebbe Nachman, acquired emotional ills stem from breaches in personal holiness.

The Zohar says that a person who throws away his mind falls into a state of poverty - not only financial poverty, but poverty of the intellect as well. He won't believe in Hashem, and his lack of faith will manifest itself in emotional maladies such as depression, sadness and anger. With continued unholiness and immoral behavior, he exposes himself to severe bodily illness, all of which originate from his sins.

Since primary holiness is *emuna*, when one severs oneself from holiness, his *emuna* deteriorates. This has an immediate effect on his emotional and physical health, his marriage, and his income, all of which take a turn for the worse. In time, such a person finds himself in a downward spiral of negative emotions.

Immorality is Judaism's number-one enemy, explaining why the wicked Bilaam advised Balak to try to weaken the People of Israel by tempting them with immorality. Hashem despises immorality. The essence of Judaism is the desire to cleave to Hashem, a goal that depends on one's personal holiness. Immorality is the opposite – the strong lust to cling to an animal-like body and yearning for the act of an animal, devoid of any holy intent such as marital bliss and procreation. He who yearns for the animal-like loses all his love and yearning for Hashem, as well as the desire to learn Torah and fulfill the mitzvoth. He distances himself from prayer and *hitbodedut*, which are the essential expressions of *emuna*.

The Zohar teaches that one's main test in this world to attain *emuna* and to overcome lust and immorality, which are dependent on one another.

Lust begins with the eyes. Guarding one's eyes is a prime manifestation of true *emuna*, showing that a person knows that the world isn't ownerless. Some things belong to him, and others don't. He refrains in looking at what's not his, for when he looks not, he covets not.

Those who raise their eyes are called "high brows," for in their arrogance they think that everything belongs to them. Our sages said, "The eye sees - and the heart covets." Their keen insights are in fact laws of nature, for we see that as soon as the eye sees, immediately the heart covets. One who covets that which is not his violates the Ten Commandments, the foundation that the entire Torah stands on.

We can now understand the notions of the "evil eye" and damaged sight which are mentioned in the Gemara. When a person covets that which is forbidden to him, he blemishes the spiritual essence and vitality of that same object, because he disconnects that object from its Divine vitality.

King David strived to attain a constant level of cleaving to Hashem. "I am always with you" (Psalm 73:23). "My eyes are always towards Hashem" (Psalm 25:15). King David's efforts in cleaving to Hashem and in guarding his eyes both had the aspect of continuance, never ceasing. He was thefore able to declare, "I place Hashem before me always" (Psalm 16:8), indicating that his focus was always on Hashem, the highest level of cleaving to Hashem.

When one refrains from physical gazing, he can still harbor lewd thoughts and images in his mind's eye. Therefore, only when his mind cleaves to Hashem – which can't possibly be the case if one's physical guarding of the eyes is lax – can he truly focus on Hashem always.

Attaining greater holiness

Difficulty in prayer indicates insufficient holiness. In figurative terms, one might have the engine of prayer (awareness of prayer's significance and value), but his oil level is low (his personal holiness is lacking). As emphasized previously, the power to pray comes from guarding one's personal holiness.

We indeed have a very great power in our hands, a power with which we can conquer all our wars, spiritual and otherwise. This is a power that can enable us to redeem ourselves and the entire world. Good things don't come easy; we must strive tenaciously for personal holiness - particularly for guarding the eyes – in order to merit the power of prayer.

Leaving the bad and doing good

The *Yetzer Hara* traps a person in two areas - "leaving the bad" and "doing good." The primary "do good" of the person is prayer. The primary "leave bad" of the person is guarding personal holiness, especially the eyes. It's no coincidence that these two matters depend on one another, since the power of prayer comes from guarding personal holiness and the essence of guarding personal holiness depends on prayer.

We learned in this book the value of prayer and the paths in which to attain it. We should remind ourselves constantly how much we need to pray to attain prayer itself. This chapter has summarized the foundation to correcting personal holiness, which prayer depends on. Needless to say, we must pray incessantly for guarding our personal holiness.

Chapter Ten:
I Call to You All Day Long

Before we conclude, we'll discuss a special type of *hitbodedut*, used in emergency situations when someone needs a major salvation quickly. Severe sickness, large debts, marital strife, or an urgent problem with a child are the types of situations that require super-charged prayer, namely, a six-hour *hitbodedut* session.

The six-hour session has a spiritual power guaranteed by the great *Tzaddikim* that's capable of moving mountains. However, one must be patient. This six-hour *hitbodedut* session must be repeated occasionally. But most of the time, people who have done the six-hour *hitbodedut* even once see salvation if they only wait patiently. We're not referring to six hours of deep meditation, but merely praying for one request in a simple and innocent fashion for six hours, even if one repeats the words again and again during the entire session.

Many people can testify about the miraculous salvations they've merited in praying for six hours straight. All the more so, if you're inspired to occasionally do six-hour *hitbodedut* for spiritual requests, your efforts will certainly be effective.

Hashem's Rule

A fundamental law of creation is that one is required to pray for everything in life; otherwise, he remains on the spiritual level of an animal, whose sustenance is provided without prayer. Our forefathers' achievements described in the Torah came through prayer, as did the achievements of all subsequent *Tzadikim*.

We too must follow their ways.

The six-hour personal prayer session, or "six-hour *hitbodedut*", is therefore a means of attaining wondrous salvations. With my own eyes, I've seen how penniless married students in our Yeshiva obtained expensive apartments in Jerusalem – debt free – after doing a six-hour-*hitbodedut*.

If the six-hour-*hitbodedut* works in invoking material blessings, it's certainly powerful in the spiritual arena, where we should place the main focus of our prayers. If you spend six consecutive hours requesting that Hashem meet a spiritual need, you will certainly be granted your request. Hashem derives great satisfaction in seeing someone who is yearning so strongly for a spiritual endeavor that he or she is willing to invest the concerted effort of six consecutive hours of prayer to attain it.

Rebbe Natan writes about Rebbe Nachman and says (*Likutay Moharan* II:96): "He spoke a lot about *hitbodedut*, giving a long, wonderful talk using many different expressions. He encouraged and urged us very strongly about doing a lot of *hitbodedut* and speaking to Hashem. At one point, he said that he would want us to spend the entire day in *hitbodedut*. Understanding that not everyone can keep to that, he can only order us to do it for at least one hour a day, which is also very good. But anyone who feels a strong relationship with Hashem and wants to truly accept upon himself to serve Hashem, he would want that person to do a full day of *hitbodedut*, as the *Gemara* says (tractate *Berachot* 26A), 'May it be that people pray all day long.'"

We learn from this that even though a full day of *hitbodedut* on a regular basis would be too difficult for most people, any increased *hitbodedut* has its wonderful virtues. However, if you have a strong will to truly serve Hashem, or if you're in a situation where you have an urgent need, or there's something specific that you want very badly to achieve, your *hitbodedut* should be as lengthy as possible. You should perform *hitbodedut* as it was really meant to be. As Rebbe Nachman said, "Anyone who feels a strong relationship with Hashem and wants to truly accept upon himself to serve Hashem, he would want that person to do a full day of *hitbodedut.*" In our generation, this concept has become a wonderful *segulah,* or spiritual key, and better than any red string or amulet. If you do *hitbodedut* in this way, be assured that your prayers will be effective.

Pray and Wait

Once, a student who did a six-hour *hitbodedut* and didn't see results asked me whether he should repeat it. I told him that while he could certainly repeat it if he'd like to, he should know that the first session had already achieved results. It's just that the response to prayers is not always apparent immediately. It can take months, or even a year, but it will definitely come. It's analogous to someone applying for a visa and receiving a visa with an effective date several months away. Similarly in Heaven, there is a program and accounting for everything, so everything has an exact moment when it occurs. The main thing is to believe that prayer is *always* effective– **prayer pierces the heavens!**

The Easy Way

Another time, a young man asked me how to deal with his staggering debts. His wife had suggested that he travel to the U.S. to ask for charity, but he wasn't keen on doing that. He asked my opinion, and I answered that I had nothing against him going to America, but I had a much better suggestion. My idea, I said, doesn't require the expense of a plane trip, takes much less time than traveling to the U.S., and will solve your debt problem once and for all: simply do a six-hour *hitbodedut* in regard to your debts!

"With your plan," I told him, "you'll be spending 20 hours on the flight going and 20 hours returning, incurring major expenses for food and lodging, and trudging from one place to another while depending on people's kindness. With all that, you'll be lucky to break even and not sink even further into debt! And even if a miracle happens, and you do manage to cover your debts, you still won't have addressed the *root* of the problem. You'll almost certainly have to return to the U.S. again and again or look for other debt solutions."

All of a sudden, the idea of a six-hour *hitbodedut* became much more appealing to the young man. It beat 20 hours on the plane and in the airport, it would cost nothing, and it didn't entail the repeated humiliation of asking for a handout. Best of all, extended prayer includes penitence, which would uproot the root cause of the debt: sin. In that way, a six-hour *hitbodedut* would assure that he would never fall into debt again.

"It's up to you," I concluded. "Would you rather travel abroad to ask for handouts, or would you prefer a day in a field, the woods, or a secluded beach talking to The One Who can truly solve all of your problems?"

"If you choose the right way," I continued, "I'll coach you on how to pray in the most effective way.

The young man now eagerly agreed, so we began our lesson.

"To start with," I instructed him, "thank Hashem for all the kindness He has done for you until now, for all the times He has helped you manage, despite your debts, and for everything else that He's done for you, both materially and spiritually.

"Next - and this might seem strange - you must thank Hashem for the debts themselves. As He does with everything else, Hashem put you in debt *for your own good*. The proof is that as a result of being in debt, you are now standing before Hashem planning to do an extensive *hitbodedut*, something you wouldn't be doing were it not for the debts."

I then taught him the most important things he should say to Hashem in his circumstances.

First, I told him, he should acknowledge Hashem's justice as follows: "Hashem, I understand that if I'm suffering and in debt, it's because I sinned. As the Gemara says, 'There is no suffering without prior transgression.' Hashem, whatever has happened to me is Your action and is just. Not only do You act in truth, but I have no doubt that You have been magnificently merciful with me, compared to what I truly deserve according to my actions. I therefore understand and accept my debts and my financial difficulties and thank You for Your righteous judgments."

Acknowledging Hashem's justice, I taught him, is a cogent way to invoke Divine compassion.

Next, I told him, he should ask Hashem to show him the way of repentance. "Master of the world, everything is revealed before You, so You know exactly what I need to correct myself spiritually. Enlighten my brain and heart so I can identify the root cause of the debts, and please help me correct what I need to correct." "In this manner," I told the young man, "beg Hashem to help you rectify your misdeeds and uproot the core reason that led you to transgress in the first place. Ask Hashem to bring you closer to Him and beg Him to forgive you of all your sins, especially those that led to you financial difficulties. Those sins require a special prayer effort."

"Once you've acknowledged Hashem's justice and have done *teshuva*, pray for *emuna*, that you should have a complete and stalwart belief that Hashem is the Sole Provider. He doesn't need your help in providing for you; in actuality, your efforts are superfluous. Pray for trust in Hashem so you should never worry about having sufficient income, or anything else. Ask for the solid faith that whatever Hashem does with you is the very best for your ultimate welfare. Pray for the privilege to tithe whatever you do receive and to give to charity with a willing heart."

"Pray for your family. Beg Hashem to have mercy on you and your wife and children. State your case to Hashem. Argue that it's difficult to concentrate on serving Him without an ample livelihood. Say, 'Hashem, please give me a means of livelihood so I can channel my energies into more Torah learning and prayer, rather than in trying to cover my debts.' Ask Hashem to give you a livelihood as a free, undeserved gift. It's good to use the argument that Rebbe Natan of Breslev made: 'Hashem, I really want to become a righteous person, but You know that takes a long time. In the meantime, give me sustenance so I'll have the time and mental composure to work on my soul correction.'"

"Commit to becoming a better person. Increase the time and effort you invest in prayer and Torah learning. Above all, never let a day go by without at least an hour of *hitbodedut*, because it's impossible to be righteous without daily personal prayer and self-evaluation. When Hashem sees that you're doing your best, trying to do *teshuva* and act in the proper manner, He'll wipe away your debts. Know full well that to get out of debt, you must do sincere *teshuva*. Hashem constricted your livelihood in the first place as a wake-up call to bring you closer to Him. If you react by seeking solutions that will distance you further from Hashem, such as traveling overseas to appeal to flesh-and-blood, you won't solve your problems. On the contrary, they'll get worse."

I summed things up by saying, "Six hours is a long time to pray, but you must beg again and again for all the things we spoke about, as well as for whatever else Hashem in His infinite goodness may bring to your mind. You will surely see great salvation!

In addition, even after the six-hour *hitbodedut*, you must continue doing a special daily hour of *hitbodedut* devoted to the topic of livelihood along the same lines as the six-hour *hitbodedut*. During that hour, you must thank Hashem and acknowledge His justice, repenting for the sin that caused you to fall into debt, praying for *emuna*, and asking that Hashem grant you a livelihood as an undeserved gift until you do *teshuva* and become righteous. In this way, you will be assured that you will solve all your problems at the root, and they will never return."

The young man heard everything I said, yet he still seemed nervous. "Honored Rabbi," he asked, "how can I do a six-hour *hitbodedut*? I barely manage to speak to Hashem for a few minutes!" I replied, "If you aren't ready to do six hours, you apparently don't grasp the severity of your situation. **If you did, you would do 20 hours straight!**"

The six-hour template

My conversation with the young man in debt should arouse everyone, regardless of what difficulties you may currently be experiencing. My coaching of the young man provides a template for speaking to Hashem in any circumstance.

Once again, here are the main steps in the six-hour *hitbodedut*, to be done when you or someone else needs an urgent salvation or solution:

1. Thank Hashem for the current difficulty and acknowledge His justice.

2. Repent for the sin that is the root of the difficulty.

3. Pray for *emuna*.

4. Ask Hashem for a free gift.

Using this four-step template, you can plug in whatever problem you may have. Try it! If you or someone else needs a soul mate, or a blessing for a child, or recovery from sickness - or anything else - speak to Hashem in the same way that I taught the young man with the debts.

The main reason that people don't make spiritual gain is that their lives are far from holiness, from Torah, from prayer, and from *emuna*. They think they can get along without Hashem.

If you would realize that you have no option *other* than seeking Hashem - for Hashem alone determines your fate - you would pray limitlessly until you perfected yourself.

Golden opportunity

You come to this world for a single purpose: to pray! Hashem prods you with difficulties. Otherwise, your entire life might go by while you remained in a deep spiritual slumber. So when Hashem places you in a difficult situation, it's a golden opportunity to wake up and turn to Hashem! If you mistakenly believe there's any other option - such as the young man in the story who considered looking for handouts in the U.S. to solve his debt problem - you're only fooling yourself.

Why wait until Hashem is forced to teach you the hard way? You'd be much smarter to realize on your own that *you have no other option*. Why waste time on imaginary solutions? Time is so precious! Sooner or later, you'll have to do *teshuva*. Why not do it now, before the problems and tribulations become worse than they already are?

Spiritual Perfection

Many people choose what seems to be the path of least resistance in spiritual matters and resign themselves to a life of spiritual mediocrity and uncorrected blemishes. Then one day, all of a sudden, a "ton of bricks" trial or tribulation comes crashing down on their head. Yet even *this* is Hashem's loving-kindness. Otherwise they'd have arrived in the Heavenly Court after 120 years on this earth with all their blemished spiritual baggage.

The six-hour *hitbodedut* is the chance to break the chains of spiritual mediocrity and uncorrected blemishes, while finding a light at the end of the dark tunnel of whatever deep trouble in which you may find yourself.

If you don't feel capable of crying out to Hashem for six hours, then you don't realize what deep trouble you're in. A spiritual flaw is indeed a serious problem in itself, but if you're unable to sense that you're in major trouble, that's your biggest problem of all!

The great *Tzaddikim* viewed their tiniest misdemeanor as an intolerable fault, for which they cried out to Hashem in non-stop *teshuva*. Why? They had "spiritual eyes" and could see the far-reaching consequences of every action! They lived with the truth that one day they would leave the world and be held accountable for every tiny blemished thought, utterance, and deed.

If you *don't* seek Hashem and arouse yourself to *teshuva*, you will pay a dear price in the end for trying to circumvent your true duty on earth.

Generally speaking, people perpetuate their imperfections because they lack faith that the power of prayer can achieve literally any salvation. If only people had simple faith, they would pray and thereby correct all their shortcomings.

This doesn't apply to those who sincerely seek Hashem, no matter what their level of observance may be. I have seen my own students who, in their first steps to becoming observant Jews, could barely understand the most basic Torah study and whose knowledge of Judaism was virtually nil. Yet they heard lessons on prayer and took them to heart, strengthening themselves in *emuna* and praying with devout innocence, attaining salvations in ways that were nothing less than incredible!

I've seen people attain miraculous salvations in the area of relationship with their children. For example, once at the end of a class, I asked, "Who is willing to undertake a daily hour of *hitbodedut*?" Of course, there were many takers. Afterwards, a woman approached me and explained that at a previous class, she had made a commitment to doing *hitbodedut*. Since then, she'd been doing an hour every day and a six-hour *hitbodedut* once a month. She told me that all her children had unfortunately left the path of Torah, so she began dedicating the six-hour *hitbodedut* each month to a different child. As a result, she said, miracles had been occurring before her eyes. She was already able to convince one of her adult daughters to attend the class, and the daughter was now dressing modestly, as is proper for a Jewish woman.

Such is the power of any woman, as simple as she might be, who is a believer in the power of prayer: her own!

I'm OK

Perhaps you're a "Mister OK." You're OK in your own eyes, convincing yourself that you're fine the way you are, with no need to pray, learn Torah, or do *teshuva*. After all, you believe, as long as you don't rob banks or eat pork, what's to correct? This is a sign of deep spiritual slumber that's always accompanied with a rude awakening.

In order to avert that fate, you must plead to Hashem, "Master of the World! Have mercy on me! Even in the straits you placed me in, I continue to slumber. Have mercy on me that I should awaken and begin to call Your Name. Don't let me be silent. Don't let me reconcile myself to mediocrity. Help me get close to You. Have mercy on me!"

I can't – but Hashem can!

You may lack motivation in seeking Hashem because you're ignorant of Hashem's power to help you. You can become discouraged if you can't see how your problems can be solved. You may shrug your shoulders, sigh, and say, "I can't solve this problem," falling into despair. But this is tantamount to amnesia: you have forgotten that *Hashem can do anything*!

On the other hand, if you're someone with *emuna*, you can smile and declare, "I can't – but Hashem can!" For Hashem, *anything is possible*. You can therefore attain anything by appealing to Hashem in prayer, the more prayer, the better.

Rebbe Natan of Breslev would pray for things that were logically beyond reach. He prayed to understand the loftiest concepts that Rebbe Nachman spoke of, to grasp the deepest secrets of Torah, and to be able to spread Rebbe Nachman's teachings around the globe. His opponents scoffed that he wouldn't be able to publish even a tiny pamphlet in the remote Ukrainian hamlet where he lived. Rebbe Natan suffered greatly at the hands of those who did their best to make life miserable for him. He was well aware of the obstacles that were in his way that appeared to be insurmountable. Yet he wouldn't give up; he begged Hashem to help him attain his goals.

The perspective of history testifies to the success resulting from Rebbe Natan's prayers. Today Rebbe Nachman's teachings have spread to the four corners of the globe, and Breslever books and CDs circulate in the tens of millions!

I was once invited to a very special housewarming. The new homeowner had at one time come to me to ask for advice, for he couldn't even afford to rent an apartment. I told him to do a six-hour *hitbodedut* and ask Hashem not for rent money, but for the opportunity to buy a home in Jerusalem. Mind you, even for someone who has cash in hand, finding an available home in Jerusalem requires many miracles, because the demand greatly exceeds the supply. Imagine the miracles needed to purchase a home for someone who didn't even have the money to rent an apartment!

The young man did the six-hour *hitbodedut*. Some time afterward, he came back to me and said with a worried tone, "Rabbi, we were evicted from our apartment and are now living in a hotel." I told him to do another six-hour *hitbodedut*. Some time after that, he came back again and reported with an even more worried tone, "Rabbi, we now have to live with my in-laws!" I told him to do another six-hour *hitbodedut*.

The man did as instructed and ended up doing six-hour *hitbodedut* a total of four times. His prayers were answered and, as a result, he was able to buy a house in Jerusalem, paying cash! It doesn't matter how it came about. The point is that he bought a house, whereas he had started without a penny to his name.

On another occasion, on the way to a lecture, I stopped in Bnei Brak for evening services. Bnei Brak is a city located just east of Tel Aviv, whose population is comprised predominantly of observant Jews. As I left the synagogue, a married *yeshiva* student came up to me and said, "Rabbi, in our *kollel*, everyone studies your book, *The Garden of Emuna*. Many of us did six-hour *hitbodedut* sessions and were able to buy houses! The man was not a Breslever, or even a Chassid at all.

People all over the world can speak to Hashem and know that anything is possible through prayer– anything!

I have seen a myriad of miracles in my own life, as the result of simple prayer. I personally have had multiple miracles related to dwellings, including receiving a home in Jerusalem for free, as the outcome of prayer. When I was first engaged to be married, I spoke to Hashem about providing a place to live. I said, "Master of the World, please see that I want to continue studying in *yeshiva*. The entire world belongs to You. Please give me a home and furnishings. I don't place my hopes in anyone else besides You. I direct all my heart's wishes to You only. I don't know anyone else. I once relied on another human being, and I repented for doing that."

Not long after that, a mathematics professor who was studying in the *yeshiva* came up to me. He said, "I heard that you're engaged. *Mazel Tov*! I have a one-year lease that I took on an apartment, but my wife doesn't like it. You can live there for the year, and I'll give you the keys." Meanwhile, someone else offered me a flat where I could live for free indefinitely. I told both of them I would ask my fiancée and do what she wanted. That is how I began married life: with a choice of two free dwellings! I also received furniture for free, but that's another story.

Some people mock miracle stories such as these. But in truth, the ones who ridicule are those who don't believe in Hashem. Believing in Hashem is not funny at all. I simply believe in Hashem, so I speak to Him about everything. I am Hashem's spoiled child, and what's wrong with letting Hashem spoil me? Why not?! What greater satisfaction is there for Hashem? Would He prefer that I go to work for 10 hours a day, spending my time in a factory or a fish market, instead of spending that time learning and praying? Certainly not!

Detraction or enhancement?

Anyone who has a problem should do a six-hour *hitbodedut* and not hide behind the excuses that doing so would detract from Torah study, or that there isn't enough time.

I spoke to an upright father whose son fell into a bad crowd and began to use drugs. I told him that to save his son, do six-hour *hitbodedut.* He did-- three separate times-- and the boy repented! **Eighteen** hours of *hitbodedut*, the numerical equivalent of the Hebrew word *chai ("life")*, and the boy repented! If the father hadn't taken the time to do the *hitbodedut*, how much would his son's spiritual nosedive have ended up detracting from the father's Torah study, or from his son's Torah study, or from subsequent generations' Torah study?

So looking at this from a long-term perspective, the so-called "detraction" from Torah was actually a mega-*enhancement* of Torah!

You may still wonder, "Is it right to take away so much time from Torah study to do *hitbodedut*?" You should re-think that question. As explained earlier, extended prayer doesn't *detract* from Torah learning, but rather *enhances* it by helping bring to fruition the Torah you learn! Our sages in the Gemara remarked that one who learns Torah without the intent to fulfill it would have been better off not being born. It's unfortunate that today we are all so far from properly observing Torah-- with constant introspection, prayers, confessions, and repentance-- so there is no chance that we'll put to good use all that we learn.

You may even question whether the practice of *hitbodedut* is meant to be done in modern times at all. You may feel that it was designed for the spiritual greats of previous generations, such as the disciples of the holy Baal Shem Tov. You may believe that the whole idea doesn't pertain to "plain folk" like us today and only detracts from Torah study. Heaven help you from such misconceptions!

Rabbi Levi Yitzchok Binder used to say that while it's true that the *Tzaddikim* of yesteryear would do *hitbodedut* to reach high spiritual levels, in our times, we need it even **more**, just to maintain our Judaism.

The darkness in today's world has become so strong that without *hitbodedut*, it's impossible to remain a proper Jew, even on a simple level.

Rebbe Nachman's remarked, "From the great to the small, it is impossible to be a truly righteous person without doing *hitbodedut*." The greater a person grows, the greater his evil inclination grows. As you reach higher levels, you must be ever more careful to beg Hashem for mercy and assistance in overcoming your evil inclination.

All your excuses *not* to do *hitbodedut* are merely a cover-up for the fact that you don't believe in the power of prayer. One who does believe prays and achieves salvations as a result. If you don't believe in prayer, you lack belief in Hashem.

For example, let's look at the man mentioned earlier who prayed 18 hours for his son. If he had believed that doing the *hitbodedut* would be a detraction from learning Torah and had not done it, how much additional anguish would the man have suffered, as a result? How much Torah study time would he likely have lost in bailing his son out of trouble, running with him to counseling, or trying to get him into drug rehabilitation? What effect would one drug-using child have had on his other children? Where would the vicious, downward cycle have ended?

Imagine the additional ramifications: What about the boy's lost soul? How much tension between the parents would the boy's presence create in the home, with guilt trips and each accusing the other of the boy's downfall? And how could this father ever concentrate on his own Torah learning knowing that his son might at that moment be in danger in some dark alley? The same argument can be made for many other problems that require prayer as the solution.

Can anyone still argue that praying detracts from Torah study? Only someone who is extremely distant from true Judaism could say that. When Moses prayed for 40 days and nights, was he wasting Torah study time?

You may ask, "What's there to say for six hours?" Just by asking that question, you also show that you are distant from prayer. Even the *Gemara* states, "One who prays at length, his prayer is not returned unfulfilled." If you ask that question about six-hour *hitbodedut*, you could just as well ask it about the *Gemara*: "What is there to spend time on in prayer?"

Prayer can achieve *anything*. Why not acknowledge that you can achieve your own salvation? It makes no sense wasting time running to free-loan funds or working 15-hour days. Instead, why not live a pleasant life? With prayer, and specifically a six-hour *hitbodedut* when needed, you will live a nice life!

How can prayer for spiritual gain be considered a waste of Torah time? Anyone who hasn't had success in Torah-learning who does six-hour *hitbodedut* will see dramatic results. If he doesn't, let him do another six-hour *hitbodedut*.

Others ask, "What is there to pray six hours for?" Again, the question is inane. In spiritual matters alone, any Yeshiva student, and certainly any married scholar, should know enough Talmudic and ethics teachings to be able to pray for 24 hours straight!

All these questions indicate either a lack of faith or a gross lack of spiritual awareness. If you are someone who does have these questions, please review this book repeatedly and study its lessons in depth until they become second nature. You must plead with Hashem constantly, "Give me *emuna*! Give me *emuna* in the power of prayer, which is really *emuna* in You."

Listening to a Rebbe: how hitbodedut saves marriages

Hitbodedut **can help with any sort of problem, including marital discord, and promotes** *shalom bayit* **(peace in the home). Here's one example.**

The Rebbe of Rostov practiced six-hour *hitbodedut*. He once told his followers to travel to a certain town for the holiday of *Succot*, far away from eastern Poland where they lived. He implored them to heed him, regardless of any hardships involved.

One of the Rebbe's young followers informed his wife that he wouldn't be with her for the holiday: Rebbe's orders! It never occurred to him to ask *her* opinion. In his mind, if the Rebbe said to do something, there was nothing to discuss. His wife told him she didn't want him to go away for the holiday and was hurt that he would even consider leaving her.

The young husband was upset. His Rebbe had explicitly told him to cast aside all obstacles and implement the directive, no matter what. So what if his wife didn't agree? Did he need her permission? Whose wish is more important, he asked himself: that of the Rebbe, whose every word comes from Hashem, or that of my wife, who only thinks about this mundane world, her convenience, and what the neighbors will say?

And so, the student went away without his wife's consent.

He returned home to discover that his wife was now hostile toward both him and his Rebbe. She was no longer the loving wife he had known. She bad-mouthed him and his Rebbe, refused to go to the *mikva* any longer, and made his life miserable in any way she could.

A year went by, and the young husband became preoccupied with the dilemma that would again face him regarding the upcoming *Succot* holiday, when he would again be instructed by the Rebbe to leave home. Who knew, he wondered, where his situation would lead this time?

But Hashem had mercy on him and manipulated events so that he ran into Rabbi Shlomo, his teacher from his youngest days in *cheder* (elementary school). Rabbi Shlomo was a man of simple faith, wonderful character traits, and decades of experience. When he heard about the young man's marital strife, he said, "My son, this is not the right way. When the Rebbe told you to travel to that town, he did not intend for you to destroy your home for it. He meant for you to act wisely and succeed both in fulfilling his directive and maintaining peace at home."

The young man asked, "How can I do both? Even last year, when we were getting along well, she wouldn't hear of it. Now that I've already gone once without her consent, and she's so angry at me, she certainly won't be willing to allow me to go this time. I have no choice but to 'overcome the obstacles,' as the Rebbe said, and go with dedication on the trip."

The rabbi answered, "No, my son. That's not what the Rebbe meant. That is foolishness, not dedication. Listen to your teacher who knows you from childhood: Go to your wife and tell her you were mistaken. Tell her that this year, you won't go without her consent. Hand her your travel papers, tell her to hold them, and say that you're not going anywhere if she doesn't want you to go. Tell her that last year, you were given bad advice by some people, and now you regret it. Tell her that she's more important than this trip. Improve your overall behavior toward her and your relationship with her, and give her the feeling that *she's* more important to you than anyone or anything else."

Rabbi Shlomo continued, "Then set aside a day and go out to a secluded, quiet area. Make it a day of prayer and supplication, at least six hours. This is a proven *segulah* for salvation. King David alluded to it in Psalm 86: 'Show me favor, Hashem, because I shall call You all day long.' Ask Hashem to forgive you for hurting your wife and also to instill in her heart a willingness to forgive you. You must also ask Hashem's forgiveness for approaching the Rebbe's directive with arrogance, rather than with the humility of husbandly consideration that your wife deserves."

"After you've made this lengthy prayer, go back to your wife. Wait for the right moment of love and tranquility when you can speak to her about making the trip. Turn to her gently and begin by letting her know that the decision is hers. Then calmly tell her about the blessings that you and your family may realize from this trip. Ask her permission to allow you to make the trip this year. If you sense the slightest opposition on her part, don't push it. If that does occur, understand that Hashem is showing you that you need another day of lengthy prayer, so go and do another long prayer session as before. Know with certainty that the moment you have prayed sufficiently, your wife will willingly send you on the trip."

The young man trusted that his childhood rabbi only wanted the ultimate best for him. He appreciated Rabbi Shlomo's profound wisdom and great faith, so he did exactly as told. His faith and prayers paid off. Just as the Rabbi had promised, when *Succot* arrived, the young man's wife readily agreed to send him on the pilgrimage.

Given the student's strong personality, he could have again chosen that time to be decisive and uncompromising. But such obstinacy could have ended in divorce. He needed to learn how to present the matter properly, how to approach his wife so that she didn't feel that the trip was competing with his attention to her. **He should have understood that** *his wife's* **"No" was really** *Hashem's* **"No." For that, he needed more prayer, character refinement, and the counsel of his former teacher.**

There's a lesson here for any husband who encounters his wife's opposition to something he wants. You must reassure her that *she* comes before anything, or anyone, else. Otherwise, she'll be even more adamant in her opposition. Then you must take the steps needed to get Heaven to say, "Yes." If peace in the home deteriorates, the answer is to increase *hitbodedut* to at least six hours, because this spiritual remedy overcomes all difficulties. Most of all, you should show your wife that she is unconditionally your first priority.

King Solomon, the wisest of all men said (Proverbs 16:7), "When Hashem is pleased with a man's ways, his adversaries will reconcile with him." Our sages of the Talmud tell us, 'his adversaries' includes his wife.

If your wife is opposed to your service of Hashem, what it really means is that there must be some outstanding Heavenly Judgments and other impediments manifesting themselves as your wife's opposition. The only way for you to mitigate these judgments is through prayer to Hashem and enhanced kindness toward your wife. Pressuring her will only complicate matters and have the opposite effect. Once you act with prayer and kindness, you will succeed, and the severe judgments will become "sweetened" into merciful blessings. *Amen.*

Chapter Eleven:
Take Your Words Along

Rebbe Natan tells about a dispute between Hashem and the Jewish People that has delayed the final redemption. Hashem said (*Malachi* 3:10), "Come back to Me, and I will come back to you".

Hashem wants us to take the initiative, awaken ourselves, and repent. Then He will come back to us and redeem us.

But The Jewish People said (*Lamentations* 5:21), "Bring us back to You, and we shall return." They wanted the opposite to occur: first Hashem should bring them back and redeem them, and then they would repent. In other words, Hashem should take the initiative.

Even today, Hashem wants us to make the first move, but we want Hashem to initiate. This dispute is continuing to hold up the redemption!

The Jewish People may have seemed justified in their claim. Hashem must take the initiative, they argued, because no one can repent without Hashem's help. They supported this claim with words from the *Gemara* (tractate *Succa* 52b): "Every day the evil inclination incites a person, and without help from Hashem, the person would not have been able to withstand the temptation."

They were partially correct in their assertion that without Hashem's assistance, one is unable to repent. The question is, "Does Hashem require *us* to initiate repentance *first*?"

Rebbe Natan resolved this apparent contradiction between the passage in *Malachi* that tells The Jewish People to initiate *teshuva* and the passage in *Lamentations* that calls for Hashem to take the first step. He explained that Hashem doesn't demand anything we are incapable of doing. The Jewish People were arguing because they didn't understand Hashem's intention when He said, "Come back to Me."

In truth, Hashem simply wants us to call out to Him constantly, saying: "Bring us back to You." He wants us to have the *desire* to repent and get closer to Him.

50th gate

The Jewish People are mistaken in thinking that Hashem is demanding something they are not capable of. The reason for this misconception, as Rebbe Natan teaches, is because the fiftieth gate of holiness is hidden from us. The current exile is the exile into the fiftieth gate of impurity, and only through the fiftieth gate of holiness shall we emerge from the exile. The marvelous wisdom of the fiftieth gate of holiness is that every person will know the need to call out Hashem's name and yearn to return to Him. This is all Hashem demands – "call out to Me and ask to return" – and He'll take care of the rest.

Hashem is fully aware that you don't have the power on your own to do true penitence. All you need to do is call His name and ask to return, and He will meet you more than halfway. "*Teshuva*" literally means "to return." Anyone can do that! **If you take the initiative and simply call out to Him, it's considered by Him as if you've taken the first step in initiating *teshuva*. What a bargain! The minute you shout to Hashem, "Help me repent," it's as if you had already repented!**

Psalms and personal prayer

The current exile has been perpetuated because we are in The 50th Gate of Impurity, may Hashem save us! To escape, we must attain The 50th Gate of Holiness, the wisdom of calling Hashem's Name and asking to return. We can attain this wisdom in two ways: by saying psalms with devotion and personal prayer.

Daily personal prayer is our call asking to return to Hashem. We may beg Hashem to help us repent with many different expressions and ways. One person may say, "Forgive me, help me repent." Someone else pleads with Hashem and asks for His help in correcting a bad character trait. A third yells for an entire hour, "Hashem, only You can help me overcome this powerful lust." A fourth person begs Hashem to help him stop smoking so he can have the strength to observe the Sabbath. A fifth person, a young woman in college, begs Hashem for the inner strength to withstand social pressure and dress modestly.

Each person, in his or her individual way, can call to Hashem and fulfill the obligation of "Come back to Me." That's all the initiative Hashem wants.

Practically speaking, the 50th Gate of Holiness is personal prayer. The *Moshiach* will fully reveal this light of prayer and personal prayer. Our holy Rebbe Nachman said that when *Moshiach* comes, everybody will devote an hour to personal prayer each day. Rebbe Natan, in turn, commented, "If that's the case, then my *Moshiach* has already arrived!" He truly understood the need to call Hashem's Name constantly in personal prayer and did so every single day from the time he was 22 years old (when he first met Rebbe Nachman) to his last day on earth at age 65.

Since this wisdom has been mostly concealed until now, the world has yet to attain its correction. But, now that Rebbe Nachman has revealed this wisdom to us, whoever will follow it will merit his individual redemption and will also help expedite the universal redemption.

King David testifies (Psalm 109:4), "And I am prayer." He, Hashem's anointed, taught us prayer and showed us the path of repentance, which is prayer and incessant dialog with Hashem, pleading for His salvation and thirsting to be close to Him. This is the path that will soon bring Moshiach - the light of the fiftieth gate of holiness - which rectifies everything!

You can talk

You distance yourself from Hashem when you say, "I'm not capable of repenting; I'm spiritually incompetent! If Hashem wants me, let Him stimulate me to repent, because I simply can't." As in the old debate about the chicken and the egg, some folks think that Hashem has to start the process, so until then, it's business as usual for them.

In a way, they're right. Someone with strong lusts, hefty bodily appetites, lewd desires, and bad character traits who lives in pitched spiritual darkness has trouble finding the way to the light. What can he do? Can he change his life in one minute? He doesn't believe he can, so he says, "If Hashem wants me, let Him awaken me! I don't have the power to change and repent at this stage of my life."

So when that person says to Hashem, "I do not have the power to change and repent," Hashem tells him, "You are right."

And when a person says, "I am not capable of changing and repenting," Hashem also tells him, "You are right."

But another person says, "Look how far I have fallen. My whole lifestyle is one big set of transgressions! The evil inclination burns inside me and incites me like a fiery furnace. I have tried many times to repent, but I couldn't. I have no idea where to begin even..."

Hashem tells this person, "You are right, but you can speak to Me with the same ease that you talk to the whole world on your cell phone. Simply talk to Me for one hour a day and ask for My help in overcoming your evil inclination."

Hashem knows that you can't overcome the evil inclination on your own. He knows your strengths, weaknesses, and current spiritual level and certainly does not demand more than what you're capable of. Hashem's demand of "Come back to me" is a simple call for you to take the first step and motivate yourself OR wake yourself up somewhat. It's simple: all you have to do is to ask Hashem, "Please help me repent."

Hashem doesn't ask much from you. He says (*Midrash Raba, Shir HaShirim* 5:3), "Open Me an opening the size of a pinhead, and I'll open for you an opening through which entire horse-drawn wagons can enter." **If you make the first, tiniest move of setting aside time to speak to Hashem in personal prayer, Hashem will do the rest.**

Hashem tells us, "I know that you don't have the power to repent on your own. I'm only asking for something that you're capable of: speech! Come speak to Me for one hour a day!"

That is the precise reason that this book was written: to stimulate you to talk to Hashem daily.

Now you can understand The Prophet's intention when he said (*Hosea* 14:3), "Take your words along with you and return to Hashem." Our sages explain that Hashem wants your words, your personal prayer. The *Tzaddikim* in all the generations knew that the only power a person has to repent is through talking. And Rebbe Nachman of Breslev knew that our individual and universal redemption depend on every single man and woman performing a daily hour of personal prayer.

Not only Breslev promotes hitbodedut

At this point, you may argue, "The *Tzaddikim* in all the generations, where did they mention *hitbodedut*? Isn't that a Breslever concept?"

By no means!

The holy Alshich in his elaboration of Exodus 24:10 says, "Of course one needs *hitbodedut*!"

Rabbi Moshe Chaim Luzzato writes (The Path of the Just," Chapter 15): "Loftier than anything is *hitbodedut*, for as a person turns his gaze from worldly matters, he frees his heart from lust. King David already spoke in praise of *hitbodedut* when he said (Psalm 55:7), "O that I had the wing of a dove that I would fly away and find rest; behold, I would wander afar in the wilderness." The Prophets Elijah and Elisha frequented the mountains in personal prayer, and our early sages of blessed memory walked in their footsteps, for they found this the most conducive avenue to perfection and withdrawal from the vanities of their contemporaries."

Rabbi Yisroel Meir HaCohen from Radin, the holy "Chafetz Chaim," writes (*Chafetz Chaim, Likutei Amarim,* Ch. 11): "If we would pray and would pour out before Hashem, certainly our prayers and supplications would not return empty. And it's not enough for a person to pray the *Shemona Esrei* three times a day, rather a few times per day, **a person needs to pour out prayers and supplications in solitude**, in his house, from the depths of his heart. Because the three prayers (*Shemona Esrei*) are already fixed in his mouth and he doesn't take them to heart so much. But if a person would contemplate in solitude and make a cheshbon hanefesh on his personal situation, his great poverty and his many toils, and for all this to live on crusty bread and water, then he will pour out his heart like water in front of Hashem, and the prayer will go out with deep *kavana* and with a broken heart and a lowly spirit. A prayer like this will certainly not return empty..."

The *Orchut Tzaddikim* (Gate of Truth) says that by *hitbodedut*, one strengthens the mind and clings to Divine light, thereby getting closer to Hashem.

Rebbe Yonatan Aibshitz says (*Yaarot Dvash*, II:12) that when Adam sinned, he did 98 straight days of *hitbodedut* to repent.

Rebbe Elimelech of Lizensk writes (*Noam Elimelech, Beshalach*) that *hitbodedut* is the beginning of service of Hashem.

The *Yismach Moshe* writes (*Parshat Ki Tavo*), "All the holy books exalt the virtue of *hitbodedut*.

The *Aravei Nachal* (*Parshat Haazinu*) learns that the Talmud demands a person to perform one 24-hour *hitbodedut* a month!

Rebbe Aaron the Great of Karlin is more stringent – he requires a person to devote an entire day to *hitbodedut* once a week (see *Seder Yom*).

Rebbe Moshe Leib of Sassov (*Hanhagot, 49*) requires a person to perform 2 hours of *hitbodedut* a day.

The above sources are only a few examples of many. In light of the above directives, Rebbe Nachman's instruction for us to do a mere one hour daily of *hitbodedut* is quite lenient.

This is also from Hashem

Here's a concept that, on the surface, appears to be a paradox: Rebbe Natan says that even the words we speak to Hashem, which are considered the product of our awakening, also come from

Hashem. King David said (*Psalm 10*:17), "You prepare their heart; may Your ear listen." Hashem prepares your heart to pray to Him, and afterwards He listens to your words as if you had produced them yourself.

So if Hashem gives us our words, how do *we* get credit for making even the tiniest step in initiating *teshuva*? Our first step must be the **desire** to talk to Him. Having that desire will fulfill the requirement of making the first step. In truth, though, our desire also comes from Hashem, as well. We are the ones who yearn deep in our hearts to speak to Hashem, but that is because He has prepared our hearts and given us the desire. It's mind-boggling just to ponder the wonderful loving-kindness Hashem does, and is willing to do, for any person who wants to return to Him.

A weak claim

If you believe that you can't do *teshuva* until Hashem comes down and personally wakens you, there's a fallacy in your thinking. After you leave this world, The Heavenly Court will ultimately demand, "If you knew that your repentance comes from Hashem, then why didn't you ask Hashem to help you repent? You claim that you didn't know how to repent, and that only Hashem could awaken you to repent."

It's true that *teshuva* – like everything else – comes from Hashem. But we have to take the first step and call out to Hashem. Rebbe Natan says that *hitbodedut* is essentially very easy and is something that anyone can do.

Nothing can uplift you from the abyss of personal exile like speaking to Hashem in personal prayer.

In essence, your only hope – and power – is to yearn for Hashem, anticipate His salvation, and call out to Him.

People today are tragically so far away from Hashem simply because they don't take the first step, and to paraphrase Hosea the Prophet, **we must take our words along with us and return to Hashem**.

Hashem doesn't expect you to make overnight, revolutionary changes in your life. You don't have to don the garb of a particular group or exchange your baseball cap for a Borsalino black hat. Your jeans and sweatshirt don't make you any less beloved in Hashem's eyes.

You don't have to know Biblical Hebrew or Oxford English to talk to Him. Hashem loves hearing your own jargon, your own slang, and your own Texas twang or Irish brogue. Hashem will stop everything He's doing just to listen to the voice of a coal miner from the depths of the earth in West Virginia.

Anybody can call His Name. Anytime, anywhere. You never need an appointment, 24/7. Could there be greater loving-kindness?

The gift of Hashem's words in your very own mouth is waiting for you right now. Go ahead and talk to Him! You can even put your own intellect aside, and Hashem will illuminate your brain, just wait and see!

Our task is to simply set aside a daily time slot for personal pray and Hashem will do the rest. Why then is it so difficult for people to do personal prayer?

The reason stems from Rebbe Natan's teaching mentioned earlier, that the source of *hitbodedut* is the 50th Gate of Holiness, which is both lofty and concealed. For that reason, human intellect doesn't comprehend the logic of personal prayer and cannot grasp its significance. That is why many people question and scoff at the notion of personal prayer.

Nevertheless, as soon as you feel the tiniest spark of insight, realizing that *teshuva* comes from Hashem, and that all you have to do is to make the first tiny step, then your soul will be kindled with an indescribable desire to speak to Hashem!

The end of sin, not sinners

The *Gemara* in tractate *Berachot* tells a story about a gang of hoodlums who were making life miserable for Rebbe Meir. Rebbe Meir prayed that they would all drop dead. His wife, Bruria, objected, saying that he should pray for the end of *sin*, not the sinner. Rebbe Meir heeded her advice and prayed that the hoodlums should return to Hashem. Shortly thereafter, they did *teshuva*!

This story teaches us how powerful and beneficial the prayers for *teshuva* can be. If prayers for another person can be that effective, even though no person has the ability to control anyone else's free choice, imagine how powerful your *teshuva* prayers for yourself would be! Not only that, you should take the *Gemara*'s lesson to heart and pray that your family, friends, fellow countrymen, and the whole world all return to Hashem.

As we say in the *Aleynu* prayer after morning, afternoon, and evening prayer services every day of the year, including Sabbath and holidays, the full correction of the entire world will occur when "...every living flesh shall call Your name."

The *Gemara* in tractate *Sanhedrin* tells a similar story to that of Rebbe Meir, this time about Rebbe Zeira. Hoodlums lived in his neighborhood, as well, but he prayed that they would return to Hashem. Rebbe Zeira reached out to the hoodlums, befriended them, and treated them kindly to the dismay of the generation's rabbinical leaders. When Rebbe Zeira died, the hoodlums cried, "Until now, Rebbe Zeira has saved us from Divine judgment. Who will save us now?" As a result, their hearts were kindled with a spark of *teshuva*, and they ultimately repented completely for their sins.

Despite Rebbe Zeira's outreach efforts, the hoodlums didn't do *teshuva* during his lifetime. Yet his efforts were not in vain and eventually bore fruit. He believed in what he was doing, despite the opposition from the rabbinical establishment. If the wise men of his time had emulated Rebbe Zeira, our people would have been redeemed long ago.

The Prophet says (*Ezekiel* 18:32) that Hashem gets no gratification from giving the death penalty to an evil person. He'd much rather see that person mend his ways and do *teshuva*. As such, your prayers for the penitence of your loved ones, acquaintances, nation, and the general populace are ever-so-dear to Hashem.

Nevertheless, we ourselves can't ignore Hashem's call, "Come back to Me, and I will come back to you" (*Malachi* 3:10). Each one of us must make our own concerted effort to return to Hashem and not wait for others to pray for us.

Even if you have already "come home" to Hashem, you certainly shouldn't stagnate, for when it comes to spirituality practice, lack of steady gain actually results in regression. Your duty is therefore to **take your words along with you**-- every single day, for at least an hour a day. As a result, you will be returning to Hashem each day on a spiritually-higher rung. As time goes by, you'll look back and see that you've made fantastic progress in getting closer to Hashem.

By returning to Him, we're guaranteed that *He'll* return to *us* - big time - by providing us with *Moshiach*, the ingathering of the exiles, and the full redemption of our people. *Amen.* Postscript

Rebbe Chanina says (*Gemara*, tractate *Bava Kama* 38a), "One who is commanded and fulfills is greater than one who is not commanded and fulfills." The *Gemara* holds that a person who fulfills a commandment out of *obligation* is on a higher level than a person who fulfills a commandment *voluntarily*.

It's wonderful to devote an hour to personal prayer daily because you understand how vital it is. But did you know that it's even greater to set aside an hour a day for speaking to Hashem because Rebbe Nachman emphatically instructed us to do so?

It's therefore spiritually beneficial to recite the following *Hitkashrut* Prayer. *Hitkashrut* is a spiritual connection to *Tzaddikim* that enhances our prayer and performance of *hitbodedut*.

Here is the accepted text that Breslevers use:

Before *Hitbodedut*, say:

I hereby connect myself through this session of *hitbodedut* to all the true Tzaddikim in this generation and all the true Tzaddikim who have departed, "the holy ones interred in the earth", and especially our holy Rebbe, tzaddik, foundation of the world, the "flowing brook, source of wisdom", Rabbi Nachman the son of Feiga, who instructed us to do an hour of personal prayer every day, may his merit protect us, amen.

Say also: I hereby commit myself to the commandment of "Thou shalt love thy neighbor as thyself."

After *Hitbodedut*, say:

Thank You, Hashem, for granting me the privilege of devoting an hour (or however much time you devoted) to *hitbodedut*. Please help me do the same tomorrow and every other day of my life. I hereby declare a new beginning, and from today, I hereby attach myself to You, beloved Father in Heaven!

Glossary

Amida (Hebrew, literally "standing") – the Eighteen Benedictions prayer said three times a day, while standing in silence.

Amalek (Biblical) – evil grandson of Esau; nickname for the *Yetzer Hara*, the evil inclination

Baal Tshuva (pl. *Baalei teshuva*) (Hebrew) – spiritually awakened Jew

Bitachon (Hebrew) – trust in G-d

Brit mila (Hebrew) – ritual circumcision

Chassid (pl. Chassidim) (Hebrew) – literally "pious person", but alludes to the disciples of the Chassidic movement, founded by Rabbi Yisroel Baal Shem Tov in the early 18th Century CE

Chattan (Hebrew) – bridegroom

Cheshbon (Ha)Nefesh (Hebrew) – literally, "accounting of the soul", denotes self-evaluation or soul-searching

Chuppa, or chupah (Hebrew) – marital canopy

Derech eretz (Hebrew) – literally "way of the land", denotes proper behavior and manners

Dinim (Hebrew) – the spiritual forces of severe judgments that are created by a person's misdeeds.

Emuna (Hebrew) - the firm belief in a single, supreme, omniscient, benevolent, spiritual, supernatural, and all-powerful Creator of the universe, who we refer to as God

Emunat Chachamim (Hebrew) - the belief in our sages

Epikoris (Greek) – skeptic, heretic

Epikorsis (Greek) – heresy, skepticism

Gemara (Aramaic) – The 2nd-5th Century CE elaborations on the Mishna, which serve as the foundation of Jewish law

Gett (Aramaic) – Jewish writ of divorce

Geula (Hebrew) – the redemption process of the Jewish people

Halacha (Hebrew) –Jewish religious law

Hashem (Hebrew) - literally means "the name," a substitute term for The Almighty so that we don't risk using God's name in vain.

Hitbodedut (Hebrew) – personal prayer

Kabbala (Hebrew) - Jewish esoteric thought

Kavanna (Hebrew) – heartfelt intent in prayer, or undistracted concentration

Kedusha (Hebrew) – holiness

Kelipot (Hebrew) – literally "husks," denotes forces of spiritual impurity, the opposite of holiness

Ketuba(h) (Hebrew) – Jewish marital contract

Likutei Halachot (Hebrew) – Rebbe Natan of Breslev's elaboration on the Code of Jewish Law based on the teachings of Rebbe Nachman of Breslev

Likutei Moharan (Hebrew) - A compilation of Rebbe Nachman of Breslev's classic teachings

Likutei Tefillot (Hebrew) - A compilation of prayers by Rebbe Natan of Breslev based on Rebbe Nachman of Breslev's classic "Likutei Moharan." The prayers in "Likutei Tefillot" ask Hashem to help us implement Rebbe Nachman's teachings in every aspect of our daily lives

Maariv (Hebrew) – daily evening prayers

Malchut (Hebrew) – monarchy; in Kabbalah, the seventh sphere

Middot (Hebrew) – character traits

Midrash (Hebrew) – collection of Jewish homiletic literature, mostly from Talmudic sources

Mikva(h) (Hebrew) – Jewish ritual bath

Mincha (Hebrew) – daily afternoon prayers

Minyan (Hebrew) – a quorum of ten men for prayer or ceremonial occasion

Mishna (Hebrew) – The oral elaboration of the Torah as given from Hashem to Moses, finally codified by Rabbi Akiva, his pupil Rabbi Meir, and his pupil Rabbi Yehuda HaNassi, 1st-2nd Century, CE

Mitzva(h) (Hebrew) – a commandment of the Torah; good deed.

Mitzvot(h) (Hebrew, pl.) – literally, the commandments of the Torah; good deeds

Moshiach (Hebrew) – Messiah

Nefesh (Hebrew) – basic life force, the outer portion of the three parts of the soul

Neshama (Hebrew) – the loftiest and innermost part of the soul

Onaat Devorim (Hebrew) – a transgression of Torah where one person insults, saddens, humiliates, or misleads another person

Parnassa (Hebrew) – income, livelihood

Pgam Habrit (Hebrew) – literally "a blemish of the holy covenant", connotes a breach in personal holiness

Rav (Hebrew) – an ordained rabbi

Rebbe (Hebrew) – spiritual guide and leader

Ruach (Hebrew) – the spirit, the middle of the three parts of the soul (see also *Nefesh*, *Neshama*)

Ruach Hakodesh (Hebrew) – holy spirit

Sandek (Hebrew) – godfather

Segula (Hebrew) – literally, something of great value or exceedingly cherished; connotes a means for effecting or invoking spiritual or material gain

Shabbat (Hebrew) – Sabbath, day of rest

Shacharit (Hebrew) – daily morning prayers

Shadchan (pl. shadchanim) (Hebrew) - matchmaker

Shalom Bayit (Hebrew) – literally "peace in the home", marital bliss

Shechina (Hebrew) – The Divine Presence

Shidduch (pl. shidduchim) (Hebrew) – a match between a man and a woman for the sake of marriage

Shlemazel (Yiddish) – literally, a person with no luck. Refers to someone clumsy and inept

Shlit'a (Hebrew) – suffix used after a contemporary rabbi's name, acronym for "may he merit long and good days"

Shmirat Habrit (Hebrew) – literally "guarding the covenant"; male holiness in thought, speech, and deed, particularly the use of one's reproductive organs only in the performance of a mitzvah

Shmirat Eynayim (Hebrew) – "guarding the eyes," or refraining from looking at forbidden objects, particularly at a woman other than one's wife

Shmona (Shemona) Esrei (Hebrew) – literally "eighteen", refers to the Eighteen Benedictions prayer said three times a day during weekdays

Shulchan Oruch (Hebrew) – Code of Jewish Law, compiled by Rabbi Joseph Caro of Tzfat, late 16th Century CE

Simcha (Hebrew) - a deep inner sense of true joy

Sitra Achra (Aramaic) – literally, "dark side", the opposite of holiness, denotes the forces of the Satan that fight against and resist holiness

Siyata D'shmaya (Aramaic) – Divine assistance

Tallit (Hebrew) – prayer shawl

Talmud (Hebrew) – Jewish oral tradition, comprised of the Mishna and the Gemorra

Tanna (Aramaic) – Mishnaic sage, 1st – 2nd Century CE

Tefillin (Aramaic) - phylacteries

Tefilla (Hebrew) – prayer

Teshuva (Hebrew) – literally "returning," the term that refers to the process of atoning for one's misdeeds

Tikkun (Hebrew) – correction of the soul **Pgam Habrit** (Hebrew) – literally "a blemish of the holy covenant", connotes a breach in personal holiness

Tikkun Habrit (Hebrew) – literally "correction of the holy covenant", connotes a state of personal holiness

Tikkun Klali (Hebrew) – A compendium of ten Psalms (16, 32, 41, 42, 59, 77, 90, 105, 137, 150) revealed by Rebbe Nachman of Breslev which are conducive to purification of the soul and personal holiness

Tikkunim (Hebrew) – plural for tikkun

Tzaddik (Hebrew) – extremely pious and upright person

Tzaddikim (Hebrew) – plural for tzaddik

Tzedakka (Hebrew) – charity

Yesod (Hebrew) – literally "foundation"; in Kabbalah, the sixth sphere that represents personal holiness

Yetzer Hara (Hebrew) – evil inclination

Yetzer Tov (Hebrew) –inclination to do good

Yir'at Shamayim (Hebrew) – literally "the fear of Hashem," a term for sincere piety

Yishuv HaDa'at (Hebrew) – self-composure

Zohar (Hebrew) - the 2nd-Century C.E. esoteric interpretation of the Torah by Rebbe Shimon Bar Yochai and his disciples

Did you enjoy this book? If so, please help us spread the message of *emuna* around the world. Send your contributions to:

Chut Shel Chesed

POB 50226

Jerusalem, Israel

Tel:

972-52-2240696

Or:

972-2-5812210

In lovin memory of our first teachers, our
Parents

Douglas D. Cooper

&

Joyce B. Friedman

It is with tremendous gratitude to Hashem for
giving Us our current teachers. There are a daily
inspiration. We are blessed to have them in our
lives.

Yizhak and Rachel Yablonski

&

Rabbi Gavriel Kleinerman

Karen, Peter, Rachel and David Cooper